Human-Computer Interaction Series

Human-Computer Interaction is a multidisciplinary field focused on human aspects of the development of computer technology. As computer-based technology becomes increasingly pervasive - not just in developed countries, but worldwide - the need to take a human-centered approach in the design and development of this technology becomes ever more important. For roughly 30 years now, researchers and practitioners in computational and behavioral sciences have worked to identify theory and practice that influences the direction of these technologies, and this diverse work makes up the field of human-computer interaction. Broadly speaking it includes the study of what technology might be able to do for people and how people might interact with the technology.

In this series we present work which advances the science and technology of developing systems which are both effective and satisfying for people in a wide variety of contexts. The human-computer interaction series will focus on theoretical perspectives (such as formal approaches drawn from a variety of behavioral sciences), practical approaches (such as the techniques for effectively integrating user needs in system development), and social issues (such as the determinants of utility, usability and acceptability).

Author guidelines: springer.com > Authors > Author Guidelines

Also in this series

Gill, S. (Ed.)
Cognition, Communication and Interaction –
Transdisciplinary Perspectives on Interactive
Technology
ISBN 978-1-84628-926-2, 2008

Law, E., Hvannberg, E., Cockton, G. (Eds.)
Maturing Usability – Quality in Software,
Interaction and Value
ISBN 978-1-84628-940-8, 2008

Lieberman, H., Paternò, F., Wulf, V. (Eds.)
End User Development
Vol. 9, ISBN 978-1-4020-4220-1, 2006

Lieberman, H., Paternò, F., Wulf, V. (Eds.)
End User Development
Vol. 9, ISBN 978-1-4020-5309-2, 2006 (softcover)

Seffah, A., Gulliksen, J., Desmarais, M.C. (Eds.)
Human-Centred Software Engineering –
Integrating Usability in the Software Development
Lifecycle
Vol. 8, ISBN 978-1-4020-4027-6, 2005

Ruttkay, Z., Pelachaud, C., (Eds.)
From Brows to Trust – Evaluating Embodied
Conservational Agents
Vol. 7, ISBN 978-1-4020-2729-1, 2004

Ardissono, L., Kobsa, A., Maybury, M.T. (Eds.)
Personalized Digital Television – Targeting
Programs to Individual Viewers
Vol. 6, ISBN 978-1-4020-2147-3, 2004

Karat, C.-M., Blom, J.O., Karat, J. (Eds.)
Designing Personalized User Experiences in
eCommerce
Vol. 5, ISBN 978-1-4020-2147-3, 2004

Ivory, M.Y.
Automating Web Site Evaluation – Researchers'
and Practitioners' Perspectives
Vol. 4, ISBN 978-1-4020-1672-1, 2004

Blythe, M.A., Overbeeke, K., Monk, A.F., (et al.)
(Eds.)
Funology – From Usability to Enjoyment
Vol. 3, ISBN 978-1-4020-2966-0, 2004 (softcover)

Blythe, M.A., Overbeeke, K., Monk, A.F., (et al.)
(Eds.)
Funology – From Usability to Enjoyment
Vol. 3, ISBN 978-1-4020-1252-5, 2003

Schreck, J.
Security and Privacy in User Modeling
Vol. 2, ISBN 978-1-4020-1130-6, 2003

Chi, E.H.
A Framework for Visualizing Information
Vol 1, ISBN 978-1-4020-0589-2, 2002

Gustavo Rossi • Oscar Pastor • Daniel Schwabe •
Luis Olsina
Editors

Web Engineering: Modelling and Implementing Web Applications

 Springer

Gustavo Rossi
Technical University of Valencia
Valencia, Spain

Oscar Pastor
Technical University of Valencia
Valencia, Spain

Daniel Schwabe
PUC-Rio
Brazil

Luis Olsina
National University of La Pampa
Argentina

British Library Cataloguing in Publication Data
A catalogue record for this book is available from the British Library

Library of Congress Control Number: 2007935105

Human-Computer Interaction Series ISSN 1571-5035
ISBN: 978-1-84628-922-4   e-ISBN: 978-1-84628-923-1

Printed on acid-free paper

9 8 7 6 5 4 3 2 1

Springer Science+Business Media
springer.com

PREFACE

In this first part of the 21st century, a large portion of the global data infrastructure is built upon World Wide Web technology. This network of data users and providers has become as critical a part of our everyday lives as those networks that provide our electrical power and communications. We are informed, educated, and entertained by Web applications and services. The Web provides us with an international mall where we can shop for every imaginable item.

This infrastructure is held together by a complex interconnection of hardware, software, international standards, aesthetics, and accepted practices. Its intricacy is not unlike that found in the engineering and design of highway systems, buildings, and bridges. To address the growth of Web systems and to ensure their efficiency, reliability, and maintainability, the discipline of Web Engineering was defined. Web Engineering combines traditional project management and software development practices with a process that will evolve just as Web technology evolves into the future via such innovations as the Semantic Web and Web 2.0.

Modeling and Implementing Web Application is a definitive book on all of the crucial elements of Web Engineering by the international researchers and practitioners who are shaping the discipline. There is no other book available at this time that covers Web Engineering so comprehensively. As the field evolves, this book will certainly always be viewed as a fundamental reference. Its completeness illustrates the premise that Web Engineering is an important and critical engineering practice for designing, implementing, and maintaining Web services and applications. The book will provide a valuable resource for Web professionals, researchers, and students at the undergraduate and graduate levels.

Bebo White
Stanford Linear Accelerator Center (SLAC)
Stanford, California
April 2007

CONTENTS

Part III: Quality Evaluation and Experimental Web Engineering

LIST OF CONTRIBUTORS

Peter Barna
Technische Universiteit
Eindhoven, PO Box 513, 5600
MB Eindhoven, The Netherlands
Email: *p.barna@tue.nl*

Hubert Baumeister
Informatik og Matematisk
Modellering, Danmarks Tekniske
Universitet, Lyngby, Denmark
Email: *hub@imm.dtu.dk*

Davide Bolchini
TEC-Lab, Faculty of
Communication Sciences,
University of Lugano, Via G.
Buffi 13 6900 Lugano,
Switzerland
Email: *davide.bolchini@lu.unisi.ch*

Marco Brambilla
Dipartimento di Elettronica e
Informazione, Politecnico di
Milano, P.zza L. da Vinci 32,
20133, Milano, Italy
Email: *mbrambil@elet.polimi.it*

Jeen Broekstra
Technische Universiteit
Eindhoven, PO Box 513, 5600
MB Eindhoven, The Netherlands;
and Aduna, Prinses Julianaplein
14b, 3817 CS Amersfoort,
The Netherlands
Email: *j.broekstra@tue.nl*

Sven Casteleyn
Vrije Universiteit Brussel,
Pleinlaan 2, 1050 Brussels,
Belgium
Email: *Sven.Casteleyn@vub.ac.be*

Sara Comai
Dipartimento di Elettronica e
Informazione, Politecnico di
Milano, Piazza L. da Vinci 32,
20133, Milano, Italy
Email: *sara.comai@polimi.it*

Olga De Troyer
Research Group WISE,
Department of Computer Science,
Vrije Universiteit Brussel,
Pleinlaan 2, 1050 Brussel,
Belgium
Email: *Olga.DeTroyer@vub.ac.be*

Zoltán Fiala
Technische Universität Dresden,
Mommsenstr. 13, D-01062,
Dresden, Germany
Email: *zoltan.fiala@inf.
tu-dresden.de*

Joan Fons
Research Group OO-Method
Department of Information
Systems and Computation,
Valencia University of
Technology, Camí de Vera s/n,
E-46022, Valencia, Spain
Email: *jjfons@dsic.upv.es*

Flavius Frasincar
Erasmus Universiteit Rotterdam,
PO Box 1738, 3000 DR
Rotterdam, The Netherlands
Email: *frasincar@few.eur.nl*

Piero Fraternali
Dipartimento di Elettronica e
Informazione, Politecnico di
Milano, P.zza L. da Vinci 32,
20133, Milano, Italy
Email: *fraterna@elet.polimi.it*

Martin Gaedke
Chemnitz University of
Technology, Faculty of Computer
Science, Distributed and
Self-Organizing Systems Group,
Straße der Nationen 62,
09111 Chemnitz, Germany
Email: *martin.gaedke@informatik.
tu-chemnitz.de*

Franca Garzotto
HOC (Hypermedia Open Centre),
Department of Information and
Electronics, Politecnico di
Milano, Milan, Italy
Email: *garzotto@elet.polimi.it*

Geert-Jan Houben
Technische Universiteit Eindhoven,
PO Box 513, 5600 MB Eindhoven,
The Netherlands; and Vrije
Universiteit Brussel, Pleinlaan 2,
1050 Brussels, Belgium
Email: *Geert-
Jan.Houben@vub.ac.be*

Alexander Knapp
Institut für Informatik, Ludwig-
Maximilians-Universität
München, Munich, Germany
Email: *knapp@pst.ifi.lmu.de*

Nora Koch
Institut fur Informatik,
Ludwig-Maximilians-Universität
München, and F.A.S.T. GmbH,
Munich, Germany
Email: *kochn@pst.ifi.lmu.de*

Maristella Matera
Dipartimento di Elettronica e
Informazione, Politecnico di
Milano, Pizza L. da Vinci 32,
20133, Milano, Italy
Email: *matera@elet.polimi.it*

Johannes Meinecke
Chemnitz University of
Technology, Faculty of Computer
Science, Distributed and
Self-Organizing Systems Group,
Straße der Nationen 62,
09111 Chemnitz, Germany
Email: *johannes.meinecke@informatik
.tu-chemnitz.de*

Emilia Mendes
WETA Research Group,
Computer Science Department,
The University of Auckland,
Private Bag 92019, Auckland,
New Zealand
Email: *emilia@cs.auckland.ac.nz*

Hernán Molina
GIDIS_Web, Engineering School,
Universidad Nacional de La
Pampa, Calle 9 y 110, (6360)
General Pico, LP, Argentina
Email:
hmolina@ing.unlpam.edu.ar

Nathalie Moreno
Dept. Lenguajes y Ciencias de la
Computación, University of
Málaga, Málaga, Spain
Email: *vergara@lcc.uma.es*

San Murugesan
Southern Cross University, Coffs
Harbour NSW 2452, Australia
Email: *san.murugesan@scu.edu.au*

Luis Olsina
GIDIS_Web, Engineering School,
Universidad Nacional de La
Pampa, Calle 9 y 110, (6360)
General Pico, LP, Argentina
Email: *olsinal@ing.unlpam.edu.ar*

Fernanda Papa
GIDIS_Web, Engineering School,
Universidad Nacional de La
Pampa, Calle 9 y 110, (6360)
General Pico, LP, Argentina
Email: *pmfer@ing.unlpam.edu.ar*

Oscar Pastor
Research Group OO-Method,
Department of Information
Systems and Computation,
Valencia University of
Technology, Camí de Vera s/n,
E-46022, Valencia, Spain
Email: *opastor@dsic.upv.es*

Vicente Pelechano
Research Group OO-Method,
Department of Information
Systems and Computation.
Valencia University of
Technology, Camí de Vera s/n,
E-46022, Valencia, Spain
Email: *pele@dsic.upv.es*

Peter Plessers
Research Group WISE, Department
of Computer Science, Vrije
Universiteit Brussel, Pleinlaan 2,
1050 Brussel, Belgium
Email: *Peter.Plessers@vub.ac.be*

José Raúl Romero
Dept. Informática y Análisis
Numérico, University of Córdoba,
Cordoba, Spain
Email: *jrromero@uco.es*

Gustavo Rossi
LIFIA, Facultad de Informatica,
Universidad Nacional de La Plata,
Calle 5° y 115, La Plata,
Argentina and Conicet
Email:
gustavo@lifia.info.unlp.edu.ar

Daniel Schwabe
Departamento de Informática,
PUC-Rio, Rua Marquês de São
Vicente, 225 RDC
CEP 22453-900 Gávea Rio de
Janeiro, Brazil
Email*: dschwabe@inf.puc-rio.br*

Victoria Torres
Research Group OO-Method,
Department of Information
Systems and Computation,
Valencia University of
Technology, Camí de Vera s/n,
E-46022, Valencia, Spain
Email: *vtorres@dsic.upv.es*

Pedro Valderas
Research Group OO-Method,
Department of Information
Systems and Computation,
Valencia University of
Technology, Camí de Vera s/n,
E-46022, Valencia, Spain
Email: *pvalderas@dsic.upv.es*

Antonio Vallecillo
Dept. Lenguajes y Ciencias de la
Computación, University of
Málaga, Málaga, Spain
Email: *av@lcc.uma.es*

Kees van der Sluijs
Technische Universiteit
Eindhoven, PO Box 513, 5600
MB Eindhoven, The Netherlands
Email: *k.a.m.sluijs@tue.nl*

Gefei Zhang
Institut für Informatik,
Ludwig-Maximilians-Universität
München, Munich, Germany
Email: *zhangg@pst.ifi.lmu.de*

PART I

WEB ENGINEERING AND WEB APPLICATIONS DEVELOPMENT

Chapter 1

INTRODUCTION

Gustavo Rossi[1], Daniel Schwabe[2], Luis Olsina[3], Oscar Pastor[4]

[1]*LIFIA, Facultad de Informatica, Universidad Nacional de La Plata (also at CONICET) Argentina,* `gustavo@lifia.info.unlp.edu.ar`

[2]*Departamento de Informática, PUC-Rio, Rio de Janeiro, Brazil,* `dschwabe@inf.puc-rio.br`

[3]*GIDIS_Web, Engineering School, Universidad Nacional de La Pampa, Calle 9 y 110, (6360) General Pico, LP, Argentina,* `olsinal@ing.unlpam.edu.ar`

[4]*DSIC, Valencia University of Technology, Valencia, Spain,* `opastor@dsic.upv.es`

This book presents the major Web application design methods currently being developed and used in both academia and industry. The book is the main result of the IWWOST (International Workshop on Web-Oriented Software Technology) series, celebrated under the auspices of the WEST project, sponsored by CYTED (a Spanish organization supporting research and development in Ibero-America).

Since 2001, IWWOST has been an international forum for discussing state of-the-art modeling approaches, methods, and technologies for Web applications. The first workshop was held in Valencia, Spain, in 2001; the second in Malaga, Spain, together with the European Conference on Object-Oriented Programming (ECOOP) in 2002; the third in Oviedo, Spain; and the fourth in Munich, Germany [both co-located with the International Conference on Web Engineering (ICWE) in 2003 and 2004, respectively]. The fifth was organized in Porto, Portugal, in the context of the International Conference on Advanced Information Systems Engineering-CAiSE 2005. Finally, in 2007 IWWOST went back to ICWE, in Como, Italy.

At the same time, many of the authors of this book got involved in the Web Engineering Network of Excellence (WEE-NET), a project funded by the European Commission under the ALFA program, which provided invaluable support for research and students meetings following the spirit of IWWOST. The project itself was another source of inspiration for the book's contents.

These workshops and meetings were historically organized in order to stimulate a discussion and an exchange of ideas and experiences. They were conceived as a place for methodologists, designers, and developers to meet and exchange their experiences in the process of building complex Web applications. Usually, all participants received a problem statement of a typical, nontrivial, Web application and were asked to fully design and, if possible, implement this application using their proposed methods.

In the workshop each group presented its solution, which was compared with other solutions and discussed among all participants. During these discussions a large number of issues that must be addressed by design methods were raised. In this way, IWWOST attendees could compare their own approaches with other colleagues', and they could discuss strengths and weaknesses of each approach, following a very fruitful theoretical and practical approach.

In the same spirit, we have put this idea into this book, presenting a common problem, selecting the most widely known methods dealing with Web Engineering issues, and asking the authors to work on this same problem from their different points of view, each supported by their own methods or design approaches.

With this strategy in mind, our objective is to provide a practical book where both students and practitioners can find a precise view on how the different approaches work and provide their corresponding solutions. We do not intend to provide new cutting-edge technical solutions but rather mature, consolidated approaches to develop complex applications.

To make the book a complete handbook on Web Engineering issues and techniques, we have included a set of chapters that address different aspects of the engineering endeavor.

The book is divided into three parts and is organized as follows. The first part contains two chapters in addition to this one: Chapter 2 by San Murugesan describes the evolution of the Web and introduces the discipline of Web Engineering. Chapter 3 by Martin Gaedke and Johannes Meinecke discusses the Web as a platform for application development, focusing in particular on distributed applications.

Part II focuses on development approaches, emphasizing design methods: Chapter 4 by Gustavo Rossi, Daniel Schwabe, Luis Olsina, and Oscar Pastor presents the most important issues Web design methods must consider and introduces the common problem to be solved. Chapter 5 by Joan Fons, Vicente Pelechano, Oscar Pastor, Pedro Valderas and Victoria Torres presents the Object-Oriented Web Solutions Approach (OOWS). Chapter 6 by Gustavo Rossi and Daniel Schwabe focuses on the use of the Object-Oriented Hypermedia Design Model (OOHDM). Chapter 7 by Nora Koch, Alexander Knapp, Gefei Zhang and Hubert Baumeister discusses the

UML-based Web Engineering approach (UWE). Chapter 8 by Davide Bolchini and Franca Garzotto presents the Interactive Dialogue Model (IDM) approach. Chapter 9 by Marco Brambilla, Sara Comai, Piero Fraternali, and Maristella Matera presents WebML, the Web Modeling Language. Chapter 10 by Geert-Jan Houben, Kees van der Sluijs, Peter Barna, Jeen Broekstra, Sven Casteleyn, Zoltán Fiala, and Flavius Frasincar presents a solution to the problem using Hera. Chapter 11 by Olga De Troyer, Sven Casteleyn, and Peter Plessers introduces the Web Semantic Design Method (WSDM) Finally in Chapter 12, Nathalie Moreno, José Raúl Romero, and Antonio Vallecillo discuss the concept of model-driven Web Engineering.

Part III deals with quality evaluation and experimental Web Engineering and the book's conclusions. It contains three chapters: Chapter 13 by Luis Olsina, Fernanda Papa, and Hernán Molina analyzes the problem of measurement and evaluation of Web software. Chapter 14 by Emilia Mendes discusses empirical methods for Web Engineering. Finally, in Chapter 15, Oscar Pastor, Gustavo Rossi, Luis Olsina, and Daniel Schwabe summarize the book and present some conclusions.

We hope you will enjoy the reading of this book as much as we enjoyed the process of writing and editing it.

Chapter 2

WEB APPLICATION DEVELOPMENT: CHALLENGES AND THE ROLE OF WEB ENGINEERING

San Murugesan
University of Western Sydney, Sydney, Australia, `san1@internode.on.net`

2.1 INTRODUCTION

The World Wide Web, more commonly known as the Web, is increasingly pervading every aspect of our lives. In the 15 years since the Web came into existence, our lives and work have been inexorably changed. It has dramatically influenced us in several ways and has matured to become a very attractive and dominant platform for deploying business and social applications and organizational information systems. It has also become a universal user interface to business applications, information systems, databases, and legacy systems. It supports document and workflow management, cooperative work, and distributed knowledge and media (photo, audio, and video) sharing.

The growth of the Web has been exponential. A recent estimate put the size of the public Web at 40 billion pages, and the size of the "deep Web"—where the pages are assembled on the fly in response to users' request—between 400 and 750 billion pages. The interaction between a Web system and its back-end information systems, as well as with other Web systems, has become tighter and complex. Many organizations have extended, and still continue to extend, the scope and functionalities of their Web-based applications and are also beginning to provide mobile and wireless access to them. As a result, Web-based systems and applications now offer an array of content and functionality to a huge population of users and serve many different purposes. The Web has become a mainstay, and it is perhaps appropriate to say that our civilization "runs" on the Web as individuals, organizations, and nations rely on a multitude of Web-based systems.

The Web, and the Internet that supports it, has become one of the most important and most influential developments not only in computing history but in the history of mankind. For instance, Web sites such as google.com, yahoo.com, myspace.com, wikipedia.org, amazon.com, ebay.com, youtube.com, napster.com, blogger.com, and saloon.com are considered as the top 10 Web sites (in no particular order) that changed the world (Naughton, 2006). Some of these sites have over 100 million users (myspace.com, ebay.com, yahoo.com), about 1 billion visits a day (wikipedia.org), and over 1 billion searches per day (google.com).

Users expect Web applications to be more usable, more reliable, and more secure, personalized, and context-aware. As our dependence and reliance on Web-based applications have increased dramatically over the years, performance, reliability, quality, maintainability, and scalability of Web applications have become paramount importance. And most Web-based systems are tightly integrated with other, traditional information systems such as databases and transaction processing systems. Some of the newer applications are also linked with other Web applications/services that facilitate information exchange. As a result, the design, development, deployment, and maintenance of Web-based applications have become inherently complex and challenging. The complexity of Web-based systems is, however, not apparent, as the Web interface presents an illusion of simplicity by hiding the complexity.

But most Web developers don't recognize and take into consideration many multifaceted, unique requirements of Web applications. They also fail to recognize that characteristics and requirements of Web-based systems significantly differ from traditional software, and so does their development. They need to recognize these differences and take appropriate measures to fulfill the unique requirements of Web applications.

But many developers and their clients still continue to view Web development as just simple Web page creation using HTML or Web development software such as *Front Page* and *Dreamweaver*, embodying few images and hyperlinking documents and Web pages, or as Internet/Web programming (scripting). They overlook system-level requirements and key design considerations and don't make use of Web design and development methodologies and processes. Further, they also mistakenly carry out Web systems' development in the same manner as software development. Many Web development projects are carried out in ad hoc manner and fail to adopt sound design methodologies, resulting in poor design of Web systems. As a consequence, they fail to successfully and effectively develop Web-based systems that are complex and/or demand high performance.

Of course, there is more to Web application development than visual design and user interface. It involves planning, selection of an appropriate Web architecture, system design, page design, coding, content creation and its maintenance, testing, quality assurance, and performance evaluation. It also involves continual update and maintenance of the Web system as the requirements change, new functionalities are introduced, and usage grow, as well as post-launch operational review of the system.

To successfully build complex Web-based systems and applications, both large and small, Web developers need to adopt a disciplined development process and sound design methodologies and use better development tools.

The discipline of Web Engineering advocates a holistic, disciplined approach to successful Web development, taking into account the unique characteristics and requirements of Web-based systems. Web Engineering "uses scientific, engineering, and management principles and systematic approaches to successfully develop, deploy, and maintain high-quality Web systems and applications" (Murugesan et al., 1999). The essence of Web Engineering is to successfully manage the diversity and complexity of Web application development and, hence, avoid potential failures that could have serious implications.

Web Engineering is receiving greater interest and significance as Web-based systems become mainstream and we increasingly rely on them. While Web Engineering shares with software engineering some common objectives, goals, and general principles and, where appropriate, adopts soft engineering techniques, it is aimed at addressing characteristics and requirements that are unique to Web applications.

This book comprehensively deals with a key aspect of Web Engineering — design of Web systems and applications. It describes various Web design methodologies that developers could use, such as OOHDM and the OO method, and illustrates them using one common example.

This chapter outlines the role of Web Engineering in the design and development of Web applications. It traces the evolution of Web applications and discusses key challenges in developing Web applications as well as some of the key aspects that differentiate development of Web applications from other types of software or computer applications. It also examines the problems and limitations of current Web development practices and their implications and provides an overview of Web Engineering. It then briefly describes key elements of Web Engineering processes and discusses the role of Web design in successful Web application development.

2.2 EVOLUTION OF THE WEB
AND WEB APPLICATIONS

The Web has evolved beyond anyone's imagination within a short span of 15 years, since Tim Berners-Lee conceived and publicized, on August 6, 1991, a system for turning the Internet into a publishing medium for sharing and dissemination of scientific data and information, which he called the "World Wide Web." It has become indispensable and essential to many people and organizations around the world.

The evolution of the Web has brought together some disparate disciplines such as media, information science, and information and communication technology, facilitating the easy creation, maintenance, sharing, and use of different types of information from anywhere, any time, and using a variety of devices such as desktop and notebook computers, pocket PCs, personal digital assistants (PDAs), and mobile phones.

The evolution of the Web could be traced and discussed along a few different dimensions and from a few different perspectives: the growth (number) of Web sites and Web pages; the number of Web users; the number of Web visits; the functionality and interactivity that Web applications offer; the technologies used for the creation of Web applications; the social and business impact of the Web; or a combination of these.

While the scope of this chapter is not to comprehensively discuss the evolution, in the context of Web design, it is helpful to classify Web systems and applications based on their key features and technology used for their creation as follows (see Figure 2.1):

1. the Shallow Web (Static Web)
2. the Deep Web (Dynamic Web)
3. the Wisdom Web (Web 2.0)
4. the Mobile Web
5. the Semantic Web

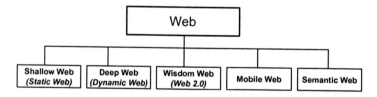

Figure 2.1. Classification of the Web.

2.2.1 Web 1.0

The Shallow Web, also known as the Static Web, is primarily a collection of static HTML Web pages providing information about products or services offered. To start with, most Web sites were just a collection of static Web pages. After a while, the Web became dynamic, delivering Web pages created on the fly. The ability to create Web pages from the content stored on databases enabled Web developers to provide customized information to visitors. These sites are known as the Deep Web, or the Dynamic Web. Though a visitor to such Web sites gets information tuned to his or her requirements, these sites provide primarily one-way interaction and limited user interactivity. The users have no role in content generation and no means to access content without visiting the sites concerned. The Shallow Web sites and Deep Web sites, which have no or very little user interaction, are now generally termed as Web 1.0.

2.2.2 Web 2.0: The New Face of the Web

In the last few years a new class of Web applications, known as Web 2.0 (or Service-Oriented Applications), has emerged. These applications let people collaborate and share information online in seemingly new ways—examples include social networking sites such as myspace.com, media sharing sites such as youtube.com, and collaborative authoring sites such as wikipedia.

The new- (second-) generation Web, also known as the *Wisdom Web* (Levy and Stone, 2006), the *People-Centric Web*, and the *Read/Write Web*, offers smart user interfaces and built-in facilities for users to generate and edit content presented on the Web and thereby enrich the content base. Besides leveraging the users' potential in generating content, Web 2.0 applications provide facilities to keep the content under the user's own categories (tagging feature) and access it easily (Web feed tool). These new breeds of Web applications are also able to integrate multiple services under a rich user interface.

With the incorporation of new Web technologies such as AJAX (Asynchronous JavaScript and XML), Ruby, blog, wiki, social bookmarking, and tagging, the Web is fast becoming more dynamic and highly interactive, where users can not only pick content from a site but can also contribute to it. The Web feed technology allows users to keep up with a site's latest content without having to visit it. Another feature of the new Web is the proliferation of Web sites with APIs (application programming interfaces). An API from a Web service facilitates Web developers in collecting data from the service and creating new online applications based on these data.

The Web 2.0 is a collection of technologies, business strategies, and social trends. The Web 2.0 is a highly interactive, dynamic application platform than its predecessor, Web 1.0, for fielding new kinds of applications. Recently, a wide array of Web 2.0 applications has been launched (for a list of these applications, refer to www.listible.com/list/complete-list-of-web-2-0-products-and-services; www.econsultant. com/web2/index.html; www. koolweb2.com).

For further information on Web 2.0, see Murugesan (2007a, b), O'Reilly (2005), and articles available at en.wikipedia.org/wiki/Web_2.0, www. whatsweb20.com, and www.readwriteweb. O'Reilly (2006) also defines four levels of Web 2.0 features.

2.2.3 Mobile Web

Advances in mobile computing and wireless communications and widespread worldwide adoption of mobile devices, such as smart mobile phones, PDAs, and Pocket PCs, are enabling a growing number of users to access the Web using handheld devices.

Mobile phones may soon challenge personal computers as the dominant platform for accessing the Web/Internet. According to a survey by Ipsos (2006), 28% of mobile phone owners worldwide browsed the Internet on a wireless handset in 2005, up from 25% in 2004. Almost all wireless device activities—information access and search, mobile commerce (i.e., purchasing a product or service via a mobile device), conducting financial transactions, mobile ticketing, etc.—experienced growth in 2005. Accessing the Internet on a wireless handheld device is becoming a common everyday occurrence for many people in some advanced and developing countries. This will become increasingly prevalent as high-end (smart) mobile phones and Pocket PCs become affordable, a higher number of people start using these more capable handheld devices, and more Web applications migrate to the wireless/mobile Web. Considering the adoption of mobile Web and its huge potential, the World Wide Web Consortium has established a new initiate called the Mobile Web.

Mobile Web applications could offer some additional features compared to traditional desktop Web applications such as location-aware services, context-aware capabilities, and personalization. Mobile Web applications have, however, some unique requirements and pose additional challenges, as outlined later in this chapter.

2.2.4 The Semantic Web

In current Web applications, information is presented in natural language, which humans can process easily. But computers can't manipulate natural language information on the Web meaningfully. The Semantic Web is aimed at overcoming this barrier.

The Semantic Web is an extension of the current Web in which information is given a well-defined meaning, better enabling computers and people to work in cooperation (Berners-Lee et al. 2001). It intends to create a universal medium for information exchange by putting documents with computer-processable meaning (semantics) on the Web. Adding semantics radically changes the nature of the Web—from a place where information is merely displayed to one where it is interpreted, exchanged, and processed. Associating meaning with content or establishing a layer of machine-understandable data enables a higher degree of automation and more intelligent applications and also facilitates interoperable services.

The ultimate goal of the Semantic Web is to support machine-facilitated global information exchange in a scalable, adaptable, extensible manner, so that information on the Web can be used for more effective discovery, automation, integration, and reuse across various applications. The three key ingredients that constitute the Semantic Web and help achieve its goals are semantic markup, ontology, and intelligent software agents. For further information on the Semantic Web, refer to Antoniou and Harmelen (2004), Berners-Lee (2001), and Shadbolt (2006).

2.2.5 Rich Internet Applications

Rich Internet applications (RIA) are Web-based applications that run in a Web browser and do not require software installation, but still have the features and functionality of traditional desktop applications. The term "RIA" was introduced in a Macromedia whitepaper in March 2002. RIA represents the evolution of the browser from a static request-response interface to a dynamic, asynchronous interface. Broadband proliferation, consumer demand, and enabling technologies, including the Web 2.0, are driving the proliferation of RIAs. RIAs promise a richer user experience and benefits—interactivity and usability that are lacking in many current applications. Some prime examples of RIA frameworks are Adobe's Flex and AJAX, and examples of RIA include Google's Earth, Mail, and Finance applications.

Enterprises are embracing the promises of RIAs by applying them to user tasks that demand interactivity, responsiveness, and richness. Predominant techniques such as HTML, forms, and CGI are being replaced by other programmer- or user-friendly approaches such as AJAX and Web services.

Building a Web application using fancy technology, however, doesn't ensure a better user experience. To add real value, developers must address users' real needs and implement structured testing techniques to understand and validate the appropriate use and design of RIAs.

2.3 UNIQUE ASPECTS OF WEB APPLICATIONS

The Web is different. Hence, a good understanding of the characteristics and demands placed on Web applications is essential for designing better Web systems and applications.

Web applications have certain unique intrinsic characteristics that make Web development different and perhaps more challenging compared to traditional software development. Web applications' operational environment and their development approach and the faster pace in which these applications are developed and deployed differentiate Web applications from those of traditional software. Further, greater emphasis is placed on the security of Web applications, which are more susceptible to security breaches than traditional computer applications. Key characteristics of Web applications are (Murugesan and Ginige, 2005)

- Most Web applications are evolutionary in their nature, requiring (frequent) changes of content, functionality, structure, navigation, presentation, or implementation. They particularly evolve in terms of their requirements and functionality (instability of requirements), especially after the system is put into use. In most Web applications, frequency and degree of change are much higher than in traditional software applications, and in many applications it is not possible to specify fully their entire requirements at the beginning. The frequency and degree of change of information content can be quite high. Thus, successfully managing the evolution, change, and newer requirements of Web applications is a major technical, organizational, and management challenge—more demanding than traditional software development.
- Web applications are meant to be used by a vast, diverse, remote community of users who have different requirements, expectations, and skill sets. Therefore, the user interface and usability features have to meet the needs of a diverse, anonymous user community. Furthermore, the number of users accessing a Web application at any time is unpredictable and could vary quite considerably, creating performance problems—there could be a "flash crowd" triggered by major events or promotions.
- Web-based applications demand presentation of a variety of content— text, graphics, images, audio, and/or video—and the content may also integrated with procedural processing. Hence, their development

includes the creation and management of the content and their presentation in an attractive manner, as well as a provision for subsequent content management (changes) on a continual basis after the initial development and deployment.

- Web-based systems, in general, demand good aesthetic appeal—"look and feel"—and easy navigation.
- Web applications, especially those meant for a global audience, need to adhere to many different social and cultural sentiments and national standards—including multiple languages and different systems of units.
- Security and privacy needs of Web-based systems are in general more demanding than those of traditional software. Hence, there is a greater demand on the security of Web applications.
- Web applications need to cope with a variety of display devices and formats and support hardware, software, and networks with vastly varying access speeds.
- Ramifications of failure or dissatisfaction of users of Web-based applications can be much worse than conventional IT systems. Also, Web applications could fail for many different reasons.
- Web applications' development timeframes are shorter, and this significantly influences the design and development methodology and process, if any, that are adopted for their development.
- Proliferation of new Web technologies and standards and competitive pressure to use them bring its own advantages and also additional challenges to development and maintenance of Web applications.
- The evolving nature of Web applications necessitates an incremental developmental process.

For a detailed and comprehensive discussion on differences between Web development and software development along 12 dimensions, see Mendes et al. (2006).

2.4 WEB SYSTEM DEVELOPMENT: CHALLENGES

Web system design and development is a complex and a challenging activity, as it needs to consider many different aspects and requirements, some of which may have conflicting needs (Cloyd, 2001; Ivory and Hearst, 2002; Siegel, 2003).

Scalability refers to how well a system copes with the new requirements and features, increases in content, increases in usage and the number of users, and higher security needs. Developing Web applications that scale well is a challenge. As Web sites grow and new functionalities are added, failures (reliability problems), usability problems, and security breaches could creep in. Today's Web-savvy consumers don't tolerate failures or slow responses.

Any system slowdown, failure, or security breach might result in loss of its customers—probably permanently. As Web applications are becoming mission-critical, there is a greater demand for their improved reliability, performance, and security.

On the Web there is virtually no control over visitor volumes and when and how visitors access a Web system. This makes developing Web applications that exhibit satisfactory performance even under a sudden surge in the number of users a nebulous and challenging task and calls for capacity planning.

Meeting the diverse expectations and needs of many different users with varying skills is hard. When users find a site unfriendly, confusing, or hard or that presents too much information or they are unable to find the information they need, they will leave that site feeling frustrated. The features that determine Web usability are (Becker and Berkemeyer, 2002) design layout, design consistency, accessibility, information content, navigation, personalization, performance, security, reliability, and design standards (naming conventions, formatting, and page organization). User feedback reveals features such as search functionality, consistent navigation structure throughout, site maps, and answers to frequently asked questions (FAQ) aid most sites' usability.

The need to making the majority of Web sites universally accessible—accessible by both the able and disabled users—places additional development challenges. However, very little has been done in practice to aid disabled Web users, such as the visually impaired (those who are blind or color blind), and there is a growing number of retired surfers who seek design features such as color contrasts, text-to-speech, and resizable text. Though there have been standards and technologies to support disabled Web users, their adoption is slow. There have been lawsuits against enterprises and Web developers for not providing Web access to the visually impaired. Several countries have legal requirements to make most public Web sites accessible to the visually impaired. Web developers need to meet the legal requirements in terms of Web accessibility.

Localization of Web applications is the process of adapting Web pages/applications (often written in English and targeted for users in a particular country) for use in other countries, considering their culture, standards, regulations, and technological conditions. It is more than just language translation and Web applications that need to be specifically designed to accomplish this multifaceted requirement.

Terms like scalability, reliability, availability, maintainability, usability, and security are used to describe how well the system meets current and future needs and service-level expectations. These *ilities* characterize (Williams, 2000) a Web system's architectural qualities. In the face of increasingly complex systems, these system qualities are often more daunting to understand and to incorporate.

Web systems should be up and running 24 hours a day, 7 days a week, and each day of the year—24/7/365. Furthermore, Web applications should function properly when accessed from diverse browsers. This necessitates that Web sites must adopt their presentation and code to work with all major browsers and client computers.

Design and development of Web applications for mobile and device-independent operations is very complex and challenging, as it needs to address many additional aspects compared to traditional Web applications. Testing and validation of Web applications for access by mobile devices is a challenge, as there are many types of devices with varying shapes and sizes. We need to make sure that applications work as intended on many different makes and models of mobile devices and evaluate their usability. Design guidelines and usability methods that work for desktop systems do not necessarily work for mobile systems. New approaches might be required to test and validate mobile Web applications. For a detailed discussion on the challenges of mobile Web application development, see Murugesan and Venkatakrishnan (2005).

Thus, the challenge is to design and develop sustainable Web systems for better

- usability, interface design, and navigation
- comprehension
- performance (responsiveness)
- security and integrity
- evolution, growth, and maintainability
- testability
- mobility

A Web-based system also has to satisfy many different stakeholders besides the diverse range of the system's users: persons who maintain the system, the organization that needs the system, and also those who fund the system development. These may pose some additional challenges to Web-based system design and development.

2.4.1 Web System Complexity

Complexity is an omnipresent phenomenon in many Web systems. A Web application fits the general characteristics of a complex system—consists of a large number of heterogeneous, highly interacting components, interactions among the components result in nonlinear behavior, and the systems often evolve. Many factors contribute to the complexity of Web systems, as shown in Figure 2.2.

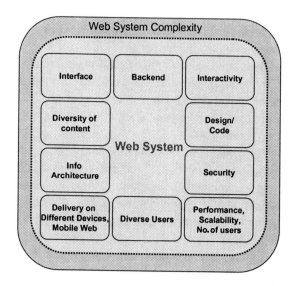

Figure 2.2. Landscape of Web systems.

Web applications become more complex as they deal not only with technological issues but also with organizational issues largely beyond a Web project team's control. Developers need to understand the dimensions of Web project complexity and how they affect project outcome. Complexity could be addressed by taking a holistic, engineering approach. Web developers need to simplify the system, meeting the given requirements rather than increasing its complexity.

2.5 STATE OF PRACTICE OF WEB DEVELOPMENT: CONCERNS

Web development has a very short history, compared to software development, information system development, or other computer application development. But within a period of a few years, a large number of Web systems and applications have been developed and put into widespread use. The complexity of Web applications has also grown significantly—from information dissemination [consisting of simple text and images to image maps, forms, common gateway interface (CGI), applets, scripts, and style sheets] to online transactions, enterprise-wide planning and scheduling systems, Web-based collaborative work environments, and now multilingual Web sites, Web services, and mobile Web applications.

Nevertheless, many pursue Web development primarily as an authoring work (content/page creation and presentation) rather than an application development requiring planning, system/architecture design, coding, Web page creation, navigation design, and testing and evaluation. They often get carried away by the myth that Web development primarily deals with "media manipulation and presentation". Sure, Web development has an important artistic side, but Web developers need to follow a disciplined and systematic process during the entire life cycle of a Web project, rather than simply "hacking" together a few Web pages.

Several attributes of quality Web-based systems such as usability, navigation, accessibility, scalability, maintainability, compatibility and interoperability, security, and reliability are not given the due consideration they deserve during development. Many Web applications also fail to address cultural and regional considerations and privacy, moral, and legal obligations and requirements. Most Web systems also lack proper testing and evaluation and design documentation.

Many developers, while designing and developing a Web application, fail to acknowledge that Web systems' requirements change and evolve, and hence don't take this into consideration while developing Web systems. Web-based systems development is not a one-off event as perceived and practiced by many; it is a process with an iterative life cycle.

Another problem is that most Web application development activities heavily rely on the knowledge and experience of individual (or a small group of) developers and their individual development practices rather than standard practices.

Poorly developed Web-based applications have a high probability of low performance and/or failure. In enterprise applications, a system failure can propagate broad-based problems across many functions, causing a major Web disaster. Bad design, shabby development, poor performance, and/or poor content management for Web-based applications could have serious implications.

Thus, there are concerns about the manner in which complex Web-based systems are created as well as the level of performance, quality, and integrity of these systems.

The primary causes of these failures are a lack of vision, short-sighted goals, a flawed design and development process, and poor management of development efforts—not technology (Ginige and Murugesan, 2001a). The way we address these concerns is key to successful deployment and maintenance of Web applications.

2.6 WEB FAILURES

Web failure is defined as the inability of a Web application to correctly function or deliver information or documents required by the users. While the success of a Web application hinges on whether or not it is usable and serves the intended purpose, Web failures could arise due to many different reasons. They include

- not meeting functionality and the users' needs
- poor usability
- poor performance
- security breaches
- not functioning properly, including errors and crashes
- poor maintainability
- poor scalability
- schedule and cost over-runs
- abandoned projects—poor project management

The Web system/application failures could also be caused by failure of a supporting infrastructure such as host hardware or software, network, and browser, or Web software/application failure such as information source failure or individual page failures.

There is a need for a better way of doing things, a Web design and development methodology—an established way of delivering projects that meet the client's needs on time and on budget. Performance problems could be caused by any number of things: a poorly designed Web architecture, poorly designed Web software or Web page, an underpowered CPU, limited network bandwidth, or a combination of several factors. A higher load can easily overwhelm a system's resources and cause performance problems. For instance, in September 2006, when news of the "crocodile hunter" Steve Irwin's sudden and bizarre death broke, too many people logged on to news Web sites, these sites showed signs of strain, and some, including the CNN and Australian ABC Web sites, had to switch to a "lite" mode, in which bandwidth-hungry elements on the home page were removed in order to cope with the surge in usage. However, a higher volume is not always required to cause performance problems. Poorly designed software that does not handle resource allocation and contention properly can easily cause deadlocks that eventually lead to performance problems even at a normal load.

Although performance problems can have many causes, the outcome is always the same—slow response. To resolve such problems, a holistic approach—also known as an all-out systems approach—is needed where the application software, the network, and the underlying computing hardware are all considered and evaluated.

Web project failures are often attributed to projects running overtime, budgets blowing up, and applications not meeting the intended purpose and failing to meet the business needs. There could be many reasons for failure, including developers interpreting a client's requirements differently from the client's own interpretation, underestimation of work required to do the project, poor project management, poor staffing, ad hoc development strategy, underdeveloped or non-existent design paradigm, and poor or no code reuse within a project or between projects.

Many Web sites have suffered site crashes, performance failures, security breaches, and outages—resulting in irate customers, lost revenue, devalued stocks, a tarnished reputation (bad publicity, lack of customer confidence), permanent loss of customers, and lawsuits (Williams, 2000). Stock prices have become inextricably linked to the reliability of a company's e-commerce site. There are also legal implications when Web applications go bad; refer to Verdon (2006) for details.

2.7 WEB ENGINEERING

Ad hoc methods are no longer capable of delivering high-quality complex Web applications, which are becoming more and more important and mission-critical. Complex interdependencies of Web systems challenge our ability to comprehend, create, maintain, and control these systems. Also, as failure of a Web application could be costly, there is a growing demand for methodologies, models, and tools that can improve Web design and the Web quality and reliability. There is also a pressing need for better methodologies, techniques, and tools for testing Web applications.

In the absence of a disciplined approach to Web-based systems development, we will find sooner or later that:

- Web-based applications are not delivering required functionality and desired performance and quality.
- The Web application development process becomes increasingly complex and difficult to manage and also expensive and grossly behind schedule.

Can adding engineering rigor to Web development address the challenges facing developers in developing and deploying complex Web systems and applications? We and many other researchers and practitioners believe it will, and practical experience and evidence support this claim.

Web Engineering seeks to address the problem of Web application development by building a foundation for the systematic creation of Web-based systems. This foundation will consist of a body of theoretical and empirical knowledge for development, deployment, and support of continual evolution of Web applications.

Web Engineering is the application of scientific, engineering, and management principles and disciplined and systematic approaches to the successful development, deployment, and maintenance of Web-based systems and applications (Murugesan et al., 1999; Kappel et al., 2006). It is a systematic way of managing the complexity and diversity of Web applications. It is also concerned with the development and organization of new knowledge about Web application development and application of that knowledge to develop Web applications and to address new requirements and challenges facing Web developers.

A Web-based system is a *living* system—it grows, evolves, and changes. An appropriate infrastructure is necessary to support the growth of a Web-based system in a flexible and controlled manner. Web Engineering helps to create an infrastructure that will allow evolution and maintenance of a Web system and also support creativity.

Web Engineering could also be viewed as a holistic and proactive approach to the development of complex Web-based systems. In a holistic approach, all aspects of the development processes, functional requirements, the application's operational environment, the supporting IT and other infrastructure, and the linkages and interactions among them are identified, analyzed, prioritized, implemented, and evaluated. It is important for developers to understand "the wider context in which a Web-based system or application will be used, and design an architecture that will support the development, operation and maintenance as well as evolution of the Web application in that context, addressing the key issues and considerations" (Murugesan and Ginige, 2005).

Web development is a process, not simply a one-time event. Thus, Web Engineering deals with all aspects of Web-based systems development, starting from conception and development to implementation, performance evaluation, and continual maintenance. Web Engineering, therefore, covers a range of areas: requirements elicitation and analysis; Web system modeling; Web architecture; Web system design; Web page design; scripting/coding; interface with databases, ERP systems, and other Web-based systems; Web quality; Web usability; Web security; Web system performance evaluation; Web testing; Web development methodologies; Web development process; Web metrics; and Web project management.

"Contrary to the perception of some professionals, Web Engineering is not a clone of software engineering although both involve programming and software development" (Ginige and Murugesan, 2001a). While Web Engineering uses software engineering principles, it encompasses new approaches, methodologies, tools and techniques, and guidelines to meet the unique requirements of Web-based systems. In many respects, development of Web-based systems is much more than traditional software development. As highlighted in previous sections, there are subtle differences in the nature and life cycle of Web-based systems and traditional software systems and the way in which they are developed and maintained.

The nature and characteristics of Web-based applications and their development demand Web Engineering to be multidisciplinary, encompassing inputs from diverse areas such as systems analysis and design, software engineering, hypermedia/hypertext engineering, requirements engineering, human-computer interaction, user interface, information engineering, information indexing and retrieval, testing, modeling and simulation, project management, and graphic design and presentation (Deshpande et al., 2002).

A well-engineered Web system (Murugesan and Ginige, 2005)

- is functionally complete and correct
- is usable
- is robust and reliable
- is maintainable
- is secure
- performs reasonably even under flash and peak loads
- is scalable
- is portable, where required (perform across different common platforms), compatible with multiple browsers
- is reusable
- is interoperable with other systems
- has universal accessibility (access by people with different kinds of disabilities)
- is well-documented

Since its origin and promotion as a new discipline in 1998, Web Engineering has been receiving growing interest among researchers, developers, academics, and clients.

2.8 WEB DEVELOPMENT

Development of high-quality Web applications is not an accident; it calls for a systematic plan for development and implementation as well as architectural design, testing, and evaluation, incorporation of security safeguards, and adoption of sound implementation polices. The design and analysis of Web systems, however, presents a significant challenge: Systems need to be understood at many different levels of abstraction and examined from many different perspectives. Web systems modeling and architecture play an important role in the development of today's complex Web systems.

2.8.1 Web Architecture

Following the IEEE Standard 1471-2000 definition of software architecture, Web architecture may be defined as "the fundamental organization of a system, embodied in its components, their relationships to each other and the environment, and the principles governing its design and evolution." It uses abstractions and models to simplify and communicate complex structures.

Architecture presents a framework, describes the structure, and makes the system understandable. It helps in making the transition from analysis to implementation (Eichinger, 2006). Architecture of some high-volume Web sites is presented by Dantzing (2002).

In Web system architecture design, various components of the system and how they are linked are decided.

Web subsystem architecture is composed of the following:

- an overall system architecture that describes how the network and the various servers such as Web servers, application servers, and database servers interact
- an application architecture that depicts various information modules and the functions available
- a software architecture that identifies various software and database modules required to implement the application architecture

Several factors influence the choice of a Web architecture, including the following:

- functional requirements
- quality, security, and performance considerations
- technical aspects
- experience

2.8.2 Web Design

Design plays an important role in the development of high-performance, high-quality Web applications. Web design has to cater to many different requirements, some of which might pose conflicting demands:

- design for usability—interface design, navigation
- design for comprehension
- design for performance—responsiveness
- design for security and integrity
- design for evolution, growth, and maintainability
- design for testability

- design for universal accessibility
- design for localization
- graphics and multimedia design
- Web page design

Design methodologies and models described later in this book are aimed at helping developers tackle the complexity of Web application development and achieve the above multifaceted goals.

2.8.3 Web Security

As more and more applications—everything from email and buying and selling to banking and business-to-business interactions and their associated data—are now running on the Web, hackers and criminals are increasingly targeting Web applications. Hence, Web security is under the spotlight. Information is one of the very important assets in almost all organizations. Once the internal networks of those organizations are connected to the Internet and Web, it becomes a potential target for cyber attacks. The number of Web-based vulnerabilities keeps increasing; in the first half of 2005, for the first time, reported Web-based vulnerabilities (61% of vulnerabilities) outpaced those of all other platforms (www.symantec.com/enterprise/threat report).

Data and information have to be protected from unauthorized access as well as from malicious corruption. A recent article (Meier, 2006) looks at the Web from an empirical perspective and, using a direct "do's and don'ts" approach, identifies security-specific activities that developers can integrate throughout the Web development life cycle. It also presents basic concepts to focus on while developing Web applications.

Programming flaws top the list of Web application security problems (Mimoso, 2003). No matter how good your process or design is, bugs will slip into the code—it's up to quality assurance (QA) and testing to weed them out. For a good survey of Web application security assessment tools, see Curphey and Araujo (2006).

A wide range of legal and regulatory issues surrounds Web development, including the need to protect sensitive business and consumer information. A good set of security policies and practices will limit Web security breaches and unintended exposure of information. A good review of several real-world security incidents, of how the law and regulations view such incidents, and how the right kind of policies and best practices can provide legal coverage for a company if (or when?) someone breaches its Web application is provided by Verdon (2006). For a discussion on who is liable for bugs and security flaws in the Web, refer to Cusumano (2004).

Glisson (2006) supports the need to establish a comprehensive security improvement approach (SIA) for Web applications and identifies six security criteria for Web application development based on empirical evidence:

1. active organizational support for security in the Web development process
2. proper controls in the development environment
3. security visibility throughout all areas of the development process
4. delivery of a cohesive system, integrating business requirements, software, and security
5. prompt, rigorous testing and evaluation
6. trust and accountability

2.8.4 Web Testing and Evaluation

Testing plays a crucial role in the overall Web development process. However, more often than not, testing and evaluation is a neglected aspect of Web development. Many developers test the system only after the system meets with failures or after limitations have become apparent, resorting to what may be called *retroactive testing*, whereas what is desired in the first place is *proactive testing* at various stages of the Web development life cycle. Benefits of proactive testing include assurance of proper functioning and guaranteed performance levels, avoidance of costly retroactive fixes, optimal performance, and lower risk.

Testing and validating a large complex Web system is a difficult and expensive task. Testing shouldn't be done only near the end of the development process. Developers and their managers need to take a broader view and follow a more holistic approach to testing—from design all the way to deployment and maintenance and continual refinement.

The test planning needs to be carried out early in the project's life cycle. A test plan provides a road map so that the Web site can be evaluated through requirements or design statements. It also helps to estimate the time and effort needed for testing, establishing a test environment, getting test personnel, and writing test procedures before any testing can actually start.

Lam (2001) groups Web testing into the following broad categories and provides helpful practical guidelines on how to test Web systems:

1. browser compatibility
2. page display
3. session management
4. usability
5. content analysis
6. availability

7. backup and recovery
8. transactions
9. shopping, order processing
10. internalization
11. operational business procedures
12. system integration
13. performance
14. login and security

Experience shows that there are many common pitfalls in Web testing (Lam, 2001), and attempts should be made overcome them. Testing and evaluation of a Web application may be expensive, but the impact of failures resulting from a lack of testing could be more costly or even disastrous. A chapter in this book is devoted to a framework for measurement and evaluation of the quality of Web applications.

While rich Internet applications (RIAs) promise improved experiences for users, they are newer and more complex than their HTML counterparts, making them vulnerable to well-known—and potentially undiscovered— usability flaws. To ensure that RIAs don't frustrate users with problems that could have been avoided, designers should look for common pitfalls and test their applications—in the context of the full site experience—throughout the design and implementation phases of an RIA.

2.9 KNOWLEDGE COLLABORATION

The creation of large Web systems requires knowledge from a wide range of domains such as Web programming, Web architecture, Web design, multimedia, Web security, and Web performance and usability. Since hardly a few Web developers may have all the required knowledge, the development of Web-based systems is no longer confined to an individual but has to rely on a group of people who can collaboratively work on developing and implementing a Web system or a Web application. Knowledge collaboration has thus become an important aspect of Web development.

Development of a Web application requires a team of people with diverse skills and backgrounds: programmers, graphic designers, Web page designers, usability experts, content developers, database designers and administrators, data communication and networking experts, and Web server administrators. A Web development team is multidisciplinary and must be more versatile than a traditional software development team.

2.10 WEB PROJECT MANAGEMENT

The purpose of project management is to ensure that all the key processes and activities work in harmony. Building successful Web-based applications requires close coordination among various efforts involved in the Web development cycle. Successfully managing a large, complex Web development is a challenging task requiring multidisciplinary skills and is, in some ways, different from managing traditional IT/software projects.

Various aspects of Web project management and how Web project management differs from software/IT project management are outlined in Mayr (2006).

2.11 WHY DO WEB PROJECTS FAIL?

Many studies reveal that poor project management is the major cause of Web failures both during development and subsequently in the operational phase. Poor project management will defeat good engineering; good project management is a recipe for success. The 10 most common factors that contribute to Web project failure, in no particular order, are (adopted from Charette, 2005)

1. unrealistic, unarticulated, poorly articulated project goals and requirements
2. inaccurate estimate of time, effort, and resources needed for development of Web applications
3. sloppy development practices and lack of development methodology (a road map from conception to deployment)
4. poor communication among developers and between developers and clients
5. inability to handle the project's complexity
6. poor project management
7. use of immature technology
8. stakeholder politics
9. commercial pressures
10. poor reporting and monitoring of project progress

Project managers need to address these project management problems.

2.12 STEPS TO SUCCESSFUL DEVELOPMENT

Ten key steps for successful development and deployment of Web applications are (Ginige and Murugesan, 2001c)

1. Understand the system's overall function and operational environment, including the business objectives and requirements, organization culture, and information management policy.
2. Clearly identify the stakeholders—that is, the system's main users and their typical profiles, the organization that needs the system, and who funds the development.
3. Elicit or specify the (initial) functional, technical, and nontechnical requirements of the stakeholders and the overall system. Recognize that these requirements may not remain the same; rather, they are bound to change and evolve over time during the system development.
4. Develop an overall system architecture of the Web-based system that meets the technical and nontechnical requirements.
5. Identify subprojects or subprocesses to implement the system architecture. If the subprojects are too complex to manage, further divide them until they become a set of manageable tasks.
6. Develop and implement the subprojects.
7. Incorporate effective mechanisms to manage the Web system's evolution, change, and maintenance. As the system evolves, repeat the overall process or some parts of it, as required.
8. Address the nontechnical issues such as revised business processes, organizational and management policies, human resources development, and legal, cultural, and social aspects.
9. Perform periodic post-implementation audit. Measure and evaluate the system's performance, analyze the usage of the Web application from Web logs, and review and address users' feedback and suggestions.
10. Refine and update the system.

2.13 CONCLUSIONS

As Web applications continue to grow in importance and extend into new territories, a disciplined approach to their development becomes mandatory. With advances in various aspects of Web Engineering, we know now how to do Web applications well. It is time to act on what we know. This book and other publications in Web Engineering would help Web developers in this important endeavor.

To successfully develop and implement a large, complex Web application:

- Adopt a sound strategy and follow a suitable methodology to successfully manage the development and maintenance of Web systems.
- Recognize that, in most cases, development of a Web application is not an event, but a process, since the application's requirements evolve. It will have a start, but it will not have a predictable end as in traditional IT/software projects.
- Within the continuous process, identify, plan, and schedule various development activities such that they have a defined start and finish.
- Remember that planning and scheduling of the activities are very important to successfully manage the overall development, allocate resources, and monitor progress.
- Consider the big picture during context analysis and planning and designing of the Web application. If you do not, you may end up redesigning the entire system and repeating the process all over. If you address the changing nature of requirements early on, you can build into the design cost-effective ways of managing change and dealing with new requirements.
- Recognize that the development of a large Web application calls for teamwork and shared responsibility among the team members, and motivate a team culture.

REFERENCES

Antoniou, G.F., and Harmelen, F., 2004, *A Semantic Web Primer*. The MIT Press, Cambridge, MA.

Becker, A.S., and Berkemeyer, A., 2002, Rapid application design and testing for usability. *IEEE Multimedia*, October–December, pp. 38–46.

Berners-Lee, T. et al., 2001, The semantic Web. *Scientific American*, May, pp. 34–43.

Charette, R.N., 2005, Why software fails. *IEEE Spectrum*, September, pp. 36–43. http://www.spectrum.ieee.org/print/1685.

Cloyd, M.H., 2001, Designing user-centered Web applications in Web time. *IEEE Software*, January, pp. 62–69.

Curphey, M., and Araujo, R., 2006, Web application security assessment tools, *IEEE Security & Privacy*, July–August, pp. 32–41.

Cusumano, M.A., 2004, Who is liable for bugs and security flaws in software? *Communications of the ACM*, March, **47**(3): 25–27.

Dantzing, P., 2002, Architecture and design of high volume Web sites. *Proceedings of International Conference on Software and Knowledge Engineering*, 2002, Ischia, Italy.

Deshpande, Y. et al., 2002, Web Engineering. *Journal of Web Engineering*, **1**(1): 3–17.

Eichinger, C., 2006, Web application architecture. In *Web Engineering: The Discipline of Systematic Development of Web Applications*, Kappel, G. et al. (eds.)., John Wiley and Sons, New York, pp. 65–84.

Ginige, A., and Murugesan, S., 2001a, Web Engineering: An introduction. *IEEE Multimedia*, January–March, **8**(1): 14–18.

Ginige, A., and Murugesan, S., 2001b, The essence of Web Engineering: Managing the diversity and complexity of Web application development, *IEEE Multimedia*, April–June, **8**(2): 22–25.

Ginige, A., and Murugesan, S., 2001c, Web Engineering: A methodology for developing scalable, maintainable Web applications. *Cutter IT Journal*, July, **14**(7): 24–35.

Glisson, W.B., 2006, Web Engineering security: A practitioner's perspective, *Proceedings of the International Conference on Web Engineering*, pp. 257–264.

Ipsos, 2006, Mobile phones could soon rival the PC as world's dominant Internet platform. Online version: www.ipsosna.com/news/pressrelease.cfm?id=3049.

Ivory, M.Y., and Hearst, M.A., 2002, Improving Web site design. *IEEE Internet Computing*, March–April 2002, pp. 56–63.

Kappel, G. et al. (eds.), 2006, *Web Engineering: The Discipline of Systematic Development of Web Applications*. John Wiley and Sons, New York.

Lam, W., 2001, Testing e-commerce systems: A practical guide. *IT Professional*, March, pp. 19–27.

Mayr, H., 2006, Web project management. In *Web Engineering: The Discipline of Systematic Development of Web Applications*, Kappel, G. et al. (eds.), John Wiley and Sons, New York, pp. 171–195.

Meier, J.D., 2006, Web application security engineering. *IEEE Security & Privacy*, July–August, pp. 16–24.

Mendes, W. et al., 2006, The need for Web Engineering: An introduction. In *Web Engineering*, E. Mendes and N. Mosley (eds.), Springer, Berlin, pp. 1–27.

Mimoso, M.S., 2003, Top Web application security problems identified. Online version: searchsecurity.techtarget.com/originalContent/0,289142,sid14_gci873823,00.html?NewsE L=9.25.

Murugesan S. et al., 1999, Web Engineering: A new discipline for development of Web-based systems. *Proceedings of the First ICSE Workshop on Web Engineering*, Los Angeles, pp. 1–9.

Murugesan, S., and Ginige, A., 2005, Web Engineering: Introduction and perspectives. In *Web Engineering: Principles and Techniques*, W. Suh (ed.). Idea Group Publishing, Hershey, PA.

Murugesan, S., and Venkatakrishnan, B.A., 2005, Addressing the challenges of Web applications on mobile handheld devices. *Proceedings of International Conference on Mobile Business*, pp. 199–205.

Murugesan, S., 2007a, Business uses of Web 2.0: Potential and prospects. Cutter Business-IT Strategies Executive Report, **10**(1), January.

Murugesan, S., 2007b, Understanding Web 2.0, *IEEE IT Professional*, July–Aug., **9**(4).

Naughton, J., 2006, 10 Web sites that changed the world. Good weekend. *The Sydney Morning Herald*, September 9, p. 38.

O'Reilly, T., 2006, Levels of the game: The hierarchy of Web 2.0 applications. Online version: radar.oreilly.com/archives/2006/07/levels_of_the_game.html.

O'Reilly, T., 2005, What is Web 2.0? Design patterns and business models for the next generation of software. Online version: www.oreillynet.com/pub/a/oreilly/tim/news/2005/09/30/what-is-web-20.html.

Shadbolt, N., 2006, The Semantic Web revisited. *IEEE Intelligent Systems,* May–June, **21**(3): 96–101.

Siegel, D.A., 2003, The business case for user-centred design: Increasing your power. *Software,* **18**(1): 62–69.

Verdon, D, 2006, Security policies for the software developer. *IEEE Security & Privacy,* July–August, pp. 42–49.

Wikipedia-1, Web 2.0, http://en.wikipedia.org/wiki/Web_2.0.

Wikipedia-2, Rich Internet applications, http://en.wikipedia.org/wiki/Rich_Internet_application.

Williams, J., 2000, Correctly assessing the "ilities" requires more than marketing hype. *IT Professional,* November, **2**(6): 65–67.

Williams, J., 2001, Avoiding the CNN moment. *IT Professional,* Nov–Mar., **3**(2): 72, 68:70.

Chapter 3

THE WEB AS AN APPLICATION PLATFORM

Martin Gaedke and Johannes Meinecke
Chemnitz University of Technology, Faculty of Computer Science, Distributed and Self-Organizing Systems Group, Straße der Nationen 62, 09111 Chemnitz, Germany

3.1 PARADIGM SHIFT IN WEB HISTORY

When Tim Berners-Lee invented the Web in 1990 at the European Particle Physics Laboratory (CERN) (Berners-Lee, 1990), he did so in the context of a development that had started long before. One idea that considerably influenced the nature and intended purpose of the early Web had its roots in the concept of *hypertext,* which had come up about half a decade before. Coined by Ted Nelson, the term "hypertext" can be understood as "nonlinear writing," i.e., creating documents that can be read not only from the beginning to the end, but rather in an order that is preferred and controlled by the reader, who navigates through the text by following associative links. On Web pages, the associative link is reflected by the concept of the anchor tag <a> used in HTML. As a precondition for realizing a large-scale hypertext system, Tim Berners-Lee first proposed a unique addressing scheme for all documents at CERN to be linked universally, the Universal Document Identifier (UDI). With this concept, he created the predecessor of the Web's Uniform Resource Identifiers (URI) and their prominent subset, the Uniform Resource Locators (URL), which provide a means of locating resources by describing their primary access mechanisms (Berners-Lee et al., 2005). As a result of the hypertext roots, everything about the early Web was characterized by a focus on documents, including HTML and the first Web browser prototype. More precisely, the intension was to support the publication and exchange of documents by scientists, who initially were the main audience.

What followed during the next 10 years was a period of continuous growth. As the scope of application quickly exceeded CERN, its popularity contributed greatly to the advance of the Internet as a whole, of which it became the major driving application. Along with the increase in available sites and servers, more and more end users started to join the Web with an Internet-capable computer. The content, which was originally published by scientists, was now also coming from professional enterprises as well as private individuals, who established their Web presence in the form of homepages, covering a wide variety of topics. Consequently, Web technology advanced to meet the requirements of the new emerging scenarios, which included, in particular, commercial applications. As a means for reaching vast numbers of consumers with comparatively low investments, the Web partially changed its focus from a forum for the publication of information toward an electronic marketplace. While overrated expectations and lack of concentration on business values during the new economy boom of the late 1990s resulted in disillusion and crashing stock prices, market consolidation followed and the Web has now returned to its period of growth.

Due to the described evolution of the Web and its manifold applications, its shape has been influenced by different, partially competing perspectives on how it is or should be used. In 1995, Guay distinguished between several *publishing paradigms* present in the early Web. The print paradigm, for example, is reflected in sites that do not make use of hypertext concepts at all and instead present their linear content in ways similar to how it is traditionally presented in print media. This approach, which was partially a result of a transitional phase toward the Web as a new medium, is gradually being replaced by the mentioned hypermedia paradigm. Another development impacting the Web is the multimedia paradigm, which took advantage of the increase in bandwidth as well as improving hardware capabilities to deliver not only text, but all sorts of media, including images, audio, and video. Ted Nelson's docuverse (Nelson, 1987) can be seen as a paradigm for the Web, describing the idea of a global library of interconnected documents. Finally, the interactive paradigm recognizes the potential of users influencing the sites they visit beyond merely deciding upon where to navigate next. Whereas formerly the author supplied information and the reader controlled the flow of information, now the author provides application logic and the reader controls the program flow.

As the interaction paradigm began to spread and the Web technology adjusted to the new requirements, new forms of Web sites evolved, which resembled applications more than documents. While many aspects of these applications can be compared to conventional software programs, there are also a number of characteristics typical for the Web platform that distinguish them from other platforms (Deshpande et al., 2002). These characteristics are challenging for the process of developing applications, but also offer innovative opportunities for business and society as a whole that were impossible to realize before. An important factor is the potential audience of the software, which, once deployed, can be accessed by millions of users from whole different regions, countries, or cultures. At the same time, this also applies for the competition, making user satisfaction a vital success factor. Unlike on other platforms, software on the Web is always operating and does not depend on time-consuming processes of rolling out new releases. Hence, scenarios can be supported that require constantly up-to-date information. In addition, there is an evolving set of technologies and standards that opens new advantages to applications that adopt them, including many specifications recommended by the World Wide Web Consortium (W3C). In contrast to common applications, the Web is also repeatedly influenced by emerging trends that encourage (if not enforce) a large number of sites to follow them. Together, these factors, among many others, have led to the emergence of a huge variety of different applications and as such contribute to the still ongoing growth of the Web.

3.2 WEB APPLICATION CONCERNS

In order to develop software for the Web platform with respect to its specific nature, a number of engineering issues have to be addressed every time an application is constructed. For the sake of clarity, such problems can be allocated to multiple concerns (Dijkstra, 1982) that may then be treated separately in design and implementation. In the following sections we distinguish between concerns related to the data being processed (Data), the interface experienced by the user (Presentation, Navigation, Dialogue), and the distributed system acting in between (Process, Communication) (Gaedke, 2000). The concerns reappear in the Web Engineering methods presented in this book that comprise approaches to deal with them in a systematic, disciplined, and quantifiable way.

3.2.1 Data

From the viewpoint of the early Web's paradigms, the data are the content of the documents to be published. Although content can be embedded in the Web documents together with other concerns like presentation or navigation, the evolution of Web applications often demands a separation, using data sources such as XML files, databases, or Web services. Traditional issues include, for example, the structure of the information space as well as the definition of structural linking. In the context of the dynamic nature of Web applications, additional dimensions have to be considered. For instance, one can distinguish between static information that remains stable over time and dynamic information that is subject to changes. Depending on the media type being delivered, either data can be persistent, i.e., accessible independently of time, or it can be transient, i.e., accessible as a flow, as in the case of a video stream. Moreover, *metadata* can also describe other data, e.g., following the de facto standard of the Dublin Core Metadata Initiative (Andresen, 2003). Such descriptions facilitate the usefulness of the data within the global information space established by the Web. The machine-based processing of information is further supported by Semantic Web approaches that apply technologies like the Resource Description Framework (RDF) to make metadata statements (e.g., about Web page content) and express the semantics about associations between arbitrary resources worldwide.

3.2.2 Presentation

Besides the question of what to publish, an import matter is also how to present it, especially in the context of the large number of competing information sources on the Internet. The task of communicating content in an appropriate way combines artistic visual design with engineering disciplines. Usually, there are numerous factors to be considered, many of them related to the assumed audience of the Web site. For example, in the international case, cultural differences may have to be accounted for, affecting not only languages but also, for example, the perception of color schemes. Further restrictions may originate from the publishing organizations themselves that aim at reflecting the company's brand with a corresponding corporate design or legal obligations with respect to accessibility [The World Wide Web Consortium (W3C), 1997]. Although presentation technologies have advanced over time, such as in terms of multimedia capabilities, the core technology of the Web application platform, the Hypertext Markup Language (HTML), has remained relatively stable. Consequently, application user interfaces have to be mapped to document-oriented markup code, causing a gap between design and implementation.

3.2.3 Navigation

Given the data and the presentation methods to communicate it, an additional challenge lies in the task of making the information easily accessible to the user. Because of the potential complexity of arbitrarily linked resources on the Web, a lack of systematic design may result in what it referred to as the "lost in hyperspace" syndrome. This holds true even though the Web makes use of only a subset of the rich capabilities of hypertext concepts, e.g., allowing only unidirectional links. Over time, a set of common patterns has evolved [cf. repositories like Lowe (1999)] that, being familiar to many users, aids them in navigating through new Web sites they have not visited before. Applied to Web application development, navigation concepts can be extended for accessing not only static document content, but also application functionality. Today, there are several Web Engineering approaches with a hypermedia background that cover navigational aspects with dedicated models and methodologies.

3.2.4 Dialogue

As expressed within the interaction paradigm, the execution of a Web application is usually characterized by a degree of user control that goes beyond the free choice of navigation. Interactive elements in Web applications often appear in the shape of forms that allow users to enter data that are used as input for further processing. More generally, the dialogue concern covers not only interaction between humans and the application, but rather between arbitrary actors (including other programs) and the manipulated information space. The flow of information is governed by the Web's interaction model, which, due to its distributed nature, differs considerably from other platforms. The interaction model is subject to variations, as in the context of recent tendencies toward more client-sided application logic and asynchronous communication between client and server, for example. This trend, based on technologies referred to as *AJAX* (Asleson and Schutta, 2006), focuses on user interfaces that provide a look and feel that resembles desktop applications.

3.2.5 Process

Beneath the user interface of a Web application lies the implementation of the actual application logic, for which the Web acts as a platform to make it available to the affected stakeholders. The *process* concern relates to the operations performed on the information space that are generally triggered by the user via the Web interface and whose execution is governed by the business policy. Particular challenges arise from scenarios with frequently changing policies, demanding agile approaches with preferably dynamic wiring between loosely coupled components. In case the application is not distributed, the process concern is hardly affected by Web-specific factors, allowing for standard non-Web approaches to be applied, such as

Component-Based Software Engineering (CBSE) (Heineman and Councill, 2001). Otherwise, service-oriented approaches account for cases where the wiring extends over components that reside in different locations on the Web, as covered by the next section.

3.2.6 Communication

Due to the Web's foundation on the Internet with its distributed and heterogeneous architecture of clients and servers, communication is obviously the underlying success factor for the Web as well as a major source of complexity challenging Web application development. To begin with, this applies to the message exchange between user agents (e.g., browsers) and server-sided applications. In this context, issues to be addressed are closely related to the dialogue concern and include, for example, caching strategies as well as session handling to overcome the stateless nature of the underlying communication protocols. More complexity arises when applications are involved that go beyond isolated monolithic sites, connected only on the surface via HTML links. Such application-to-application communication scenarios allow multiple distributed autonomous and loosely coupled services to interact with each other within the scope of a *service-oriented architecture* (SOA) (Booth et al., 2003). Together with the means to describe, publish, and find services, this architecture paves the way for extending the application idea on a global scale.

3.3 PLATFORM FOR DISTRIBUTED APPLICATIONS

As mentioned before, the Web is still growing in size and simultaneously changing in terms of how it is put to use. In order to highlight some recent paradigm shifts, this section elaborates solely on the communication aspect to show how the Web is increasingly turning into a platform for distributed applications, whereas the following chapters mainly focus on the remaining five aspects.

3.3.1 Technological Trends

Many concepts found in the state of the art of distributed Web applications are not completely new, but can also be found in earlier approaches. Pre-Web communication standards like message-oriented mechanisms or remote procedure call (RPC) have been applied by technologies such as CORBA or (D)COM. As an equivalent specification for the Web, the

Simple Object Access Protocol (SOAP) (Box et al., 2000) emerged, governing the invocation of *Web services*. Being an application of the XML, this protocol is independent of platform technology and transport mechanism, as required by the heterogeneous environment of the Web. A diversity of transport alternatives, including HTTP over port 80, mail, or even fax, makes it suitable for innovative end-to-end communication scenarios involving the invocation of services worldwide. As such, SOAP, together with WSDL as a specification to define service interfaces, and UDDI as a specification of a registry service for advertising these, provide a basic infrastructure for distributed applications on the Web. To account for additional messaging needs, further specifications have been developed as protocol extensions, covering issues such as message security, reliability, and transactions.

The first fields of application for the Web service concept were mostly restricted to the intranet of individual companies. Seen as a means for integrating legacy systems that may be distributed over multiple platforms and company sites, this technology can be applied to rigidly connect applications that may not be related to the Web at all. From the perspective of the Web as a platform, more interesting scenarios involve a larger number of services that are as publicly available as Internet Web sites and that are combined to create additional value. Today, tendencies in the Web to this end, together with many other emerging concepts, can collectively be referred to as Web 2.0 (O'Reilly, 2005). As a simple form of service, the XML-based RSS feed has already become relatively popular, often in the shape of Weblogs (short form: blog). The resulting kinds of applications are characterized by a new style of collaborative development, e.g., Wikipedia or interorganizational business applications. In this context, a growing number of Web services are published that give access to massive data stores or process logic as a new business concept, such as the functionality belonging to Amazon or Google. The sum of available services, also referred to as the API-Cloud, has the potential to add value to other Web applications that could not provided by locally deployed components.

3.3.2 Selected Aspects of Distributed Web Applications

Returning to the matter of Web application development with special emphasis on distribution and the mentioned technological advances, this section presents some problem aspects of corresponding applications. For the purpose of visualization, architecture illustrations are given for each case, using the notations of the WebComposition Architecture Model (WAM) (Meinecke and Gaedke, 2005). WAM is specialized on the description of distributed interorganizational Web applications and comprises an easy-to-communicate

Web
Portal
1

Figure 3.1. WAM symbol for a single Web application.

"pen & paper" graphical notation. Figure 3.1 contains, as the most basic case of a Web application model, the symbol for a single Web portal that is not distributed in any way.

In the subsequent sections, this abstract example is gradually extended to outline a selection of possibilities that arise from the integration of distributed artifacts over the Web. More specifically, the presented subjects of integration are services, access policies, federation partners, and devices.

3.3.3 Service Integration

As a first alternative of distribution, a Web portal can invoke Web services that either offer functionality formerly included in the monolithic Web application or serve as access points to external data sources and systems. Hence, the service-oriented approach offers a way of decomposing functionality into reusable parts with defined interfaces. The invoked services may in turn invoke others to perform the requested operation and afterwards combine the obtained results. This is also the case in the scenario in Figure 3.2, in which a composite Web service aggregates the functionality of three atomic services.

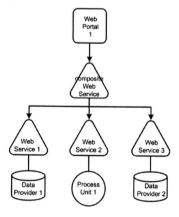

Figure 3.2. Example involving the integration of legacy data sources and process units.

Depending on the concrete realization, service composition may vary from a hardwired approach up to a completely loosely coupled binding of exchangeable services. On a higher detail level, one can distinguish between the service and the component that provides the actual functionality to be integrated. In the example, there are two data providers that, from the model's point of view, only act as components for storing and retrieving data, as well as a process unit that, when triggered by the wrapping Web service, performs additional operations.

3.3.4 Identity and Access Management

The need for identity and access management arises in situations where the offered services and applications are not intended to be publicly available in an uncontrolled manner. For example, payment might be charged for the usage of a service, up to the point where a company's business model depends exclusively on rendering services over the Web. Other reasons include the necessity of confidentiality due to legal obligations or the need for an established identity to enable service personalization. Unlike, for example, an operation system platform, the Web does not include the concept of a uniform user identity (Cameron, 2005). Hence, to overcome the diversity of proprietary approaches built into individual applications and services, additional security- and identity-related protocols have to be applied (Scavo and Cantor, 2005). In the example in Figure 3.3, a common security zone has been established (defining a uniform access control policy for *Company A*), surrounding all services and applications of the company.

User identities are managed with the help of an identity provider that facilitates a central login form and account database, allowing for single sign-on (SSO) across multiple portals. This concept can also be extended for

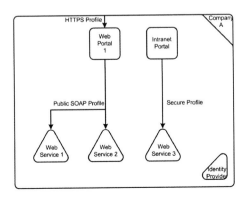

Figure 3.3. Example involving a uniform access control context (realm).

controlling accesses on Web services by obliging requestors to include security tokens (obtained from the identity provider) into their SOAP messages. Further security-related design decisions include the distinction between different access profiles that specify the allowed protocols and scope of visibility for individual services and applications.

3.3.5 Federation

Situations in which the necessity for the integration of external services (as in Section 3.3.3) coincides with requirements for established identities and access control (as in Section 3.3.4) raise a set of new problems. Among these problems, many are related to identities that have multiple accounts for accessing resources from multiple realms, causing security vulnerabilities and unnecessary administration efforts. In contrast, identity federation approaches assume only one account per identity, accepting requestors with external accounts based on explicit trust relationships between the federation partners. As one of several issues related to "portal federation," this topic is receiving growing attention in science and industry (Gootzit and Phifer, 2003). Figure 3.4 depicts the architecture of an application that extends across two companies.

Here, the two partners agreed upon a unidirectional trust relationship, allowing users at *Company A* to sign on at *Web Portal 2* with their native account as a form of interorganizational single sign-on. Furthermore, *Web Service 4*, which is otherwise not accessible to the general public, is made available. In both cases, the authorization is governed by predefined rules that map the foreign identities to locally meaningful access control decisions.

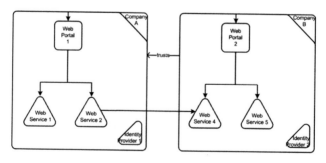

Figure 3.4. Example involving the sharing of resources from autonomous partners.

3.3.6 Device-Spanning Applications

Regarding distribution from a more hardware-oriented point of view, Web applications can be enriched by the use of nontraditional platforms other than the personal computer. To this end, the vision of the *Embedded Web* is to extend the common use of the Web by integrating Web server technology into all sorts of equipment to improve their overall intelligence, functional capability, and interactivity (Lee et al., 1997). This can take the form of Web user interfaces, integrated into car radios, for example, or Web service interfaces that expose device functionality to be integrated into device-spanning Web applications. A challenging question in this context is how the concepts and technologies targeted at the common Web can be applied to Web applications enriched with devices. As an example, Figure 3.5 describes a federated scenario in which sensors and actuators belonging to multiple organizations are being integrated as physical components into the distributed Web application, allowing for innovative kinds of business concepts.

Like in the scenario in Section 3.3.5, a foreign Web service is made available, only in this case to provide control over an underlying air-conditioning system. This allows *Company A*, which possesses a network of meteorological stations and temperature sensors providing accurate weather forecasts, to regulate the indoor climate at *Company B* very efficiently. The involved Web services are either integrated into the devices themselves or deployed on computers that are connected to the devices with non-Web technologies—allowing for these new kinds of service provider solutions.

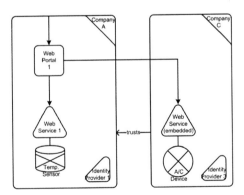

Figure 3.5. Example involving a device-spanning federation.

3.4 SUMMARY

This chapter gave an overview of the development of the Web, seen as a platform for delivering applications to users worldwide. Originally focused on the publications of documents, the Web has been used in different ways, reflected by changing paradigms such as the print paradigm, the hypertext paradigm, the multimedia paradigm, the docuverse paradigm, and the interactive paradigm. During this development, the Web application has emerged as a new form of interaction between humans and machines. For the disciplined construction of such Web applications, one can distinguish between different concerns, i.e., Web-specific aspects of the design and implementation: data, presentation, navigation, interaction, process, and communication. As the Web continues to grow, new types of applications evolve. Among the current tendencies that are often referred to as Web 2.0, one is the trend toward applications that compose functionality from distributed sources using Web service technology. Resulting from this new paradigm, applications can integrate data and software systems via service interfaces, share access policies, extend safely across organizational boundaries, and include the functionality of devices as integral parts.

REFERENCES

Andresen, L., 2003, *Dublin Core Metadata Element Set, Version 1.1: Reference Description.* http://dublincore.org/documents/dces/.

Asleson, R., and Schutta, N.T., 2006, *Foundations of Ajax.* Apress, Berkeley, CA.

Berners-Lee, T., 1990, *Information Management: A Proposal.* http://www.w3.org/Proposal.html (10.10.1998).

Berners-Lee, T., Fielding, R., et al., 2005, *Request for Comments: 3986, Uniform Resource Identifier (URI): Generic Syntax.* http://www.ietf.org/rfc/rfc3986.txt (10.05.2006).

Booth, D., Champion, M., et al., 2003, *Web Services Architecture - W3C Working Draft 14 May 2003.* http://www.w3.org/TR/2003/WD-ws-arch-20030514/.

Box, D., Ehnebuske, D., et al., 2000, *Simple Object Access Protocol (SOAP) 1.1.* http://www.w3.org/TR/2000/NOTE-SOAP-20000508/ (12.05.2000).

Cameron, K., 2005, *The Laws of Identity.* http://msdn.microsoft.com/library/en-us/dnwebsrv/html/lawsofidentity.asp (29.10.2005).

Deshpande, Y., Murugesan, S., et al., 2002, Web Engineering, *Journal of Web Engineering,* 1(1): 3–17.

Dijkstra, E.W., 1982, How do we tell truths that might hurt? *SIGPLAN Notices,* 17(5): 13–15.

Gaedke, M., 2000, *Komponententechnik für Entwicklung und Evolution von Anwendungen im World Wide Web.* Shaker Verlag, Aachen, Germany.

Gootzit, D., and Phifer, G., 2003, *Gen-4 Portal Functionality: From Unification to Federation*. Stamford, CT.

Guay, T., 1995, *WEB Publishing Paradigms*. http://www.faced.ufba.br/~edc708/biblioteca/interatividade/web%20paradigma/Paradigm.html (06.02.2006).

Heineman, G.T., and Councill, W.T. 2001, *Component-Based Software Engineering—Putting the Pieces Together*. Addison-Wesley, Boston.

Lee, B., Houtchens, S., et al., 1997, *WWW6 Workshop on Embedded Web Technologies*.

Lowe, D., 1999. *Hypermedia Patterns Repository (HPR)*. Version 1.0, http://www.designpattern.lu.unisi.ch (23/03/99).

Meinecke, J., and Gaedke, M., 2005, Modeling federations of Web applications with WAM. *Third Latin American Web Congress (LA-WEB 2005)*, Buenos Aires, Argentina, IEEE Computer Society.

Nelson, T., 1987, All for one and one for all. *Hypertext '87 Proceedings*, The Association for Computing Machinery, Chapel Hill, NC.

O'Reilly, T., 2005, *What Is Web 2.0—Design Patterns and Business Models for the Next Generation of Software*. http://www.oreillynet.com/pub/a/oreilly/tim/news/2005/09/30/what-is-web-20.html (18.10.2005).

Scavo, T., and Cantor, S., 2005, *Shibboleth Architecture—Technical Overview Working Draft 02, 8 June 2005*. http://shibboleth.internet2.edu/shibboleth-documents.html (02.11.2005).

The World Wide Web Consortium (W3C), 1997, *Web Accessibility Initiative (WAI)*. http://www.w3.org/WAI/ (10.05.2006).

PART II

WEB DESIGN METHODS

Chapter 4

OVERVIEW OF DESIGN ISSUES FOR WEB APPLICATIONS DEVELOPMENT

Gustavo Rossi,[1] Daniel Schwabe,[2] Luis Olsina,[3] Oscar Pastor[4]

[1]*LIFIA, Facultad de Informatica, Universidad Nacional de La Plata (also at CONICET) Argentina,* gustavo@lifia.info.unlp.edu.ar

[2]*Departamento de Informática, PUC-Rio, Rio de Janeiro, Brazil,* dschwabe@inf.pucrio.br

[3]*GIDIS_Web, Engineering School, Universidad Nacional de La Pampa, Calle 9 y 110, (6360) General Pico, LP, Argentina,* olsina1@ing.unlpam.edu.ar

[4]*DSIC, Valencia University of Technology, Valencia, Spain,* opastor@dsic.upv.es

4.1 INTRODUCTION

In this part of the book we will focus on design issues in Web applications development. To make the book useful both for practitioners and for researchers, we decided (following the successful style of the IWWOST series) to use a common example throughout the rest of the chapters in which each design method is presented. In the following two sections we summarize the most important aspects that development approaches should consider, and then we briefly present the example that will be solved subsequently in each chapter. The aspects we introduce in Sections 4.2 and 4.3 will be refined in each subsequent chapter of the book.

4.2 ISSUES FOR DESIGN METHODS

For discussion purposes, we have grouped the issues under four headings; in Section 4.7 we discuss some additional issues.

1. data/information, with issues relating to data representation
2. navigation, with issues relating to navigation structure and behavior

3. functionality, with issues relating to application functionality beyond navigation
4. presentation/interface, with issues relating to interface and presentation design

This order reflects to some extent the historical evolution of Web applications over time—from simple "read-only" applications to full-fledged information systems—and also reflects the nature of the methods themselves.

This is in contrast with a more software engineering-centered view, which might place "functionality" first, since it is an aspect of applications that all traditional software design methods have taken into account, followed by navigation, which was the "new" abstraction introduced by hypermedia and the Web.

The issues presented here address different aspects of Web applications, which exist to a greater or lesser extent in any such application. Any method purporting to help design Web applications should, therefore, address a significant number of such issues, if not all.

4.3 DATA/INFORMATION/CONTENT—WHAT IS THE SUBJECT MATTER OF THE APPLICATION?

Web applications, like any application, must deal with information items that constitute the problem domain, i.e., the subject matter of the application. The first aspect that a method must define is how to characterize such information items, providing a data model.

This is not a new problem; it has been dealt with in software development as well as in database design methods. Among the most popular are the entity–relationship (E/R) model and the relational model, which are clear examples of widely used extended data models. Also, the data counterparts of popular object-oriented (OO) models, such as UML and ORM, address this same problem. Although differing in details, they all provide for the definition of information items as composed of attributes, which characterize individual properties of such items. Most methods provide means to describe sets of items with the same attributes, usually through concepts such as "classes" or "entities." In addition, generalization and specialization hierarchies can typically be defined among classes or entities.

While Web-based applications do not present additional requirements for the expressiveness of such models, some methods offer additional abstraction mechanisms that allow one to deal with specific issues of the contents of Web applications, such as multimedia data types, or with multiple representations for the same information item.

Besides the information items, relations must also be represented. While some methods allow a single relation type, others provide specialized types such as aggregation and composition relations. In addition, cardinality constraints must also be expressed.

When applications must deal with extensive domains, model specification may become very large. Some methods provide modularization primitives that allow the specification to be broken into smaller parts.

The application itself may be represented in many ways. In some models, it is the union of all items; in others, there is a special element that stands for the application itself. For example, in object-oriented methods, it is sometimes called an "application singleton" since it is a single object instance of its class.

4.4 NAVIGATION

Although it might seem obvious, given the widespread experience people have using the Web, many authors do not distinguish navigation from other application functionalities or, frequently, equate it with any event that causes changes in the interface. It is clear that navigation is a salient feature of Web applications, but such authors don't consider it worthy of particular attention during application design; it is simply "another application functionality," and the notion of linking is simply ignored.

On the other hand, most current Web application design methods recognize navigation as an outstanding feature of Web applications and provide models and notations to specify it. Briefly stated, characterizing navigation aspects of a Web application entails defining the "things" being navigated and specifying how the navigation space is structured—what items are reachable from any given item. Since the semantics of navigation is better understood, it justifies providing specialized notations that help users describe this functionality on an appropriate level of abstraction.

Much in the same tradition as in the database world, design method proposers have realized that the items being navigated (variously called *nodes*, *objects*, etc.) are different from the conceptual items that make up the problem domain. Whereas conceptual items represent the information in a task- and user-independent way, navigation items are defined taking into account user requirements, providing a view over conceptual items. The idea is that this abstraction mechanism allows the hiding of unwanted details as well as the grouping of interrelated items, with respect to the user profile and the task being supported. This is analogous to the "external views" as related to "conceptual views" in traditional database design, where users actually manipulate (external) views over the conceptual objects.

Once navigation items have been characterized, methods must also allow the definition of the navigation space. For any reasonably sized application, defining the navigation space topology directly in terms of only "nodes-and-links" is too restrictive, since the amount of information quickly overwhelms both designers and users. Furthermore, descriptions at this low level miss the opportunity to exploit typically occurring regularities in the navigation space topology.

Many methods introduce higher-level abstractions that allow the navigation space to be defined in a more concise way, such as sets or (indexed, ordered) lists, navigation chains, etc. Such abstractions play an analogous role with respect to navigation topology as classes do with respect to object instances—they allow one to refer to the navigation properties of a large number of nodes (respectively, the structure and behavior properties of objects) with a single primitive (respectively, classes).

Such specifications will, in most cases, translate straightforwardly into implementation mechanisms for dynamic Web sites, where pages are not stored explicitly but are generated dynamically, on demand, combining HTML or XML templates with the appropriate data directly retrieved or computed from application data stored in databases.

The initial focus of most novice designers is on the navigation items that will be made available to users. More experienced designers have realized that equally important are the access structures that will lead users to the desired information items—there is no point in having elaborate, detailed information if the user can't reach it!

Consequently, defining the navigation space of Web applications necessarily entails defining its access structures. Once again, higher-level abstractions are necessary, such as (ordered) lists, guided tours, etc. For example, in our exemplar application described at the end of the chapter, we find indexes for accessing films by each of its specific features, such as genres or actors, or film directors, etc. More opportunistic indexes such as top-selling DVDs or today's recommendations are increasingly being used as well. Additionally, some methods also provide the means to specify items that are always accessible, i.e., items that can be reached from anywhere in the navigation space. For example, easy access to each key functionality is usually provided, for example, television movies, DVDs, access to the user's account or shopping cart, and so on.

4.5 FUNCTIONALITY (BEYOND NAVIGATION) AND TASKS

When the first applications were deployed in the WWW, they were mostly "read-only," meaning they allowed users to browse information (hence the name "Web browsers"!), but not to create or change information items. With the increased sophistication of the run-time environments of Web servers, applications have become increasingly more complex, reaching the current stage where browsers are really interfaces to full-fledged applications allowing the creation and modification of information items, often in a distributed, asynchronous fashion.

Since navigation is recognized as a special kind of functionality, most methods must allow the characterization of navigation states, i.e., the dynamic behavior of the application as the user navigates from node to node. The original browse-only applications had, therefore, only navigation states.

As additional functionality was added, the need arose to deal with its associated states and state changes. Stateful applications were already the norm outside the Web, and design methods proposed a variety of mechanisms to specify them. Web application design methods must allow the specification of such applications and integrate the application states with the navigation states. For example, the check-out operation in electronic stores represents a task that the user must fulfill; it is represented as a set of subtasks, although finally it consists of filling in a set of forms accessed as a sequence of nodes.

The added complexity arises from the combination of this functionality with navigation operations and the sometimes subtle interplay between them. For example, some application functions may only be accessed in certain navigation states, or, more generally, accessible functions may change depending on the navigation state. Conversely, certain navigation alternatives may only be available in certain functionality states; for example, personal data may only be accessed after the user has logged in.

The inclusion of states, coupled with the distributed nature of the WWW, naturally leads to the notion of non-atomic processes and transactions. Many applications allow functionality to be accessed as a sequence of steps, which may sometimes be interspersed with navigation operations. Conversely, some applications have the notion of transactions, which must be implemented over an essentially stateless run-time environment. Design methods must allow the specification of both types of run-time behavior, preferably independently of the run-time environment.

Another source of complexity is the inclusion of multimedia data, which are often combined with elaborate timing and synchronization requirements that must be integrated with the other functionalities.

To deal with these aspects, some methods propose new mechanisms, but many rely on integrating with or extending existing methods that have already been successfully applied to such aspects of application design.

4.6 INTERFACE AND PRESENTATION

Web applications are, obviously, interactive applications. Users access the application functionality, including navigation, through the interface. For some authors, the interface directly presents the conceptual information items and exposes the application functionality. In fact, applications typically react to some interface event (such as a link or button being clicked), triggering the corresponding functions, which in turn cause the interface elements to change in some way. Even for non-Web environments, many design methods already decouple interface design from functionality design as a way to modularize and reduce the complexity of the design task.

In contrast, for many design methods, a distinction should be made between interface transformations and navigation operations in Web applications. In other words, some interface events that trigger application functionality do not correspond to any navigation operation, even if the interface changes in some way. This is true even if there is access to the server as a result of the interface operation. A simple example is an update operation to an order being made, changing, for instance, the quantity of some item in the order. Even though this causes an access to the server, which triggers some script that updates the internal data structure representing the order (and possibly reflecting it in a database), there is no associated navigation—the item being "navigated" is still the same order.

Consequently, Web design methods must provide a way for the designer to specify the interface—which elements compose it and how it reacts to all possible events. The interface behavior must necessarily be tied to the application functionality, including navigation.

Web application interface design must deal with another dimension, namely graphic design. In contrast with non-Web applications, where the complete design is carried out by software engineers, the interface appearance of Web applications is mostly defined by graphic (or, in current parlance, user experience) designers, who determine the actual "look and feel" of the application. Design methods must allow the clear separation between the so-called abstract interface design, where interface functionality is defined, and the concrete design, where layout and graphical appearance are defined.

In addition, the existence of an abstract interface design is also useful because of the rapidly evolving technological platforms upon which Web applications are implemented. New standards are issued and new versions of Web browsers are released almost every six months. Having an abstract interface design allows a more stable part of the design that remains unchanged by such technological evolution to be encapsulated. Besides this type of evolution, market reasons tend to pressure many Web applications to periodically completely change their graphical appearance; the abstract interface designs also help to cope with this requirement.

The rapid introduction of new devices used to access the Web, such as palmtops and cell phones, presents yet another dimension of requirements. Since such devices provide radically different run-time environments, with more limited display and interaction capabilities, some design methods strive to identify a "device-independent" portion of the interface design that remains unchanged regardless of the device being used to access it.

4.7 FURTHER ISSUES

4.7.1 Design Process

The discussion so far has focused mostly on the representational needs of Web application design methods. Beyond that, methods must also address the design process itself. The Web environment presents additional demands on the development process, caused by factors such as

1. the specific target environment, which is a hypermedia, distributed client-server environment
2. the rapid evolution and constant change in the implementation environment
3. the accelerated design cycle
4. the broader and sometimes harder-to-characterize audience (or intended target user categories)
5. the multidisciplinary nature of the development team, involving other professional skills such as communicators, content experts, graphics designers, etc.

Some methods provide additional tools to capture or model requirements that are better suited for this environment; typically, they are also more focused on user (or stakeholder) needs, as opposed to focusing on the designer or contractor alone.

Although a very large number of applications are available on the WWW (basically, most moderately sized Web sites can be considered Web applications of some sort), it is also true that several of their characteristics can be found repeatedly across many applications. In other words, many subproblems recur, thereby presenting an opportunity for design reuse. After all, if a certain subproblem has been faced and resolved, why not reuse its solution, perhaps adapting it to the situation at hand?

There are several approaches to deal with this, some directly incorporated into the design methods themselves, others complementary to them. In this latter category, mechanisms such as design patterns are employed, allowing known problems and their solutions to be characterized in an easily used format.

On a higher abstraction level, it is also possible to recognize that certain types of applications, in given domains, also exhibit recurring structures. For example, most institutional Web sites are similar, as are many online stores. Some methods can be extended to allow the characterization of families of similar applications, effectively forming Web application design frameworks. Starting with such frameworks, it is possible to rapidly instantiate specific applications in the given domain, by appropriately instantiating the framework's hotspots.

As the number of different applications being deployed on the WWW increases, software engineers have identified a number of recurring functionalities. In addition to the various forms mentioned above, another approach to leverage this accumulated experience is to encapsulate these functionalities in components that can be composed to form a more complex application. More generally, complex applications can eventually be defined as the composition of simpler ones. In some methods, the notion of a component is available as a primitive, together with language specifying how a component can be composed.

4.7.2 Model Representation

An integral part of any method is the definition of the notation used to describe its models. Such a notation has many uses, as it must support the communication between

1. customers and designers
2. designers and end users
3. designers and other designers
4. designers and implementor
5. implementor and end users

and so on. Each of these communications poses different requirements on the notation. For example, the client–designer communication must allow the client to express himself as closely as possible to his own world and vocabulary; the designer–implementor communication must be precise and unambiguous to ensure that the implementation adheres to the specified application. Notations may be graphical, textual, or both.

Most methods propose a new notation, extend some existing notation, or use existing notation directly. The advantages of directly using or extending existing notation are that, in most cases, users do not have to relearn entirely new conventions, and existing tools may be used directly or extended as needed. On the other hand, if the existing notation is too limited in its expressive power, extending it may require so much that the additions offset these advantages, and it may be more effective to use an entirely new notation.

Since many methods propose different models for describing different aspects of the application, different notations are used, and the relations between the models must also be represented.

Other considerations for notations regard their adequacy for automated tool support and legibility in printed form.

4.7.3 Implementation

Designing and implementing applications using methods produces several documents and, as with any larger software development, is best supported by computer-aided software engineering (CASE) tools. Such tools may support only the specification and help manage the documentation but may also include the generation of the final running implementation. This may be achieved in a completely automatic fashion or may be semi-automated, requiring the designer to manually fill in implementation details that cannot be automatically determined by the CASE environment.

Most complex Web applications involve dynamic processing of information, which in turn requires extensions to the server. The CASE environment may only generate the application targeted at a specific run-time environment, for example, Apache server with PhP scripting, or may be configured to generate the application for various such environments. In some cases, run-time environments are part of a larger framework, such as J2EE.

In addition, it may be further customized to also take into account the various access devices possible, such as cellular phones or handhelds, and provide environment information to support ubiquitous applications.

Dynamic Web applications rely heavily on databases to store and manage their data. An important part of the generated application is its interface to the DBMS. Typically, this involves establishing a mapping between the information items in the application and the data items stored in the database. Once more, this interface may be automatically generated and managed by the CASE environment, or it may require the manual intervention of the designer. In some cases, the CASE environment may also provide support for performance tuning and for maintenance and evolution of the application.

However, the task of implementing Web applications is increasing in complexity day by day due to the continuous emergence of new platforms and technologies. Specific needs are also arising for the development of several kinds of Web applications: Web data systems, interactive systems, transactional systems, workflow-based systems, collaborative systems, site-oriented systems, social systems, ubiquitous systems, or Semantic Web applications.

In this context, Web Engineering methods are evolving to be properly adapted to the continuous evolution of Web system requirements and technology. Web Engineering is a domain where model-driven software development (MDSD) principles can be used to address the evolution and adaptation of Web software to new platforms and technologies in order to achieve technological independence.

The Model-Driven Architecture (MDA®) initiative from the Object Management Group (OMG™) proposes defining the software building process based on a set of models. Depending on the level of abstraction, these models are dependent or independent of technological issues. One of the major benefits that introduce this separation of concerns is that system definitions can be reused for generating the system implementation in different technologies. On the other camp, Software Factories promote the systematic reuse, the application of the product lines philosophy, the model-driven development, the definition and use of domain-specific languages, the development of frameworks, and the generation of incremental code.

Recent Web Engineering approaches have made real advances in the prospects that are offered by model-driven software development (MDSD). This becomes more evident if we consider that some Web Engineering methods have successfully adopted the MDSD principles. They address different concerns using separate models (navigation, presentation, data, etc.) and are supported by model compilers that produce most of the application's Web pages (using PHP, JSP, ASP.NET, etc.). Moreover, they also take into account the possibility of accessing these systems via different devices, such as cellular phones or handhelds, and business logic (using COM+, EJB, J2EE, Web services) based on the models. This may be achieved either completely automatically or semi-automatically, requiring the designer to manually fill in implementation details that the tool cannot automatically determine.

Several signs point out that the use of the MDSD approach is going to rapidly increase. First, MDSD has received significant support from both the

MDA and the Software Factories. Second, the proliferation of CASE tools that support MDSD-based approaches that claim to be "MDA-compliant" is widespread. Third, technologies and tools for developing "your own" DSDM tools (graphical editors, model transformers, code generators, etc.) have also become abundant. In this category of tools we can find a set of projects developed under the Eclipse Modeling Project (EMF, GMF, GMT, etc.) and the DSL tools that are integrated with the MS Visual Studio 2005 Team System Edition. In this context, companies and research groups are considering the development of their own CASE tool for supporting their own Web Engineering method (following the MDA, Software Factories, Product Lines, Generative Programming of whatever other, more specific proposal) using one of these tools.

Although current Web Engineering methods still present some limitations when it comes to modeling further concerns, such as architectural styles or distribution, the adoption of MDSD principles can help achieve a real technological independence. In this way, methods are ready to be adapted to the second (Web 2.0) or third (Web 3.0) generation of Web applications, giving support to AJAX-based (Asynchronous Javascript and XML) Rich Client applications, Mashups, folksonomies, REST or XML Web Services to integrate current Web applications with third-party services, portals, as well as legacy systems.

4.7.4 Evolution and Maintenance

The dynamic nature of the current Web environment, and of the Internet in general, means that applications evolve very rapidly, as does the environment in which they run. Some methods provide direct support for the evolution of Web applications or provide support for tracing design decisions at various levels, easing the maintenance problem.

The resilience of applications designed with such methods with respect to changes is in good part determined by the abstraction levels supported by the method. If the adequate abstraction levels have been provided, the magnitude of changes in the application should be directly proportional to the magnitude of the changes in their requirements or of their run-time environments.

4.7.5 Role of Standards

Perhaps the main reason for the success of the Web was its establishment and adherence to standards. Following this tradition, some methods adopt some of the more recent standard notations such as UML at the design level or XML at the data level, some with direct support from CASE tools. In such cases, adopting such standards may also affect the target run-time environments, since several of them already provide direct support for these standards. The adoption of these standards may also facilitate model interchange between tools supporting different methods, such as XMI for UML-based notations.

Although standards such as XML address the syntactical aspect of model specifications, it may also be possible to use other standards that advance further into the semantic realm, such as RDF, RDFS, or OWL.

4.7.6 Personalization and Adaptation

Personalization has become a very important issue in the Internet, as a consequence of the increasing sophistication of Web sites, driven by the unabated competition between sites to attract viewers. Even though almost from the beginning browsers allowed personalization of presentation features, the current ubiquity of the World Wide Web, together with the myriad of platforms that support some kind of browsing, has reshaped this problem toward building applications customized to the individual.

Designing personalized Internet applications may mean building different interfaces, customized to a particular device; providing different navigation topologies to different persons; recommending specific products according to the user's preferences; implementing different pricing policies, and so on. All these facets of personalization share the need of modeling the user and his preferences, building profiles, finding algorithms for best linking options, etc., and integrating them in a cohesive design.

Several types of personalization must be accommodated:

1. role-based personalization, where the user sees different items and has different options depending on his role
2. link personalization, where the actual navigation topology depends on the individual and her access rights
3. content personalization, where actual contents of information items change depending on the person accessing the content
4. behavior or functionality personalization, where the functions the user can activate, and their behavior, change depending on the user
5. structure personalization, where the entire application may be customized according to the user's preferences or profile
6. presentation personalization, where the appearance (look and feel) of the content is adapted to the user, not the content itself

Many methods provide primitives that directly support personalization design, whereas others provide only guidelines.

Personalization can be seen as a special case of a more general behavior, adaptation. This behavior allows Web applications to alter some of their own characteristics as a function of various possible parameters. Personalization is really adaptation in which the input parameter is the user's identity and role. Other possible parameters are geographic location, available bandwidth, input device, past browsing history, etc.

Adaptation is paramount in the case of ubiquitous Web applications, i.e., applications that can be accessed anywhere, anytime. This means that they must be context-aware, in the broadest sense—not only must the logical context be taken into account, but also the physical and geographical environments as well. Such awareness may be directly expressible by some primitives in certain methods or implemented by lower-level primitives in others.

4.7.7 Quality Assurance Issues

Current Web applications can be very complex products and critical assets for an organization, so their quality can, to some extent, determine the organization's success or failure.

Quality assurance is a key support process and strategy mainly at the organization's software project level, in order to assure high-quality products and services by providing the main project stakeholders with the appropriate visibility, control, and feedback on resources, processes, and associated products throughout the software and Web life cycle.

Quality assurance applies to evaluation not only of products, processes, and services but also of resources as development methods, development teams, among others. To be effective, the quality assurance strategy should be planned and integrated to the main processes in the early phases of a project: That is, plans, activities, and procedures that will add value to the project and satisfy functional and nonfunctional requirements should be established from the very beginning. Quality assurance as a support process deals ultimately with preventive, evaluative, and corrective actions.

To measure, evaluate, verify, and validate functional and nonfunctional requirements from the quality assurance standpoint, different classes of methods can be categorized, including, for example, testing, inspection, simulation, and surveys, among others. In turn, for each category, particular methods and techniques can be applied (e.g., feature analysis method, heuristic guidelines inspection, Web usage analyses, white box testing, and user testing, among many possibilities) regarding the specific evaluation objectives and information needs.

Functional requirements actually represent what the Web application must do and provide (i.e., the scope) in terms of functions, contents, and services for the intended users. Nonfunctional requirements actually specify the capabilities, properties, and constraints that those functions, contents, and services should satisfy under certain conditions, for the intended users and contexts of use. The former are supported by different Web development methods by providing constructors and models at the conceptual, navigational, or presentational level, etc., as introduced in earlier sections here (and illustrated throughout this book). These models usually serve as input to many evaluation, verification, and validation activities, in addition to particular models for functional testing as test cases models, among others. The latter are currently supported to some extent by a couple of Web development methods; moreover, very often methods are not well integrated with quality assurance activities.

For instance, in order to measure and evaluate the external quality or quality in use of a Web application (or its components), models for quality, or quality in use, or subcharacteristics such as usability, security, reliability, etc. should be specified. These models, which represent nonfunctional requirements, can be performed by means of characteristics and attributes, or by means of heuristic guidelines, or by categories and questionnaire items.

Therefore, as the reader can surmise, conceptual frameworks for evaluation (as we will discuss in Chapter 13) that allow specifying nonfunctional requirements at different stages, in addition to the measurement (e.g., based on metrics) and the evaluation (e.g., based on indicators) components, might be necessary in order to support the analyses and recommended actions. In fact, some of the measurement, evaluation, and verification activities may be integrated and even automated in software and Web development methods in a sounder way.

4.8 THE PROBLEM STATEMENT

We deliberately kept the specification of the example for this book simple to make it more understandable for a broad audience. The requirements of the proposed application case are just described textually to leave place for each author to express it using the corresponding method's primitives.

The goal is to model an Internet site like www.imdb.com (the Internet Movies Database). The site allows users to explore movies and television programs, their actors, directors, and producers. Movies descriptions contain director, actors, genre(s), user comments, user ratings, country of origin, qualification, etc. Information about soundtracks can also be obtained. Relationships with related movies can be explored. External links (such as the official movie Web site) are also provided. Actors and directors are described by a short bio, a photograph, and his/her filmography (as actors, producers, writers, directors, and other related roles). For example, for each actor one can explore all the movies he participated in. Photo galleries of the actor/director can also be explored. The filmography can be explored according to different criteria: awards, user's votes, genre, etc.

The site provides daily information on new movies, biographies of selected actors, and news on the world of movies. Regarding nonnavigational behaviors, it is possible to add comments to films (in the style of sites such as www.amazon.com). It is also possible to explore show times and to buy tickets in selected cinemas. In this regard it is possible to select a city and a movie (currently on exhibition) and get the list of cinemas in that city that are showing the film. It is possible to select one show time of a given cinema and buy a ticket to see the chosen movie. The site maintains a list of films currently playing, giving a short description, together with access to user comments.

In a similar sense, the site maintains a list of upcoming movies, information on festivals, awards (like Emmy, Oscar, etc.), and miscellaneous news. It is also possible to buy DVDs for some movies online, with the usual functionality for online stores. Search facilities are also provided for movies, actors, companies, etc.

Chapter 5

APPLYING THE OOWS MODEL-DRIVEN APPROACH FOR DEVELOPING WEB APPLICATIONS. THE INTERNET MOVIE DATABASE CASE STUDY

Joan Fons, Vicente Pelechano, Oscar Pastor, Pedro Valderas, Victoria Torres
Research Group OO-Method. Department of Information Systems and Computation. Valencia University of Technology. Cami de Vera s/n, E-46022, Spain, `jjfons@dsic.upr.es`

5.1 INTRODUCTION

A decade after the emergence of the Web Engineering (Murugesan and Desphande, 2001) discipline, the development of complex Web applications is still a relevant research topic. For many years, Web Engineering approaches have done an excellent job adapting software engineering (Pressman) methods that were initially conceived to support traditional (non-Web) software development to provide solutions for the development of Web applications.

All of these Web Engineering methods were based on a similar principle: Web applications must be developed by starting with a sound, precise, and non-ambiguous description of an information system in the form of a conceptual schema (CS). Then, the CS must be properly transformed into its corresponding software product by defining the mappings between conceptual primitives and software representations. To achieve this, traditional conceptual schemas, which were mainly focused on capturing the static structure and the system behavior, were extended with new models and abstraction mechanisms to capture the new aspects introduced by Web applications. There are basically two aspects: navigation aspects and presentation aspects. Some representative efforts to introduce these aspects into traditional conceptual modeling approaches are the Object-Oriented

Hypermedia Design Model (OOHDM) (Rossi and Schwabe, 2001), WebML (Ceri et al., 2002), UML-base Web Engineering (UWE) (Knapp et al., 2004), and Web Site Design Method (WSDM) (De Troyer, 2001).

In this context, recent Web Engineering approaches have made real advances in the prospects that are offered by the model-driven strategy (Mellor et al., 2003). This becomes more evident if we consider that some Web Engineering methods have successfully adopted the Model-Driven Architecture (MDA) proposed by OMG (MDA, 2004). In accordance with the MDA approach, CSs are compared to Platform-Independent Models (PIM). Then, these PIMs are transformed into Platform-Specific Models (PSM) by the application of model-to-model transformations.

Our proposal provides a very specific contribution within this context. We have adapted the Web Engineering method, Object-Oriented Web Solutions (OOWS), to be compliant with MDA. OOWS proposes a PIM that allows us to fully describe the different aspects that define Web applications. This PIM extends the conceptual schema of a traditional object-oriented development method called OO-Method (Pastor et al., 2001) by introducing new models for describing the navigational and presentational aspects that characterize Web applications.

The PIM proposed by the OOWS method provides all the information needed to perform what MDA calls an "automatic transformation." This transformation is made using a tool to transform a PIM directly into deployable code. This can be done since the PIM is computationally complete. To achieve this transformation, we extend the OO-Method code generation strategy by presenting a precise transformational process for obtaining code from the new models introduced by OOWS. This process introduces a set of correspondences between the PIM abstractions and the final software components. We have also extended the commercial tool that supports OO-Method in the code generation process (OlivaNova Model Execution, CARE Technologies) by integrating mechanisms that allow us to incorporate the transformational process into the automatic code generation process.

We also explain how the transformational process proposed to obtain code from the PIM has been defined taking into account the unique characteristics of Web applications that have not been dealt with in the past by the software engineering community. In particular, we focus on the increased emphasis on user interfaces that has emerged in the development of Web applications. In a world where success is measured in terms of number of visits, Web applications need to provide attractive user interfaces in order to engage users. Therefore, development companies need to involve not only software engineers [as occurs in traditional development projects (Reifer, 2000)] but also graphic designers who are able to design more attractive interfaces. We explain how our approach allows software engineers and graphic designers to work in a collaborative way through the entire development process.

The structure of this work is the following: Section 5.2 introduces an MDA-based view of the OOWS approach. It also describes the OO-Method foundations on which the OOWS is based. The new models that OOWS introduces in the PIM model are of special relevance. Section 5.3 presents a discussion of the model transformation strategy used to obtain code from these models. This section also presents an implementation framework that helps in the development of the final solution. Section 5.4 presents the Internet Movie Database case study in which all of these ideas are put into practice.

5.2 OOWS: AN MDA-BASED WEB ENGINEERING METHOD

OOWS is a Web Engineering method that provides methodological support for Web application development. OOWS is the extension of an object-oriented software production method called OO-Method. Nowadays, the OO-Method approach has an industry-oriented implementation named OlivaNova (OlivaNova Model Execution, CARE Technologies) that has been developed by CARE Technologies S.A.

Section 5.2.1 presents the OO-Method approach that deals with "classic" software development using model-driven techniques for software development. Section 5.2.2 presents OOWS, introducing the diagrams that are needed to capture Web-based applications requirements.

5.2.1 OO-Method Conceptual Modeling

OO-Method (Pastor et al., 2001) (see left side in Figure 5.1) is an OO software production method that provides model-based code generation capabilities and integrates formal specification techniques with conventional OO modeling notations.

OO-Method provides a PIM where a system's static and dynamic aspects are captured by means of three complementary views, which are defined by the following models:

- a **Structural Model** that defines the system structure (its classes, operations, and attributes) and relationships between classes (specialization, association, and aggregation) by means of a *class diagram*
- a **Dynamic Model** that describes the valid object-life sequences for each class of the system using *state-transition diagrams*. Object interactions

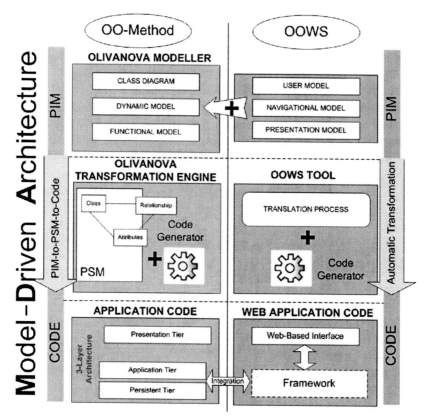

Figure 5.1. The MDA-based OO-Method/OOWS process development.

(communications between objects) are also represented by *sequence diagrams* in this model

- a **Functional Model** that captures the semantics of state changes to define service effects using a textual formal specification

OlivaNova, a commercial product, provides an operational, MDA-compliant framework, where a Model Compiler transforms a PIM into its corresponding Software Product. On one hand, the OlivaNova Modeller (OlivaNova Modeller, CARE Technologies) allows us to graphically define the different views that describe a system (the structural, dynamic and functional models). On the other hand, a set of OlivaNova Transformation Engines (OlivaNova Transformation Engines, CARE Technologies) compile these views in order to translate the conceptual primitives defined in the PIM into a specific implementation language. According to MDA, each OlivaNova Transformation Engine is a tool that automatically performs PIM-to-PSM transformations and PSM-to-Code transformations.

A three-tier architectural style has been selected to generate software applications:

- **Presentation tier:** It includes the graphical user interface components for interacting with the user.
- **Application tier:** This tier is divided into the Business façade, which publicizes the interfaces provided by the Business Logic, which implements the structure and the functionality of the classes in the conceptual schema.
- **Persistence tier:** It implements the persistence and the access to persistent data to hide the details of data repositories from the upper tiers.

As stated in Murugesan and Desphande (2001), Web applications introduce additional properties that are not addressed by software methods during the development process. In this sense, OO-Method is not an exception and requires some extensions in order to cope with them. These new properties refer to aspects such as navigation, presentation, and other advanced features such as user personalization. To achieve this, OOWS (see right side in Figure 5.1) introduces three new models into the PIM supported by the OlivaNova Modeller: the **user model**, the **navigational model**, and the **presentation model**.

These three new models allow one to fully describe Web applications at the PIM level. The code generation process implemented by the OlivaNova Transformation Engines must also be extended in order to automatically generate code from the OOWS models. However, this extension must be performed in a conservative way with respect to the transformation engines to assure compatibility with already developed software.

In order to achieve this conservative extension, we have defined a parallel translation process that generates code from the OOWS models. Then, the integration of both translation processes (OO-Method and OOWS) are performed at the implementation level.

The parallel translation process is supported by a tool that generates Web-based interfaces from the OOWS models. These interfaces are directly implemented from the OOWS models since these models contain all the necessary information to generate code. In accordance with MDA, we perform an automatic transformation.

The Web-based interface constitutes the presentation tier of the Web applications. To obtain full Web applications, this tier must be integrated with the application and persistent tiers generated by the OlivaNova Transformation Engine (the two tiers that implement the functionality of the system from the static and dynamic aspects described in the OO-Method models). To achieve this integration, we have developed a framework that allows us to implement Web-based interfaces and connect them with the services provided by the application tier generated by the OlivaNova Transformation Engine.

The following sections explain in detail the set of models introduced by the OOWS extension.

5.2.2 OOWS: Extending Conceptual Modeling to Web Environments

In order to fill the gap left by conventional software methods, the OOWS (Fons et al., 2003) approach defines the three new models mentioned above. The first model (the *User Model*) allows us to specify a categorization about the kind of users that can interact with the system as well as the inheritance relationships among these kinds of users. The second model (*the Navigation Model*) allows us to specify the system visibility (in terms of data and functionality) and the valid paths to traverse the system structure (navigational semantics) for each type of user. Finally, the third model (*the Presentation Model*) is introduced to specify presentation requirements for the elements defined in the Navigation Model.

5.2.3 User Model: User Identification and Categorization

A user diagram allows us to specify the types of users that can interact with the system. Types of users are organized in a hierarchical way by means of inheritance relationships, which allow us to specify navigation specialization (MDA, 2004). Child types of users can inherit the navigational semantics associated to their parent, which allows us to reuse navigational descriptions. This model categorizes types of users into three groups:

- *Anonymous users* (depicted with the '?' symbol). They represent users who are not logged into the system.
- *Registered users* (depicted with a pad-lock symbol). They represent users who are identified (logged) in the system as valid users.
- *Generic users* (depicted with a cross symbol). They are used to represent abstract users (users who cannot be instantiated).

An example of a graphical representation of this model is depicted in Figure 5.2. As this figure shows, the *Management Personnel* user has been defined as a *generic* user. This means that this kind of user will have an associated navigational model that will be enriched by the models defined by their inherited types of users. This inheritance mechanism allows different users to reuse navigational models.

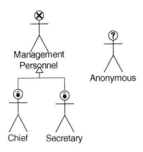

Figure 5.2. User diagram.

5.2.4 Navigational Model: Representing Navigation

The Navigational model was introduced in the OOWS approach to specify the view over the system in terms of classes, class attributes, and operations and relationships between classes for each kind of user defined in the *User Model*. This model is built in two phases. The first phase defines a global view over the navigation. This global representation is called "Authoring-in-the-large." The second phase makes a detailed description of the elements defined in the previous phase. This detailed view is called "Authoring-in-the-small."

5.2.5 The "Authoring-in-the-Large" Phase

The "Authoring-in-the-large" phase involves describing the navigation allowed for each kind of user by means a **Navigational Map.** Figure 5.3 depicts this map graphically by means of a directed graph whose nodes represent *navigational contexts* or *navigational subsystems* and whose arcs represent *navigational links* that define the valid navigational paths over the system.

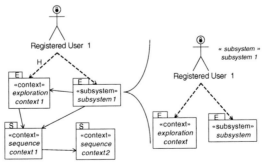

Figure 5.3. Navigational map and navigational subsystem.

Navigational contexts correspond to nodes from the navigational map and represent user interaction units that provide a set of cohesive data and operations to perform certain activities. **Navigational subsystems** are used to structure the navigational map when these get highly complex. They allow us to define subgraphs within the graph recursively.

Both *Navigational contexts* and *navigational subsystems* can be categorized depending on their reachability in

- *Exploration navigational contexts/subsystems* (depicted with an "E" label) are reachable from any other node. They define implicit navigational links. which are represented as dashed arrows pointing to these contexts.
- *Sequence navigational contexts/subsystems* (depicted with an "S" label) are nodes that can only be accessed following a predefined path. These paths are defined by linking different nodes using *sequence links*.

The *home* context (the context displayed by default when the user logs into the system) is defined as an exploration context whose implicit link is labeled with an "H."

Navigational links correspond to arcs from the navigational map and are used to define reachability paths among different nodes. There are two types of navigational links:

- *Sequence links* or *"contextual links"* (represented using solid arrows) involve a semantic navigation between two contexts and understand semantic navigation as the activity of carrying some information from a source context to a target context.
- *Exploration links* or *"noncontextual links"* (represented using dashed arrows) represent valid navigation paths through different contexts. In contrast to the navigation defined by sequence links, this navigation does not involve carrying information between contexts. These links are implicitly defined by exploration contexts or exploration subsystems.

5.2.6 The "Authoring-in-the-Small" Phase

Once navigational maps are built, the *"Authoring-in-the-small"* phase details the specification of the previously built navigational contexts. Navigational contexts are made up of a set of **Abstract Information Units** (AIU), which represent the requirement of retrieving a chunk of related information. *Contextual AIUs* (labeled with a circled C in Figure 5.4) filter this information using the information that is related to a sequence link. *Noncontextual AIUs* (labeled with a circled NC) do not depend on sequence links.

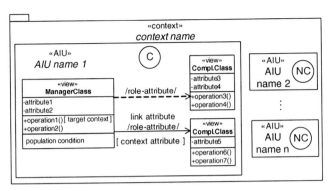

Figure 5.4. Navigational context.

AIUs are made up of **navigational classes**, which represent views over the classes defined in the Class Diagram (see Figure 5.4). These views are represented graphically as UML classes that are stereotyped with the *«view»* keyword and that contain the set of attributes and operations that will be available to the user.

Each AIU must include one navigational class (called the **manager class**) and can optionally include a set of complementary class views (called **complementary classes**) to complete the information retrieved by the manager class.

Navigational classes are related by unidirectional binary relationships called **navigational relationships**. These relationships are defined over existing association or inheritance relationships defined in the Class Diagram. To eliminate any possible ambiguity in the case of multiple relationships between two classes, navigational relationships must include the role name of the relationship (depicted graphically as /role-attribute/) as well as the attribute used as an anchor to move between navigational contexts. Moreover, depending on the navigational capability of the navigational relationship, these can be of two types:

1. A **context dependency relationship** (graphically represented using dashed arrows) represents a basic information retrieval by crossing a structural relationship between classes. When a context dependency relationship is defined, all the object instances related to the origin class object are retrieved.

2. A **context relationship** (graphically represented using solid arrows) represents the same information recovery as a context dependency relationship does plus a navigation capability to a target navigational context, creating a sequence link in the navigational map. Context relationships have the following properties:

- a *context attribute* that indicates the target context of the navigation (depicted as *[target context]*).
- a *link attribute* that specifies the attribute used as the *"anchor"* to activate the navigation to the target context. The link attribute is usually an attribute of the target navigational class. For usability reasons, it is sometimes interesting to define the anchor as a "label" (static text).

A **Service Link** defines a navigation that will automatically be performed after the execution of a navigational operation of a navigational class. Figure 5.4 shows an example of a service link in the *ManagerClass* that defines a navigation to the *target context* that will be performed each time the *"operation1()"* is executed inside this context.

Apart from attributes and operations, navigational classes can also define conditions to filter the retrieved objects. These filters are called **population condition filters** and are specified by means of OCL formulas at the bottom section of the class view primitive.

These are the core primitives for navigational specifications. However, this specification can be enriched by introducing mechanisms to help the user explore and filter the huge amount of information inside a context. The following section explains how to introduce advanced navigational features to the OOWS navigational model.

5.2.6.1 Advanced Navigational Features

Navigational contexts retrieve the population of classes defined in the conceptual schema. We define the cardinality of a navigational context as the number of instances that should be retrieved. Sometimes, the retrieved information is difficult to manage mainly due to its size. To help users browse through that amount of information, we have defined mechanisms for browsing and filtering in a navigational context. There are two main search mechanisms: **indexes** and **filters**. Those features are described in a dashed-line box at the bottom of each AIU.

An **index** is a structure that provides an *indexed access* to the population of the manager class. Indexes create a list of summarized information by using an attribute or a set of attributes. If the indexed property belongs to the manager class, it is defined as an **attribute index**. If the indexed property belongs to any complementary class, the index is defined as a **relationship index**, and the relationship must be specified. When an index is activated, a list of all possible values for the indexed attribute(s) is created. By choosing one of these values, all objects that have the same value for this property will be shown in a search view. This search view describes the information that will be available to the user to aid him in selecting an instance. This selected instance will be activated in the navigational context.

A **filter** defines a *population condition* to restrict the object instances to be retrieved. If the filter condition is applied to attributes of the manager class, it is defined as an **attribute filter**. If the filter condition is applied to attributes of complementary classes, it is defined as a **relationship filter**. There are three types of filters:

- *exact filters*, which take one attribute value and return all the instances that match it exactly.
- *approximate filters*, which take one attribute value and return all the instances whose attribute values include this value as a substring.
- *range filters*, which take two values (a maximum and a minimum) and return all the instances whose attribute values fit within the range. If we specify only one value, it is only bounded on that side (upper or lower bounded).

Moreover, it is possible to predefine the values of the filter conditions at the modeling stage. This sort of filter is called a *static population condition*. The main difference between a *population condition filter* and a *static population condition* is that the former is always active while the latter has to be activated by the user. When a static filter is activated, the instances that fulfill the condition are displayed in a search view that behaves the same way as the *exact* filter defined above.

5.2.7 Presentational Modeling

Once the navigational model is built, we must specify presentational requirements of Web applications using a **Presentation Model** (see Figure 5.1). This model is strongly dependent on the navigational model since it uses navigational contexts (system–user interaction units) to define the presentation properties.

Presentation requirements are specified by means of patterns that are associated to the primitives of the navigational context (navigational classes, navigational links, searching mechanisms, etc.). The basic presentation patterns are as follows:

Information Paging. This pattern allows us to specify information "scrolling." All the retrieved instances are broken into logical blocks so that only one block is visible at a time. Mechanisms to move forward or backward are provided. This pattern can be applied to the *manager class*, to a *navigational relationship*, or to an *index* or a *filter*. The required information is

- *Cardinality*, which represents the number of instances that make a block.
- *Access mode*, which can be defined as *Sequential*, providing mechanisms to go to the next, previous, first, and last logical block or *Random*, where the user can directly access any block.

- *Circularity*. When this property is active, the set of blocks behaves as a circular buffer.

Ordering Criteria. This pattern defines a class population ordering (*ASC*endant or *DESC*endant) using the value of one or more attributes. It can be applied to either navigational classes or access structures, specifying how the retrieved instances will be ordered.

Information Layout. We provide three basic layout patterns and one layout operator. The three patterns are: *register, tabular (vertical and horizontal)*, and *tree*. The operator pattern (*master-detail*) is applied to many-to-many relationships using one of these basic layout patterns to show the detail portion. Any of these layout patterns can be applied either to the *manager class* or to a *navigation relationship*.

These presentation patterns, together with the specified navigation features, capture the essential requirements for the construction of Web interfaces.

5.3 DEVELOPING THE WEB SOLUTION

This section presents the development strategy defined in OOWS to implement Web application interfaces extending and using the OO-Method approach. The development strategy is based on the following principles:

- *Integrating OOWS code generation with the OO-Method software solution*. Web application interfaces developed with the OOWS approach must be integrated within the OO-Method implemented applications architectural style. Section 5.3.1 explains in more detail this requirement and the software artifacts offered by the OO-Method implemented applications for integration purposes.
- *Building Web-based user interfaces*. We defined a taxonomy of Web pages and contents by analyzing many implemented Web pages. This taxonomy allows us to build Web pages using "contents" as page components. Section 5.3.2 provides more details about this approach.
- *Implementation strategy*. We implemented a framework that provides us with a more abstract interface to develop Web pages. This framework produces HTML pages that use OO-Method implemented applications. The most relevant primitives of this framework are presented in Section 5.3.6.
- *Dealing with graphical design*. To cope with the look and feel of the implemented Web interfaces, we have defined a strategy that allows us to define visualization rules to improve Web page aesthetics. These rules

are categorized within two groups of rules: domain-dependent and domain-independent. Section 5.3.9 provides detailed information about this strategy and how it is applied by the framework.

5.3.1 Integrating OOWS Code Generation with the OO-Method Software Solution

As explained in Section 5.2.1, OO-Method uses a three-tier architectural style to generate software applications: a *presentation tier,* an *application tier,* and a *persistence tier.*

The information (*persistence tier*) and functionality (*application tier*) of the Web application are generated by the OlivaNova Model Transformation Engines taking as basis the OO-Method's structural and behavioral models.

Taking into account the navigational and presentation features introduced by the OOWS models, the generation process is enriched by providing a new translation process to generate the *presentation tier* for Web applications.

Applications generated with the OlivaNova Transformation Engines provide the following two integration mechanisms:

1. *Components.* The code generated by the ONME[1] is accompanied by two types of components for each domain class: *querying* and *business logic* components. *Querying components* provide operations for querying class population (retrieving instances by their identifiers or by filtering conditions, etc.) and operations for retrieving the population of related classes. *Business logic components* provide the functional operations for each class. Depending on the target technologies, those components are COM+ (VisualBasic), .NET components (C#), and EJB3.0 (Java).

2. *Web services.* The generated Web services encapsulate the previous components. These Web services decouple integrating applications from the ONME code technology. OlivaNova generates the following Web services: (1) a Web service for each domain class, which provides an interface for querying and for accessing business logic functionality, and (2) a generic Web service (*XML_Listener*) in an SOA architectural style; the port type of this Web service is implemented using the inversion of control pattern that provides an operation for each querying and business logic domain operation (see Figure 5.5).

---

[1] Acronym for OlivaNova Model Execution strategy

```
<?xml version="1.0" encoding="UTF-8"?>
<definitions name="XML_Listener">

    <message name="XML_Listener.XMLRequestInput">
        <part name="xmlRequest" type="xsd:string"/>
    </message>
    <message name="XML_Listener.XMLRequestOutput">
        <part name="return" type="xsd:string"/>
    </message>

    <portType name="XML_ListenerPortType">
        <operation name="XMLRequest" parameterOrder="xmlRequest">
            <input name="XMLRequestRequest" message="tns:XML_Listener.XMLRequestInput"/>
            <output name="XMLRequestResponse" message="tns:XML_Listener.XMLRequestOutput"/>
        </operation>
    </portType>

    <binding name="XML_ListenerBinding" type="tns:XML_ListenerPortType">
        <soap:binding style="rpc" transport="http://schemas.xmlsoap.org/soap/http"/>
        <suds:class type="ns0:XML_Listener" rootType="ServicedComponent">
        </suds:class>
        <operation name="XMLRequest">
            <soap:operation/>
            <suds:method attributes="public"/>
            <input name="XMLRequestRequest">
                <soap:body use="encoded" encodingStyle="http://schemas.xmlsoap.org/soap/encoding/"/>
            </input>
            <output name="XMLRequestResponse">
                <soap:body use="encoded" encodingStyle="http://schemas.xmlsoap.org/soap/encoding/"/>
            </output>
        </operation>
    </binding>

    <service name="XML_ListenerService">
        <port name="XML_ListenerPort" binding="tns:XML_ListenerBinding">
            <soap:address location="http://ascalon.dsic.upv.es:80/WSIMDb/IMDbWebSpace.XML.XML_Listener.soap"/>
        </port>
    </service>
</definitions>
```

Figure 5.5. XML_Listener Web service definition provided by OlivaNova.

5.3.2 Building Web-Based User Interfaces

Before defining Web page implementation, we started by analyzing many implemented Web pages. Our objective was to define what types of Web pages are commonly implemented as well as the contents that these should include. The idea was to try to define a strategy to decompose Web pages into different types of contents and, then, to try to map conceptual modeling primitives into these different contents.

This strategy also allows us to define different types of Web pages depending on the objective of each Web page. As an example, the following subsections show that there are Web pages whose purpose is to structure navigation, such as the "*home*" Web page.

Section 5.3.3 analyzes the different types of Web pages used to implement Web applications by defining the main objectives or goals of each one. Next, Section 5.3.4 defines the different types of contents that are used to define a Web page. Finally, Section 5.3.5 relates the Web page taxonomy with Web contents by defining which types of contents should or must appear in each type of Web page.

5.3.3 Web Page Taxonomy

After analyzing many implemented Web pages, we have categorized them into three basic types of Web pages: navigation structuring, informational, and data input. Each one of these types has a different objective within the Web application.

- *Navigation structuring Web pages.* This type defines some kind of navigation organization. When a user reaches a Web page of this type, the page provides the user with a set of links to the natural navigational links that she can follow. Web pages of this type should appear when there are a lot of navigation capabilities.
- *Informational Web pages.* This type provides the user with information and functionality related to an instance or group of instances of the system. With these Web pages, the system provides the user with information about the system state and the operations that are available in that state. Also, these Web pages can define navigation capabilities to other Web pages by "clicking" on some of their contents. These Web pages are the most common pages within a Web application.
- *Data input Web pages.* Web pages of this type are related to an operation execution (whenever the system needs some data from the user). When a user invokes an operation, if this operation requires additional arguments, the system displays a Web page of this type to the user. This Web page basically contains a form that includes an input mechanism for each argument that must be introduced.

A final consideration must be made with regard to this taxonomy. As the following section shows, each Web page can provide different types of contents, for instance, navigation content. This might lead to a misconception such as the following: All Web pages that have navigation contents are *navigation structuring Web pages.* However, this is not always true. We consider that a Web page has only one main objective and may have other objectives, but those are secondary. This reasoning is explained in more detail in Section 5.3.5.

5.3.4 Web Page Contents

At first glance, the types of Web pages described above appear to include totally different contents. However, a more careful analysis shows that this is not really true; in most cases, there exist different "pieces" of Web pages that are basically the same within many other Web pages, and other "pieces" that appear in all Web pages. For instance, most Web pages have a zone[2] where a navigational menu (made of navigational links) is provided.

After defining the different types of Web pages, we analyze the different types of contents of those Web pages. Following the same approach, we encountered the following zone contents:

- *Navigation zone.* It provides the user with a set of navigable links that can be activated within the Web page.
- *Location zone.* It provides the user information about where the user is and the navigation path (sequence of navigational pages) that he has followed to reach that location.
- *Information zone.* It provides information about the system (usually in a database).
- *Services zone.* It provides access to the operations that can be activated. This zone is contained inside an information zone, and all the operations are related to that information.
- *User information zone.* It shows identification information about the logged user. This zone only appears for registered users.
- *Institutional zone.* It contains information about the institution (company, entity, organization, etc.) that is responsible for the Web application. It usually shows information regarding the name of the institution, the logo, etc.
- *Data entry zone.* It is responsible for providing the user with a form to input data to execute certain operations. Then, a submit-like button links the input data with the associated functionality.
- *Application links zone.* It contains some common Web functionalities such as Login, Logout, and Home.
- *Access structures zone.* It contains search mechanisms to help in browsing data. In fact, this zone is always related to one *information zone*. For this reason, this zone always appears inside an information zone.
- *Custom zone.* It contains information regarding other types of contents that cannot be catalogued in the other zones. This zone is normally used for domain-independent content, such as advertisements, other related Web applications, external applications, etc.

To complete the approach, these content zones should be joined to compose Web pages. The next section discusses how these contents can be appropriately combined to build Web pages.

---

[2] We refer to "Web page zone" or simply "Web zone" as a cohesive data and functionality that has a meaning of its own.

5.3.5 Relating Web Page Taxonomy to Web Page Contents

Once Web page types and content zones have been defined, a relationship between them must be established by indicating which type of contents should or must appear in each type of Web page and how many times these contents can appear. We can mark a content zone as being *mandatory, recommended, optional,* and *not recommended*. We have followed a quality strategy to define what content zones appear to ensure that this particular type of Web page provides the user with the minimum information needed to accomplish the objective of that Web page type.

Moreover, there is a basic rule that is applied: A Web page must *always* provide the user with information regarding *where the user is, how the user arrived there* (navigational path), and *the places where the user can move from there.* This rule implies that any Web page must contain navigation and location zones.

Taking into account these basic principles, we have defined Table 5.1, which combines Web pages with content zones, indicating the suitability of including each content zone within each Web page category.

Table 5.1. Web Page Taxonomy Related to Web Page Contents

✓- Mandatory   ✗- Not recommended

👌 - Recommended   ?- Optional

✱- It can appear more than once

	Information Web Page	Navigation Web Page	Data Entry Web Page
Navigation zone	✓, ✱	✓, ✱	✓, ✱
Location zone	✓	✓	✓
Information zone	✓, ✱	✗	✗
Services zone	?, ✱	✗	?, ✱
User info. zone	👌	👌	👌
Institution zone	?, ✱	?, ✱	?, ✱
Link app. zone	👌	👌	👌
Data entry zone	✗	✗	✓
Access struct. zone	?	?	?
Custom zone	?, ✱	?, ✱	?, ✱

The *not recommended* tag is intended to mark contents that can overload a type of Web page with different objectives, possibly causing the user to get confused about or deviate from the main objective of that type of Web page. For instance, in a navigation Web page, content zones regarding information or data entry are *not recommended,* so that the main objective of this Web page is only to structure navigation.

Finally, note that this table has been used to define the types of Web pages that must be implemented as well as the types of contents that these pages should have. We have built an HTML framework that implements this table (see Section 5.3.6).

5.3.6 Implementation Strategy

The OOWS Tool provides a code generator that takes two PIM models (the OO-Method model and the OOWS models) and translates them into Web application code. This code defines the interface tier for Web application environments (see Figure 5.1). The generation process is only possible by having a set of predefined transformation rules that represents abstract concepts of the PIM model into specific code.

The following subsections explain the implementation strategy based on an implementation framework in detail. This framework raises the level of abstraction of the HTML code to a set of implementation patterns that define correspondences between conceptual modeling primitives and the implementation framework components. This framework also provides facilities to integrate with the OlivaNova generated code.

5.3.7 Implementation Framework

By following a pure MDA approach, we have defined a PSM model of the HTML language, which we implemented using PHP, creating an implementation framework that allows us to implement Web pages at a more abstract level of abstraction. We have implemented this Web page definition and implementation framework applying the taxonomy of Web pages and content zones presented in Section 5.3.2. This framework basically provides us with a set of primitives for defining two types of objects: a Web application and Web pages.

The *Application* object contains all the information about the application. It needs a name and the reference to the component that implements the functionality interface (provided by OlivaNova). This object provides the following operations:

- *AddRol(User, UserAlias, ValidationMethod, inheritsFrom).* This operation defines the different types of users that can interact with the Web application. If a validation method is specified (by means of the OlivaNova generated user validation primitive), the user is registered. The final argument is used to specify user inheritance.

- *AddPageGroup(GroupName, GroupAlias, Group, User, Visibility).* This operation defines a group of pages that will only be visible when navigating inside the group. The third (optional) argument specifies the group that this group is in. The fourth argument refers to the user who owns the page. The last argument can take the following values: "always" (a Web page that is always accessible) and "fromPage" (a Web page that is only accessible through another Web page).

- *AddPage(PageName, PageAlias, Group, User, Visibility).* This operation defines a Web page (that can be inside a group) for a user. The last argument has the same meaning as in the *AddPageGroup* operation.

- *SetDefaultStyle(StyleName).* This operation specifies the default style that will be used. If no style is defined, no style will be applied. More information about Web page visualizations is included in Section 5.3.9.

- *SetHomePage(PageName, User).* This operation allows specifying the page that will be used as the user's home page.

These application primitives define the properties of the entire Web application. These primitives also implicitly define other properties. For instance, the navigational menu of every Web page is automatically created by using the *AddPage* and *AddPageGroup* operations (by using the visibility argument) and with the *AddRol* operation (for inheritance specification).

Figure 5.6 shows an excerpt of the code that implements a Web application using the proposed implementation framework. Both *AnonymousUser* and *RegisteredUser* are allowed to access the Web site (*AddRol*), and registered users also have access to the Web pages of the

```php
<?php
include_once "../Framework/ApplicationBegin.php";

    $Application = new Application("OrderThingsDemo", "SimpleOrders");

    $Application->AddRol("Anonymous","","","");
    $Application->AddRol("RegisteredUser","RegisteredUser",
                         "RegisteredUser_MVAgentValidation","AnonymousUser");

    $Application->AddFirstLevelPage("MembersList","Clients","AnonymousUser");
    $Application->AddFirstLevelPage("ItemsList","Products","AnonymousUser");
    $Application->AddFirstLevelPage("OrdersList","Client's Orders","AnonymousUser");
    ...
    $Application->AddFirstLevelPage("MembersList","Clients","RegisteredUser");
    $Application->AddPage("memberDetail","Detailed Information","RegisteredUser");

    $Application->SetDefaultStyle("UPV-like");

    $Application->SetHomePage("MembersList","AnonymousUser");
    ...

include_once "../Framework/ApplicationEnd.php";
?>
```

Figure 5.6. Example of an excerpt of a Web application definition.

AnonymousUser (through inheritance). There are five Web pages, three of which are separate and two of which are in a group. The three separate Web pages belong to the *AnonymousUser* (*MemberList*, *ItemsList,* and *OrdersList*), and the remaining two (*MemberPersonalInfo* and *memberDetail*) belong to the *RegisteredUser*. All of these Web pages are always accessible through the navigational menu. However, the *memberDetail* for the *RegisteredUser* isn't visible from the navigational menu. It can only be reached by navigating from another Web page. The *UPV-like* visualization style (*SetDefaultStyle*) has been selected. Finally, the home Web pages for the *AnonymousUser* and *RegisteredUser* are specified (*SetHomePage*).

Once each Web page has been defined, it must be described. The framework provides primitives to describe the content zones of these Web pages. Following the conclusions obtained in Section 5.3.5, the navigation and location zones must appear in every Web page. As the links in the navigation zone are derived from the Web application configuration and the location zone is derived from the user navigation path, the framework does not provide explicit primitives to define these zones. It calculates them automatically.

The framework provides a primitive to introduce the other type of content. Some examples are *AddInformationZone*, *AddInstitutionZone*, *AddUserInfoZone*, etc. The information zone is based on a manager class and provides operations for adding fields (*AddField*, class attributes), linking to other pages using a field as the anchor (*AddInternalLink*), and sorting by using a field (*SetSorted*) in "ascendant" or "descendant" mode, etc. The *AddDetailedRelationship* retrieves related data from a related class. Each one of these zones is implemented using HTML DIV containers.

Figure 5.7 presents an excerpt of the MemberList Web page definition for the *RegisteredUser*. It is made up of the following zones: (1) the navigation zone (implicit); (2) the location zone (implicit); (3) a user zone

```
<?php
include_once "../Framework/PageBegin.php";

$Page = new Page("MemberList","RegisteredUser");

$UserZone = $Page->AddUserInfoZone();

$InfoZone = $Page->AddInformationZone("MembersList","Member");
$InfoZone->AddField("Username","Name");
$InfoZone->Username->AddInternLinkTo("memberDetail");
$InfoZone->Username->AddDynamicFilter("Approach");
$InfoZone->Username->SetSorted("Ascendant");
$InfoZone->AddField("Adress","Adress");
$InfoZone->AddField("City","City");
...

$ServicesZone = $InfoZone->AddServicesZone("MemberServices","Operations for Registered Users");
$ServicesZone->AddServiceReference("RegisteredUser_create_instance","New");
$ServicesZone->AddServiceReference("RegisteredUser_MVChangePassword","Change password");
...

include_once "../Framework/PageEnd.php";
?>
```

Figure 5.7. Example of an excerpt of a Web page definition using the framework.

(*AddUserInfoZone*) in which information about the user is displayed; (4) an information zone called *MemberList* that provides information about the *Member* class and its *Username, Address,* and *City* attributes (sorted by *Username* "ascendant"). The username has been defined as an anchor to navigate to the *memberDetail* Web page (*Username->AddInternalLinkTo*). Finally, (5) the service zone has been included inside this information zone (*InfoZone->AddServicesZone*) to allow *RegisteredUser*s to execute the *RegisteredUser_create_instance* and *RegisteredUser_MVChangePassword* operations. These operations come from the OlivaNova specification (see Section 5.3.1 for more details about integration with OlivaNova).

5.3.8 Implementation Patterns Using the Framework

Finally, correspondences between the OOWS conceptual modeling primitives with the implementation framework primitives must be defined. This step is automatically applied by a model-to-code generator. The first rule always creates a Web application project by defining the application (name) and the default visualization style (see the Figure 5.6 primitive *new Application*). Then several groups of transformation rules are applied to complete this transformation process, taking the OOWS models as input.

(1) Transformation rules referring to the user diagram:

(1.1) *User rule*: For each user defined in the navigational map, an *AddRol* operation is created in the Web application definition file. If it is an anonymous type of user, the validation operation is not specified. If a user is a specialization of another user, it is specified using this *AddRol* operation.

(2) Transformation rules referring to the navigational map:

(2.1) *Page group rule*: For each navigational subsystem that appears in the navigational map, an *AddPageGroup* operation with the "always" *visibility* argument is created. It is specified to belong to the user of the navigational map in which it is defined. If it is inside a subsystem, the group that is related to that subsystem is specified.

(2.2) *Page rule*: For each exploration navigational context that appears in the navigational map, an *AddPage* operation with the "always" *visibility* argument is created. For each sequence navigational context, an *AddPage* instruction with the "fromPage" *visibility* argument is created. All these pages are specified to belong to the user of the navigational map in which they are defined. When these nodes are inside a subsystem, the group that is related to that subsystem is specified.

(2.3) *Home page rule*: A home navigational node can be defined in a navigational map. The generation process establishes this page as the home page with the *SetHomePage* operation. If no node has been defined as the home page, a new page is created using *AddFirstLevelPage* and marking *SetHomePage*. Each navigational subsystem must have a home page. The same algorithm is applied recursively, treating each navigational subsystem as if it were a navigational map.

(3) Transformation rules from the navigational node specifications

Each navigational node has been specified as a Web page by the (2.1) rule in the Web application definition file. In this step, the transformation process creates a Web page definition file for each one of these specified Web pages. Depending on the type of the navigational node, one of the following rules is applied:

(3.1) *Navigational context rule*: An informational web page (see taxonomy in Section 5.3.3) file is created. A new information zone is created for each AIU. Then an *AddField* is invoked for each navigational attribute of the manager class. A (sub)zone is created using the *AddServicesZone* if the manager class has at least one operation. This (sub)zone includes a service reference (*AddReference*) for each operation of the manager class. Finally, an *AddDetailedRelationship* operation is created for each navigation relationship. Each attribute, operation, or relationship is also defined.

(3.2) *Navigational subsystem rule*: A navigation structuring Web page file is created. As the pages inside this subsystem have already been created with the (2.1) rule, the framework automatically creates a navigation zone containing the links to all these related Web pages.

The transformation process has more rules than the ones just mentioned (for instance, it includes rules regarding the presentation model). However, for reasons of brevity, these transformation rules are not presented.

5.3.9 Dealing with the Graphical Design of Web Interfaces

The graphical design, or "look and feel," of a Web application is a requirement that must be properly managed when building Web applications. Nowadays, Web application graphical design is usually built by means of *visual styling rules* defined in specific languages such as the CSS language (cascade style sheet), which is standardized by the W3C.

The OOWS implementation strategy objective is to deal with a few basic principles with regard to graphical design:

- *Separation of concerns*. System designers should not take graphical design into account when designing the system. Only graphical designers should deal with these graphical designs.
- *Reusability*. Graphical designs should be reusable for any application.

- *Adaptability.* Graphical designs should be easily adapted for specific applications so that specific visualization rules can be defined.
- *Visualization patterns.* On the World Wide Web, visualization patterns are used now and then in Web applications. Those visualization patterns that are widely used must facilitate the graphical design description. These visualization patterns should be used.

OOWS follows this strategy to apply these principles to define Web interfaces:

1. Use specific languages for the definition of the visualization rules (CSS) and do it in separate files: None of the implemented Web pages should include visualization rules (we use XHTML to define Web pages).
2. Define a markup of Web pages based upon conceptual terms and not on implementation terms.
3. Create two files for defining visualization rules: a domain-dependent file that includes rules that can only be used in Web pages of the same domain, and a domain-independent file that includes generic rules that can be applied to any Web page, independently of the application domain.
4. Publicize a repository of graphical designs and visualization patterns. This repository should be used by the implemented Web pages to obtain the visualization rules.

The implementation framework is responsible for marking up the Web pages and linking to the two graphical design files (domain-dependent and domain-independent files). Section 5.3.10 discusses the markup strategy that must be undertaken in each implemented Web page. Section 5.3.11 explains how to define domain-independent and domain-dependent visualization rules.

5.3.10 Web Page Markup

The framework implements a Web page markup strategy that divides the tags into two groups: domain-dependent tags and domain-independent tags.

The **domain-independent tags** are based upon the OO-Method/OOWS primitives and terms that come from the Web page and content taxonomy discussed in Section 5.3.2. Each specific content zone has its own tags. This group of tags defines generic visualization rules that can be applied to every Web application implemented with the framework since the concepts they use are domain- and platform-independent.

The **domain-dependent tags** are based upon domain-specific terms. These group of tags can appear anywhere in the Web page where the term related to the tag is used. This markup defines visualization rules for that specific application. However, as the following section discusses, the visualization rules that use these tags won't be reusable.

The following list shows the most representative Web zones as well as the domain-independent (DI) and domain-dependent (DD) tags that are used within those zones. This markup is shown in Figure 5.8.

- **Web page body.** The following tags can be applied to the HTML BODY construct:

  DI tags: *Context, Subsystem*

  DD tags: the name of the context or the subsystem

- **Location zone**

  DI tags: *LocationZone, Path, PathStep, PathStepSeparator*

  DD tags: the name of the contexts or subsystems related to each *PathStep*

- **Navigation zone**

  DI tags: *NavigationZone, NavigationLink, NavigationGroup*

  DD tags: the name of the contexts or subsystems related to each *NavigationLink*

- **Information zone.** This is the most complex zone. The tags are structured into the different DIVs that define this zone.

  DI tags: *InformationZone, AIU, ManagerClass, ComplementaryClass, AttributeName, AttributeValue, Operation*, etc.

  DD tags: the *AIU* name, the name of the OOWS navigational classes related to the *ManagerClass* and *ComplementaryClass* tags, etc.

CSS provides two types of tags that can be used for marking up the HTML code: *class* and *id*. Domain-independent tags are defined using the *class* construct. Domain-dependent tags are defined with the *id* construct.

Figure 5.8 shows an example of a Web page excerpt that has been implemented using this markup strategy. This Web page has been generated using the OOWS implementation framework for the *Movie.Overview. MainDetails* Web page that appears in Section 5.4.5 (Figure 5.20).

5.3.11 Visualization Rules

The visualization rules define how elements of the Web page must be visualized, referring to their location, size, color (background, text, etc.), type, etc. depending on the element type and tag used. These rules are defined in separate files from the HTML content using CSS as its definition language.

```
<?xml version="1.0" encoding="iso-8859-1"?>
<!DOCTYPE html PUBLIC "-//W3C//DTD XHTML 1.0 Strict//EN" "http://www.w3.org/TR/xhtml1/DTD/xhtml1-strict.dtd">
<html xmlns="http://www.w3.org/1999/xhtml" lang="en-US">
<head>
<title></title>
<link rel="stylesheet" type="text/css" href="style/dd-IMDb.css" />
<link rel="stylesheet" type="text/css" href="http://ascalon.dsic.upv.es/Styles/IMDb/di-IMDb.css" />
</head>

<body class="Context" id="NC_Movie_Overview_MainDetails">

<div class="LocationZone">
 <div class="Path">
   <div class="PathStep"><a class="PathStep" id="Movie_Overview_MainDetails" href="MainDetails.php"><span
                             class="PathStep" id="NS_Movie">Movie</span></a></div>
   <div class="PathStepSeparator"><span class="PathStepSeparator"></span></div>
   <div class="PathStep"><a class="PathStep" id="Movie_Overview_MainDetails" href="MainDetails.php"><span
                             class="PathStep" id="NS_Overview">Overview</span></a></div>
   <div class="PathStepSeparator"><span class="PathStepSeparator"></span></div>
   <div class="PathStep"><a class="PathStep" id="Movie_Overview_MainDetails" href="MainDetails.php"><span
                             class="PathStep" id="NC_MainDetails">main details</span></a></div>
 </div>
</div>


<div class="NavigationZone">

<div class="NavigationGroup">
 <div class="NavigationLink" id="NC_NowPlaying"><a class="NavigationLink" id="NC_NowPlaying"
             href="NowPlaying.php"><span class="NavigationLink" id="NC_NowPlaying">NOW PLAYING</span></a></div>
<div class="NavigationLink" id="NC_MovieNews"><a class="NavigationLink" id="NC_MovieNews"
             href="MovieNews.php"><span class="NavigationLink" id="NC_MovieNews">MOVIE/TV NEWS</span></a></div>
<div class="NavigationLink" id="NC_MyMovies"><a class="NavigationLink" id="NC_MyMovie"
             href="MY Movies.php"><span class="NavigationLink" id="NC_MyMovies">MY MOVIES</span></a></div>
 ...
</div>


<div class="InformationZone">

<div class="AIU" id="AIU_Movie_Main_Details">
<table class="ManagerClass" id="Class_Movie">
 <tr><th class="AttributeName" id="Class_Movie_Title"><span class="AttributeName"
                                   id="Class_Movie_Title">Title</span></th>
     <td class="AttributeValue" id="Class_Movie_Title"><span class="AttributeName"
                                   id="Class_Movie_Title">The Godfather</span></td></tr>
 <tr><th class="AttributeName" id="Class_Movie_Year"><span class="AttributeName"
                                   id="Class_Movie_Year">Year</span></th>
     <td class="AttributeValue" id="Class_Movie_Year"><span class="AttributeName"
                                   id="Class_Movie_Year">1972</span></td></tr>
 ...
</table>
</div>

<div class="AIU" id="AIU_User_Comments">
...
</div>

...

</div>

</body>
</html>
```

Figure 5.8. Web page with both domain-dependent and domain-independent tags.

As discussed in Section 5.3.10, we define two types of visualization rules: domain-independent and domain-dependent rules, so there are two files with two groups of rules.

By combining those ideas with the markup strategy, we can define really complex visualization rules, even those that involve both domain-dependent and domain-independent tags (in this case, the rule must be considered domain-dependent).

Graphical designers focus their efforts on defining these files. There is no need to interact with system developers because the graphical designers know a priori which tags will be used to implement the Web application. In addition, it is more effective to define the visualization rules based on conceptual terms rather than defining or converting these rules into solution-dependent terms (HTML, etc.).

Here we present two examples of visualization rules:

- "Put the navigation zone of each Web page at the top of the page. Put a vertical bar between each navigational link. All IMDb Web pages must show the IMDb logo." These are three examples of domain-independent visualization rules.
- "Movie titles must appear in large-sized, bold type." This is an example of a domain-dependent visualization rule.

Figure 5.9 shows the representation of these visualization rules using CSS markup language. These visualization rules come from the IMDb visualization rules used in the implementation discussed in Section 5.4.

```
...
.Context {
        background-image: url("logo.jpg");
}

.NavigationZone {
        z-index:1;
        position: absolute; top:35px; left: 170px;
        font-weight: bold;
        font-size: 9px;
}

.NavigationGroup div.NavigationLink + div.NavigationLink {
        border-left-style: solid;
        border-width: thin;
        padding-left: 5px;
}

...
```

```
...
#Class_Movie_Title {
        font-weight: bold;
        font-size: 15px;
}

...
```

Figure 5.9. Example of domain-independent (left panel; di-IMDb.css) and domain-dependent visualization rules (right panel; dd-IMDb.css), respectively.

5.4 CASE STUDY: THE IMDB INTERNET MOVIE DATABASE

The IMDb Internet Movie Database (IMDb) is an online repository of information related to the movie world. As stated in its official Web site (www.imdb.org), it is "the Earth's Biggest Movie Database." Any kind of information regarding a specific movie can be found in the IMDb: movie details (production notes, duration, format, trailers, photo galleries, soundtracks, memorable quotes, etc.); movie participants (credited cast, directors, writers, and producers, etc.); and information about current showtimes (where those movies are being played). Moreover, registered users are allowed to introduce movie reviews and ratings, and they can also introduce their votes in the daily poll. Anonymous users can also interact with this Web application to search and browse through the movie catalogue, but they cannot introduce their opinions, votes, etc. However, they can register at any time to access this functionality.

The purpose of this section is to describe the conceptual model that leads to the implementation at www.imdb.org. Following the OO-Method approach, Section 5.4.1 describes the conceptual model of the IMDb Web application by defining (1) the structural and behavioral parts of the system and (2) the system navigational and presentation properties using the OOWS approach. Those (PIM) models are taken as the input for the development process to apply a Model-Driven Development strategy. An MDA-based code generator produces the final application by implementing a set of predefined model-to-code transformation rules. The results of this step are presented in Section 5.4.2.

Due to the size of the application, it is not possible to present all the concepts in detail. Therefore, we have selected a representative part of this system to present in depth.

5.4.1 The IMDb Conceptual Model

Following the OO-Method/OOWS approach described in Figure 5.1, the first step is to describe the structural and behavioral aspects of the Web application. These requirements are gathered by means of a class diagram, state-transition diagrams, and a functional model, which are presented in Section 5.4.2.

Section 5.4.3 presents the navigational properties of the IMDb Web system by means of a user diagram, which describes the different types of users who can use the application. This section also presents the navigational model, which is related to each kind of user and describes its accessibility through the system. Finally, Section 5.4.4 introduces some abstract presentation requirements, which are related to the specified navigational model to complete the Web interface specification.

5.4.2 The IMDb OO-Method Conceptual Model

The first step in building an OO-Method conceptual model is to describe its structural model (by means of a class diagram) and its behavioral model (using a dynamic and functional model). According to the main objectives of the IMDb Web application, the structural model must capture information about the movies, their main participants, showtimes, user reviews, ratings, and daily polls. Figure 5.10 presents the IMDb class diagram.

This figure focuses on the portion of the system that is related to movie information. As the figure shows, *Movie* is the central main class. The system provides a lot of information about a movie: its title and production year, a brief general description, the official URL Web site, its production state ("filming," "post-production," etc.), a main photo, languages, color,

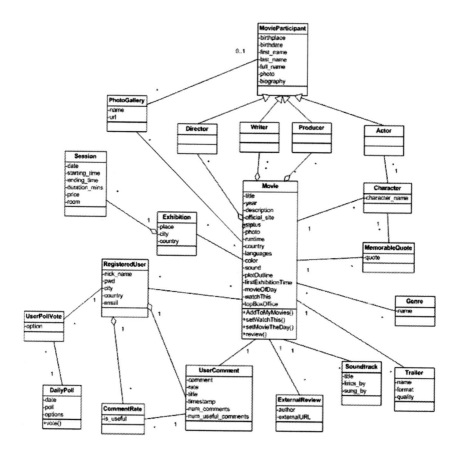

Figure 5.10. Class diagram of the IMDb Web application.

sound, etc. Also, a movie can be checked with different flags to indicate that it is the "movie of the day" or a "watch this" recommendation. By using the "firstExhibitionTime" property, the system can also dynamically derive the "coming soon" movies. Multimedia contents (soundtracks, trailers, and photoGallery) are also collected for each movie. The system organizes the movies within a set of *Genres* and lists the different places where the movies are being shown (*Exhibition*).

A movie has many participants (*MovieParticipant*), and they can play different roles in different movies. These participant roles include *Directors, Writers, Producers,* and *Actors*. For instance, Harrison Ford appears in the IMDb system as an actor, a producer, and a writer. Each time an actor/actress participates in a movie, he or she interprets a specific *Character*. This character can have a set of memorable quotes (interesting dialogue) within the movie.

The IMDb also has *RegisteredUser*s. These users are allowed to introduce comments (*UserComment*) about the movies they have seen and to rate the comments (*CommentRate*) provided by other users. With this information, IMDb provides an easy way of sharing the "non-expert" opinions of the users. Moreover, the IMDb publicizes a *DailyPoll* asking for user opinions on a certain topic, and registered users can introduce their own opinions for that specific question.

5.4.3 The IMDb Navigational Model

Once the structural and functional requirements have been determined, the next step is to specify the navigational capabilities of the system. Following the OOWS approach, the following diagrams must be specified: (1) a user diagram; (2) a navigational map; and (3) a presentation model.

There are two visible types of users: *AnonymousUser*s and *RegisteredUser*s. Both types can explore the movie database, but only *RegisteredUsers* are allowed to introduce their opinions and votes.

Figure 5.11 shows the User diagram. The *AnonymousUser*s are labeled with a "?" mark to specify that they do not need identification to access the system. *RegisteredUser*s have been specialized from *AnonymousUser*s to inherit their navigational maps (Fons et al., 2003). These *RegisteredUser*s are labeled with a padlock symbol to represent the fact that they need to be identified to enter the system. Following the OO-Method point of view, the *RegisteredUser*s are directly related to one class (*RegisteredUser* class) of the class diagram (Figure 5.10).

The next step involves the definition of a *navigational map* for each type of user. This navigational map defines the user accessibility within the system. Figure 5.12 presents the navigational map for the *RegisteredUser*s. The navigational map for the *RegisteredUser*s is made up of 18 navigational contexts and 1 navigational subsystem. Each of these navigational contexts provides a different view over the class diagram. The "*Now Playing*" navigational context shows information about the movies that are currently being shown, and the "*Showtime & Tickets*" navigational context shows where these movies are being exhibited. The figure shows a link (solid

Figure 5.11. The IMDb user diagram.

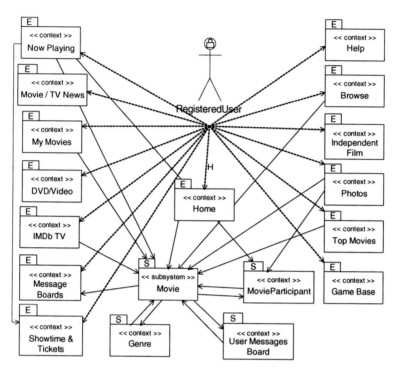

Figure 5.12. RegisteredUser navigational map.

arrow) from the "*Now Playing*" context to the "*Showtime & Tickets*" context. This link represents the capability of navigating from the "*Now Playing*" context to the "*Showtime & Tickets*" to obtain the current showtimes and ticket information.

Another example is the "*My Movies*" navigational context, which allows *RegisteredUsers* to mark their preferred movies.

Fourteen of these navigational nodes are labeled with an "E" (exploration). This means that these nodes are always accessible for *RegisteredUsers*. They appear in the navigational map as the target of a dashed arrow. The other nodes are labeled with an "S" (sequence), meaning that they are only reachable by following a predefined navigational path (solid arrows).

At the center of the navigational map is a navigational context (named *Home*) that has its explorational link (dashed-arrow) labeled with an "H." That means that this context will be the *default* node that the *RegisteredUsers* will reach when they connect to the system. This context is responsible for providing the user with information about: current movies (trailers and more), daily poll, the movies of the day, top at the box office, "opening this week," and "coming soon" movies. Figure 5.13 shows the *Home* navigational context. Due to the amount of information that this

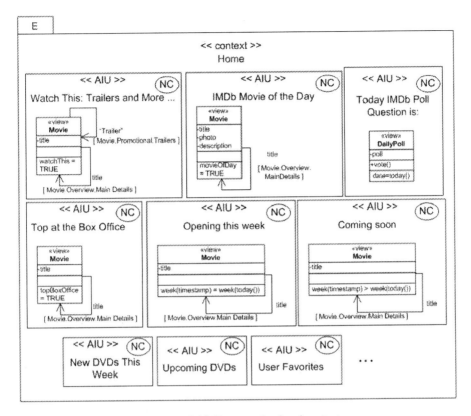

Figure 5.13. Home navigational content.

context provides, it has been defined as having a set of AIUs, each of which provides a part of the information.

The AIU "*Watch This: Trailers and More ...*" provides the users with the titles of the movies that are marked as being "*watchThis*" (see class diagram in Section 5.4.1). This requirement has been defined by specifying the Movie class view with the title attribute and a population filter condition "*watchThis = TRUE.*" Two navigational capabilities are defined within this AIU by means of two context relationships (solid arrows). The first context relationship defines a navigation capability to the *Trailer* navigational context, which is inside the *Promotional* subsystem, which is inside the *Movie* subsystem (see Figure 5.14). This capability allows users to select a specific movie to see its available trailer. The second context relationship defines a navigation capability to the *Main Details* context, which is inside the *Overview* subsystem, which is inside the *Movie* subsystem. This capability allows users to obtain more detailed information about a movie by clicking on its title (anchor).

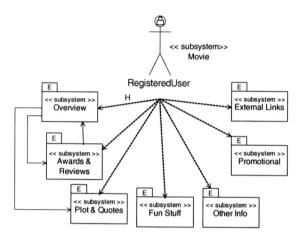

Figure 5.14. Movie navigational subsystem.

The AIU *"Today IMDb Poll Question is:"* provides the use with the *DailyPoll,* whose *date* is equal to *today().*[3] This AIU also allows *RegisteredUsers* to *vote()* for the poll.

In the same way, the other AIUs provide the users with other information of interest using different conditions (movie of the day, top at the box office, opening this week, and coming soon). All these AIUs are marked as *noncontextual* because they do not need any contextual information for filtering with. Figure 5.19 shows the final Web page that implements the *Home* context.

Since there is so much information about a movie, it has been organized inside the *Movie* subsystem of the navigational map. This subsystem is responsible for providing different views for the same movie. This subsystem has also been organized using different subsystems: *Overview, Awards & Reviews, Plot & Quotes, Fun Stuff, Other Info, Promotional,* and *External Links* subsystems (see Figure 5,15). For example, the Overview subsystem is labeled with an "H," which converts it to the default node.

An expanded view of the *Promotional* and *Overview* subsystems, which are inside the *Movie* subsystem, are shown in Figure 5.15. The *Movie.Promotional* subsystem allows users to navigate through the *Taglines, Trailers, Posters,* and *Photo Gallery* of a specific *movie* (for instance, the *Trailer* context inside the Promotional subsystem can be accessed from the *Home* context using the *"Watch This: Trailers and More..."* AIU; see Figure 5.13). The *Movie.Overview* subsystem provides the main information about a movie (it can be considered as the main part of the IMDb movie database): *Main Details, Full Cast & Crew, Combined Details,* and *Company Credits.*

---

[3] *Today()* is an environment operation that returns the current system date.

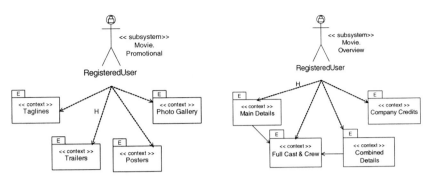

Figure 5.15. *Promotional* and *Overview* navigational subsystems
inside the *Movie* subsystem.

Within the *Movie.Overview* subsystem is the *Main Details* context, which is responsible for retrieving the main information about a movie: *title, plotOutline, runtime, country, languages,* etc. It also provides information about the *Directors, Writers,* and *Producers*. It presents the characters and memorable quotes for each actor and actress in the movie (Figure 5.16).

This *Main Details* context is made up of four contextual AIUs (depending on the selected movie) and one noncontextual AIU (*Message*

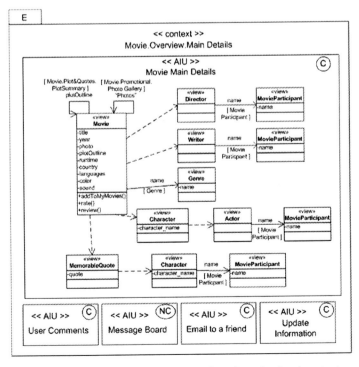

Figure 5.16. *Movie.Overview.Main Details* navigational content.

Board), which provides user comments about the movie. The *Movie Main Details* AIU is the main contextual AIU and provides information about the movie (title, year, plotSummary, run time, country, languages, color, and sound). It also allows users (1) to add movies to "*My Movies*" (remember that context at the navigational map of Figure 5.12), (2) to rate the movie, and (3) to write a movie review.

Figure 5.16 shows the *Movie.Overview.MainDetails* context, specifying how to retrieve the *name* of the *Directors, Writers,* and *Actors,* as well as the *characters, memorable quotes,* and the *name* of the involved *genres* for each movie. The name of the *genre* is the anchor for exploring more information about that genre within the *Genre* navigational context. This is the case because there is a context relationship between the *Movie* and the *Genre* view classes. In the same way, the *plotOutline* value is the anchor for exploring more details of that plot summary in the *Movie.Plot&Quotes.PlotSummary* context, and the static text "*Photos*" leads to the *Movie.Promotional.PhotoGallery* context.

5.4.4 The IMDb Presentation Model

Once the navigational model has been built, we specify presentational requirements using the *presentation model*. IMDb follows a very simple, homogeneous way for displaying the information: For each entity, all related subentities are shown in a register. One-to-one relationships also use the register pattern. One-to-many relationships use the master-detail pattern, with the detail in a register way. This leads to a basic presentation model description.

Figure 5.17 shows a representative example of the IMDb presentation model (see *Movie.Overview.MainDetails*).

5.4.5 The IMDb Implemented Web Application

This section presents the IMDb generated prototype. Figure 5.18 shows the generated application configuration file using the framework. Note that the IMDb default style has been applied in the prototype. The domain-independent version of this style has been implemented by hand so that it has the same look and feel as the real IMDb Web application.

This configuration file defines the two different roles (*AddRol*) specified in the user diagram shown in Figure 5.11. As this file shows, *RegisteredUsers* inherit from *AnonymousUsers* (see the last argument of the *AddRol* operation).

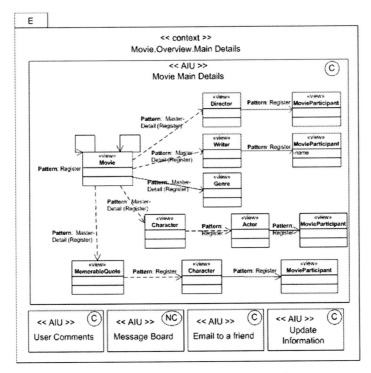

Figure 5.17. Movie.Overview.Main Details presentation context.

```php
<?php
include_once "../Framework/ApplicationBegin.php";

    $Application= new Application("IMDB","IMDB");

    $Application->AddRol("AnonymousUser","","","");
    $Application-
>AddRol("RegisteredUser","RegisteredUser","RegisteredUser_MVAgentValidation","AnonymousUser");

    $Application->AddPage("NowPlaying","NOW PLAYING","","AnonymousUser","always");
    $Application->AddPage("MovieTVNews","MOVIE/TV NEWS","","AnonymousUser","always");
    $Application->AddPage("MyMovies","MY MOVIES","","AnonymousUser","always");
    $Application->AddPage("DVD/Video","DVD/VIDEO","","AnonymousUser","always");
    $Application->AddPage("IMDbTV","IMDb TV","","AnonymousUser","always");
    $Application->AddPage("MessageBoards","MESSAGE BOARDS","","AnonymousUser","always");
    $Application->AddPage("Showtime&Tickets","SHOWTIME&TICKETS","","AnonymousUser","always");
    $Application->AddPage("GameBase","GAME BASE","","AnonymousUser","always");

    $Application->AddPage("Home","Home","","AnonymousUser","always");
    ...

    $Application->AddPageGroup("PG_BrowseMovie","Movie","","AnonymousUser","always",);

    $Application->AddPageGroup("PG_Overview","Overview","Movie","AnonymousUser","always",);
    $Application->AddPage("MainDetails","main details","PG_Overview","AnonymousUser","always");
    $Application->AddPage("CombinedDetails","combined details","PG_Overview","AnonymousUser","always");
    $Application->AddPage("FullCastAndCrew","full cast and crew","PG_Overview","AnonymousUser","always");
    $Application->AddPage("CompanyCredits","company credits","PG_Overview","AnonymousUser","always");

    $Application->AddPageGroup("PG_Awards&Reviews","Awards & Reviews","Movie","AnonymousUser","always",);
    $Application->AddPage("UserComments","user comments","PG_Awards&Reviews","AnonymousUser","always");
    ...

    $Application->SetDefaultStyle("IMDB")

    $Application->SetHomePage("Home","AnonymousUser");

include_once "../Framework/ApplicationEnd.php";
?>
```

Figure 5.18. Generated IMDb Web Application configuration file.

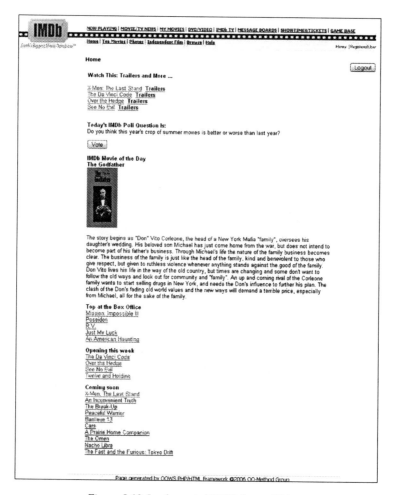

Figure 5.19. Implemented IMDb home Web page.

A Web page is created (*AddPage*) for each navigational context defined in the navigational map (Figure 5.12). A Web page group (*AddPageGroup*) is also created for each navigational subsystem. All these Web pages belong to the *AnonymousUser*. Since *RegisteredUser*s are a specialization of *AnonymousUser*s, they can also access these Web pages. The *Home* navigational context has been defined as the *Home* Web page.

As specified in its definition context (see Figure 5.13), this Web page retrieves six different types of information, each of which comes from a different AIU: Watch this, Today's poll, IMDb movie of the day, Top box office, Opening this week, and Coming soon. Following its definition, the Watch this (AIU) portion of the Web page shows the title of movies that are marked as watch this. The title is the anchor to navigate to the *Movie.Overview.MainDetails* Web page. A link named "Trailers" is attached to each title (as specified in the AIU) to navigate to the *Movie.Promotional.Trailers* navigational context.

The IMDb *Movie of the day* AIU shows the title, photo, and description of the movie with its *movieOfDay* set to true. The photo has been defined as the anchor for navigating to the *Movie.Overview.MainDetails*. If that photo is clicked on, the *MainDetails* Web page is shown.

The *MainDetails* Web page comes from the *MainDetails* navigational context, which is inside the *Overview* subsystem, which is inside the *Movie* subsystem. This requirement can be seen in the Web application configuration file (Figure 5.18). This page has been generated by the OOWS tool as shown in Figure 5.20.

```php
<?php
include_once "../../Framework/PageBegin.php";

    $Page=new Page("Movie Overview Main Details","RegisteredUser");
    $Page->AddUserInfoZone();

    $InfoZone = $Page->AddInformationZone("AIU-1","Movie Main Details.","Movie");
    $InfoZone->AddField ("title","Title");
    $InfoZone->AddField("year","Year");
    $InfoZone->AddImageField ("photo","Photo");
    $InfoZone->AddField("plotOutline","Plot");
    $InfoZone->AddField("country","Country");
    $InfoZone->AddField("languages","Languages");
    $InfoZone->AddField("runtime","Runtime");
    $InfoZone->AddField("color","Color");
    $InfoZone->AddField("sound","Sound");
    $InfoZone->plotOutline->AddInternLinkTo("Movie_Plot&Quotes_PlotSummary");
    $InfoZone->photo->AddInternLinkTo("Movie_Promotions_PhotoGallery");

    $ServiceZone = $InfoZone->AddServicesZone("movieServices","");
    $ServiceZone->AddServiceReference("Movie_AddToMyMovies","Add to my Movies");
    $ServiceZone->AddServiceReference("Movie_rate","Rate it");
    $ServiceZone->AddServiceReference("Movie_review","Add a Review");

    $InfoZone->AddDetailRelationship("Director");
    $InfoZone->RelatedDirector->AddRelatedField("name","Name","MovieParticipant");
    $InfoZone->RelatedDirector->MovieParticipant_name->AddInternLinkTo("Movie_Participant");

    $InfoZone->AddDetailRelationship("Writer");
    $InfoZone->RelatedWriter->AddRelatedField("name","Name","MovieParticipant");
    $InfoZone->RelatedWriter->MovieParticipant_writer->AddInternLinkTo("Movie_Participant");

    $InfoZone->AddDetailRelationship("Genre");
    $InfoZone->RelatedGenre->AddField("name","");
    $InfoZone->RelatedGenre->name->AddInternLinkTo("Genres");

    $InfoZone->AddDetailRelationship("Character");
    $InfoZone->RelatedActorParticipant->AddField("character_name","Character");
    $InfoZone->RelatedActorParticipant->AddRelatedField("name","Name","Actor.Character");
    $InfoZone->RelatedActorParticipant->Actor_Character_name->AddInternLinkTo("Movie_Participant");

    $InfoZone->AddDetailRelationship("MemorableQuote");
    $InfoZone->RelatedMemorableQuote->AddField("quote","Quote");
    $InfoZone->RelatedMemorableQuote->AddRelatedField("character_name","Character","Character");
    $InfoZone->RelatedMemorableQuote->AddRelatedField("name","Name","Character.MovieParticipant");
    $InfoZone->RelatedMemorableQuote->Character_MovieParticipant_name->AddInternLinkTo("Movie_Participant");

        $InfoZone = $Page->AddInformationZone("AIU-2","User Comments.","User");
        ...

include_once "../../Framework/PageEnd.php";
?>
```

Figure 5.20. Generated code for the Movie.Overview.MainDetails
with the implementation framework.

This Web page, *Movie.Overview.MainDetails,* retrieves all the information specified in its related context for the selected movie (title, year, photo, plotOutline, etc.). This is represented by the *AddField* operator to the manager class of the AIU (AIU-1). The *plotOutline* attribute is used as the anchor for navigating to the *Movie.Plot&Quotes.PlotSummary* page (*plotOutline->AddInternalLinkTo*). This page finally leads to the implemented Web page shown in Figure 5.21.

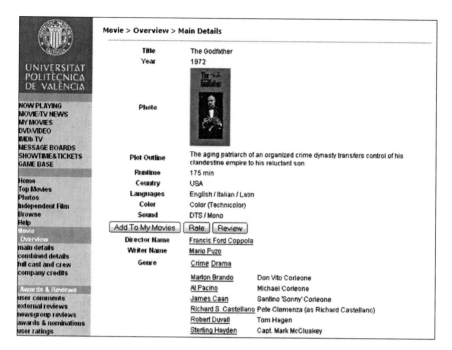

Figure 5.21. Implemented *Movie.Overview.MainDetails* Web page.

As stated in Section 5.3.11, we have manually implemented the visualization rules to recreate the IMDb look and feel (see Figure 5.9).

To demonstrate the reusability of the graphical designs, we have applied a graphical design that we had previously used in another Web application. This design implements the visualization of the UPV Web site (www.upv.es). The visualization view can be changed by simply changing the *SetDefaultStyle* in the Web application definition file to

```
$Application->SetDefaultStyle("UPV-like");
```

and a visualization like the one in Figure 5.22 will be obtained.

5.5 METHOD EXTENSIONS

During the last few years, the OOWS approach has evolved by including features to support some new extensions. These extensions cope with the following topics: *Web requirements modeling, adaptive systems modeling, business process modeling, applications of the semantic Web technologies,* and *service-oriented architectures.*

Figure 5.22. IMDb using the UPV graphical design.

5.5.1 Web Requirements Modeling

This extension proposes the use of a requirements model for Web applications development (Valderas et al., 2006). This model is based on the concept of a task that has been reoriented to capture not only structural and behavioral requirements (as happens in non-Web applications) but also navigational requirements.

This OOWS requirements model is created in three main stages:

1. In the first stage, a *task taxonomy* is created. This task taxonomy hierarchically specifies the tasks that users should achieve when interacting with the Web application. There are general and specific tasks. Structural and temporal decompositions are proposed to perform the task refinement.

2. In the second stage, each leaf task is described by analyzing the interaction that users require from the Web application. A strategy based on *activity diagrams* is used. Each activity diagram is defined using system actions and interaction points that represent the moments during a task where the system and the user exchange information (this information allows us to capture navigational semantics at the requirements level).

3. In the third stage, a set of *information templates* is described. These templates describe the information that is exchanged in each interaction point.

Then, a strategy to specify and to apply model-to-model transformations to obtain partial navigational models from the requirements model has been defined. The code generation process allows us to obtain prototypes in a multidisciplinary environment by defining the different roles (graphical designers, usability experts, etc.) and responsibilities. Model-to-model and model-to-code transformations provide us with a high level of traceability between code and requirements. This characteristic facilitates the management of volatile requirements and application evolution.

5.5.2 Adaptive Systems Modeling

Most of the research efforts in the field of adaptive hypermedia have focused on implementing adaptivity concepts to solve specific problems and on developing and improving adaptation strategies and algorithms, which are introduced at later stages of the software development process.

Providing a higher level (more general and domain-independent) perspective of adaptive hypermedia applications development, different model-driven approaches have been proposed. However, important problems are still related to the poor conceptual support to multiple adaptive techniques and to the lack of a complete methodological support.

The approach that OOWS proposes for the development of adaptive Web applications provides conceptual tools to describe different adaptive techniques, at a high abstraction level. To provide methodological support, the main parts of this OOWS extension are the following:

1. A user modeling strategy based on the description of the intended users of the application as a domain concept, considering their personal characteristics, their relationships with the application domain, and the description of their interaction with the application (Rojas and Pelechano, 2006).

2. A set of conceptual structures and properties, incorporated into the OOWS navigational model, that give support to well-known adaptive

techniques, such as link-hiding, link-ordering, or conditional fragments (Rojas et al., 2005).

3. A requirements specification approach including capabilities to define the requirements relative to the distinct users of the application (user classification, information, and functionality requirements). Furthermore, it provides us with tools to describe the set of adaptivity requirements of the application, in terms of the adaptive characteristics of the system tasks (discussed in Section 5.5.1). In this way, the decisions about adaptivity that are taken in the conceptual modeling phase are supported by their corresponding user-related and adaptivity requirements (Rojas et al., 2006).

4. A systematic approach to derive conceptual specifications of adaptivity characteristics from their corresponding requirements specifications, through the definition of mapping rules to the structures of the OOWS conceptual models (Rojas et al., 2006).

5.5.3 Business Process Modeling

The increasing widespread use of the Web service technology makes the Internet the most adequate platform for the development of business applications (many companies are already providing services to third parties by means of this technology).

Some of the challenges that arise with these kind of applications are the following: (1) Sometimes the description of these business applications is highly related to a business process (BP) definition, where the objective of these applications is not only *information management* but also *process management*; (2) real BPs do not only include automated activities and system participants; in fact, they can also include human participants (participants who require a user interface to interact with the process) and manual activities (activities that are not automated at all; for instance, "to make a phone call" or "to review a document").

From the OOWS approach, we propose the automatic generation of Web applications that give full support to the execution of BPs (Torres and Pelechano, 2006). To achieve this goal, we propose to generate from a BP definition (1) the required graphical user interface to launch and complete process activities, as well as (2) the equivalent executable definition of the process. However, this approach enforces us to revise the OOWS approach not only from the modeling point of view but also from the architectural one (in some cases the execution of the process is going to be performed by a process engine). This proposal allows us to obtain BP implementations that are totally integrated within the Web application. This integration is achieved at three levels: *data/content, functionality,* and *graphical user interface.* For this purpose we have defined an extension to the OOWS navigational model that allows us to model the graphical interfaces that are necessary to allow interaction between human participants and the business process.

5.5.4 Application of the Semantic Web Technology

In order to turn the vision of the Semantic Web into reality (Berners-Lee et al., 2006), it is necessary to provide developers with guides, methods, and tools that encourage them to make use of semantic technologies for the development of real-world applications. The development of the Semantic Web involves not only the generation of semantic content (defining specific domains using ontologies) but also the semantics of some functionality that allows external users and software agents to discover, invoke, compose, and monitor this functionality with a high degree of automation.

In this sense, Web Engineering methods should now be prepared to provide solutions that tackle the modeling of this new dimension, which refers to the view over the system from the Semantic Web point of view. This new dimension allow us to generate applications intended not only for humans, but also for automated software agents, which can understand the application contents (data and functionality) because they are expressed in a language that provides a vocabulary along with a formal semantics.

We propose generating part of the system specification that is going to be accessible through the use of the Semantic Web technology (Torres et al., 2006). This generation can be performed since the OO-Method/OOWS approach includes a set of models that specify in a sound and precise way the system structure and behavior in the form of a conceptual schema. The OO-Method/OOWS approach has been enriched with a mechanism to define—at the modeling level—the system in terms of the Semantic Web point of view. This new dimension specifies the view/access over the system for external agents by defining two models: The first model specifies the system domain (tourism, health, news, education, etc.), and the second model describes how external entities/agents should use the system functionality exposed in business settings.

5.5.5 Service-Oriented Architectures

A main objective of Service-Oriented Architectures (SOA) is to solve integration problems between heterogeneous applications in a distributed environment. Architectures of this kind provide appropriate scenarios to integrate Web applications. Web Engineering methods should provide mechanisms to apply SOA architectures to support the use of external Web services to develop new services.

In accordance with SOA, a methodological guidance to automatically design and implement fully operative Web services from OO-Method/OOWS models has been defined. In order to design and implement these Web services, the OO-Method/OOWS models are used as the key point. In this strategy, we have first determined which models are useful to identify Web services operations, and then we have proposed a guidance to design these operations (Ruiz et al., 2005, 2006).

This extension is supported by an additional tool that takes the conceptual model as input and applies the guide to obtain Web services operation descriptions. This tool finally generates the code for this Web services operation automatically (Ruiz et al., 2006).

REFERENCES

Berners-Lee, T., Hendler, J., and Lassila, O., 2001, The Semantic Web. *Scientific American*, May.

CARE Technologies. *OlivaNova Model Execution*. http://www.care-t.com, accessed 2007.

CARE Technologies. *OlivaNova Modeller*. http://www.care-t.com/products/modeler.html, accessed 2007.

CARE Technologies. *OlivaNova Transformation Engines*. http://www.care-t.com/products/transengine.html, accessed 2007.

Ceri, S., Fraternali, P., and Matera, M., 2002, Conceptual modeling of data-intensive Web applications. *IEEE Internet Computing*, **6**(4): 20–30.

De Troyer, O., 2001, Audience-driven Web design. In *Information Modeling in the New Millennium*, Eds. Matt Rossi and Keng Siau, Publ. IDEA Group Publishing, Hershey, USA, ISBN: 1-878289-77-2, pp. 442–462.

Fons, J., Pelechano, V., Albert, M., and Pastor, O., 2003, Development of Web applications from Web enhanced *conceptual schemas*. ER'2003, Springer *Lecture Notes in Computer Science*, **2813**: 232–245.

Knapp, A., Koch, N., Zhang, G., and Hassler, H.M., 2004, Modeling business processes in Web applications with ArgoUWE. UML 2004, Springer *Lecture Notes in Computer Science*, **3273**: 69–83.

Mellor, S.J., Clark, A.N., and Futagami, T., 2003, Model-driven development—Guest editor's introduction. *IEEE Software*, Sept.–Oct., **20**(5): 14–18.

Murugesan, S., and Desphande, Y., 2001, *Web Engineering. Software Engineering and Web Application Development*. Lecture Notes in Computer Science—Hot Topics, Springer, New York.

Object Management Group, 2004, Model Driven Architecture (MDA). www.omg.org/mda.

Pastor, O., Gomez, J., Insfran, E., and Pelechano, V., 2001, The OO-Method approach for information systems modeling: From object-oriented conceptual modeling to automated programming. *Information Systems*, **26**: 507–534.

Pressman, R.S., 2005, *Software Engineering: A Practitioner's Approach*. MacGraw-Hill, New York, ISBN: 0-07-285318-2.

Reifer, D.J., 2000, Web development: Estimating quick-to-market software. *IEEE Software*, Nov.–Dec., **17**(6): 57–64.

Rojas, G., and Pelechano, V., 2005, A methodological approach for incorporating adaptive navigation techniques into Web applications. *Proceedings Sixth International Conference on Web Information Systems Engineering* (WISE 2005), New York.

Rojas, G., Pelechano, V., and Fons, J., 2005, A model-driven approach to include adaptive navigational techniques in Web applications. *Proceedings Fifth International Workshop on Web-Oriented Software Technologies* (IWWOST'05) [within The 17th Conference on Advanced Information Systems Engineering (CAiSE'05)], Porto, Portugal.

Rojas, G., Valderas, P., and Pelechano, V., 2006, Describing adaptive navigation requirements of Web applications. *Proceedings Fourth International Conference on Adaptive Hypermedia and Adaptive Web-Based Systems* (AH2006), Dublin, Ireland.

Rossi, G., and Schwabe, D., 2001, Object-oriented Web applications modeling. In *Information Modeling in the New Millennium*, IGI Publishing, USA, ISBN: 1-878289-77-2, pp. 463–484.

Ruiz, M., Valderas, P., and Pelechano, V., 2005, *Applying a Web engineering method to design Web services. Proceedings Third International Conference on Service-Oriented Computing* (ICSOC), pp. 576–581.

Ruiz, M., Pelechano, V., and Pastor, O., 2006a, Designing Web services for supporting user tasks: A model driven approach. *Proceedings of Conceptual Modeling of Service-Oriented Software Systems* (CoSS).

Ruiz, M., Valverde, F., and Pelechano, V., 2006b, Desarrollo de servicios Web en un método de generación de código dirigido por modelos. *II Jornadas Científico-Técnicas en Servicios Web* (JSWEB) [in Spanish].

Torres, V., and Pelechano, V., 2006, Building business process driven Web applications. *Proceedings Fourth International Conference on Business Process Management* (BPM 2006),.Vienna, Austria, pp. 322–337.

Torres, V., Pelechano, V., and Pastor, O., 2006, Building Semantic Web services based on a model driven Web engineering method. Workshop on Conceptual Modeling of Service-Oriented Software Systems (CoSS2006), Tucson, Arizona.

Valderas, P., Pelechano, V., and Pastor, O., 2006, A transformational approach to produce Web application prototypes from a Web requirements model. Submitted to *International Journal on Web Engineering and Technology* (IJWET).

Chapter 6

MODELING AND IMPLEMENTING WEB APPLICATIONS WITH OOHDM

Gustavo Rossi[1] and Daniel Schwabe[2]

[1]*LIFIA, Facultad de Informatica,Universidad Nacional de La Plata, (also at CONICET), Argentina,* `gustavo@lifia.info.unlp.edu.ar`
[2]*Departamento de Informática, PUC-Rio, Rio de Janeiro, Brazil,* `dschwabe@inf.puc-rio.br`

6.1 INTRODUCTION

The Object-Oriented Hypermedia Design Method (OOHDM) (Schwabe and Rossi, 1998) is a model-based approach to develop Web applications. It allows the designer to specify a Web application, seen as an instance of a hypermedia model, through the use of several specialized meta-models. Each model focuses on different aspects of the application. Once these models have been specified for a given application, it is possible to generate run-time code that implements the application. The examples shown in this chapter use the HyperDE environment (Nunes and Schwabe, 2006) for this.

OOHDM uses different abstraction and composition mechanisms in an object-oriented framework to allow, on the one hand, a concise description of complex information items and, on the other hand, the specification of complex navigation patterns and interface transformations. The principles of OOHDM have also been applied in another version of the method, SHDM (Schwabe et al., 2004), in which the data model used is based on RDF and RDFS (Brickley and Guha, 2004).

In OOHDM a Web application is built in a five-step process supporting an incremental or prototype process model. Each step focuses on a particular design concern, and an appropriate model is built. Classification and generalization/specialization are used throughout the process to enhance abstraction power and reuse opportunities. We next summarize the five activities.

6.1.1 Requirements Gathering

The first step is to gather the stakeholder requirements. To achieve this, it is necessary to first identify the actors (stakeholders) and the tasks they must perform. Next, scenarios are collected (or drafted) for each task and type of actor. The scenarios are then collected to form use cases, which are represented using User Interaction Diagrams (UIDs). These diagrams provide a concise graphical representation of the information flow between the user and the application during the execution of a task. The UIDs are validated with the actors, and redesigned if necessary. In sequence, a set of guidelines is applied to the UIDs to extract a basic conceptual model.

6.1.2 Conceptual Design

In this step a conceptual model of the application domain is built using well-known object-oriented modeling principles. There is no concern for the types of users and tasks, only for the application domain semantics. A conceptual schema is built out of subsystems, classes, and relationships. OOHDM uses UML (Fowler, 1997), with slight extensions, to express the conceptual design.

6.1.3 Navigational Design

In OOHDM, an application is seen as a navigational view over the conceptual model. This reflects a major innovation of OOHDM [also adopted by other methods such as UWE (Koch and Kraus, 2002)] and WebML (Ceri et al., 2002), which recognizes that the objects (items) the user navigates are *not* the conceptual objects, but other kinds of objects that are "built" from one or more conceptual objects, to suit the users and tasks that must be supported.

In other words, for each user profile we can define a different navigational structure that reflects the objects and relationships in the conceptual schema according to the tasks this kind of user must perform. The navigational class structure of a Web application is defined by a schema containing navigational classes. In OOHDM there is a set of predefined basic types of navigational classes: nodes, links, anchors, and access structures. The semantics of nodes, links, and anchors are the usual in hypermedia applications. Nodes in OOHDM represent logical "windows" (or views) over conceptual classes defined during conceptual design. Links are the hypermedia realization of conceptual relationships as well as task-related associations. Access structures, such as indexes, represent possible ways for starting navigation.

Different applications (in the same domain) may contain different linking topologies according to the various users' profile. For example, in the Internet Movie Database (IMDB) application, a rental store view of a certain DVD may indicate for each available copy when it is due to be returned, whereas the customer view may omit this information.

The navigational structure of a Web application is described in terms of navigational contexts, which are sets of related nodes that possess similar navigation alternatives (options) and are meaningful for a certain step in some task the user is pursuing. Navigation contexts play an analogous role with respect to navigation that classes play with respect to the structure and behavior of objects—they provide a way to talk about the navigation alternatives for sets of nodes without requiring talking about individuals, the same way as classes allow talking about the structure and behavior of objects without requiring talking about individuals objects. For example, we can model the set of actors in a film, the set of films directed by a director, the set of DVD copies of a film, and so on.

6.1.4 Abstract Interface Design

The abstract interface model is built by defining perceptible objects—also called widgets—that contain information (e.g., a picture, a city map, etc.) in terms of interface classes. Interfaces are defined as recursive aggregations of primitives classes (such as exhibitors or capturers) or of other interface classes. Interface objects map to navigational objects, providing them with a perceptible appearance, or to input values. Interface behavior is defined by specifying how to handle external and user-generated events and how communication takes place between interface and navigational objects.

6.1.5 Implementation

Implementation maps interface and navigation objects to run-time objects and may involve elaborate architectures, e.g., client–server, in which applications are clients to a shared database server containing the conceptual objects. A number of DVD-ROM–based applications, as well as Web–sites, have been developed using OOHDM, employing various technologies such as Java (J2EE), .NET (aspx), Windows (asp), Lua (CGILua), ColdFusion, and Ruby (Ruby on Rails). In this chapter, we will illustrate the implementation using HyperDE, an environment based on Ruby on Rails that is freely available on the Internet (see http://server2.tecweb.inf.puc-rio.br:8000/hyperde).

In the following sections we show some details of the OOHDM notation using an example that can be considered a simplified version of the Internet Movie Database (www.imdb.com) together with an associated site such as www.amazon.com where one can buy a DVD. For the sake of simplicity, we will focus mainly on the process of finding movies, i.e., in the store catalogue; less emphasis is put in the buying and check-out process (see Schmid and Rossi, 2004). This example is somewhat archetypical as many different Web applications can be modeled using the ideas we will show next.

6.2 REQUIREMENTS GATHERING AND SPECIFICATION

6.2.1 Identifying Actors

In OOHDM we build a different navigational model for each user profile; in this application we clearly have at least two different user profiles: the customer, who is looking for a movie to buy or just for information about the movie, and the administrator, who maintains the movies database. We will mostly discuss the application for the customer profile. Once we have identified the actors, we must identify the tasks the user will accomplish using the application, in order to obtain usage scenarios.

Clearly, there are many tasks to be supported in our application scenario. Some of the typical tasks for the customer user profile are

- Find a movie given its title.
- Find a movie given an actor's name.
- Find information about an actor or actress.
- Find movies of a particular genre.
- Find recently released movies.
- Choose movies to buy given one of the above criteria.

6.2.2 Use Case Specification

We next describe the usage scenarios. A scenario represents the set of subtasks the user has to perform to complete a task. Scenarios are specified textually using the point of view of the final user, in our case a customer. Whenever possible, the user scenarios should be obtained from a sample of real users who are representative of the intended audience. When this is not possible, this role can be played by members of the design team or by other stakeholders. More than one scenario can be defined for the same task.

As an example of the first task ("Find a movie given its title"), a possible scenario would be

> "I enter the movie title or part of it, and I see a list of matching movie titles. For each movie matching the title, I get some information such as a picture of the DVD cover, the year the movie was released, and its main actors. I can get additional information such as all the actors, director, soundtrack information, user comments, etc. For some films, I can also see a short trailer."
>
> "After reading the information, I can decide to buy it or to quit."

After collecting several such scenarios, a generalization is captured in a use case, defined next. We use the following heuristics:

1.   Identify those scenarios related with the task at hand. In our case we will use the previous scenario.
2.   For each scenario, identify information items that are exchanged by the user and the application during their interaction.
3.   For each scenario, identify which data items are associated among themselves; they typically appear together in the text of the use case.
4.   For each scenario, identify those data items organized as sets. Usually, the use case text refers to them explicitly as sets.
5.   The sequences of actions appearing in scenarios should also appear in the use case.
6.   All operations on data items that appear on scenarios should be included in the use case.

After defining the data involved in the interaction, the sequence of actions, and the operations, we can specify the use case. A use case will be constructed based on the sequence of actions, detailed with the information about the data items and operations involved. Use cases can also be enriched with information from other use cases or provided by the designer. The resulting use case for the previous scenario is the following:

Use case: Find a movie given its title.

1.   The user enters the movie title (or part of it).
2.   The application returns a list of movies matching the data entered or the information about the movie (if only one movie matches, see step 4). For each movie, the title, main actor, and cover art are shown.
3.   In case the user wants to see more information on the movie, he selects it.

4. The system returns detailed information for the movie: title, cover, availability, actors' names, director, and other technical information. If the user wants to buy the movie, he can include it in the shopping cart to buy later (use case: Buy a DVD given its title). If he wants, he can watch a trailer of the movie.

5. If the user wants to know information about an actor who had a role in the movie, he can select the actor and the application will return his name, date of birth, a photograph, and a list of movies in which he participated.

The specification of other use cases follows a similar process.

6.2.3 User Interaction Diagrams

Use cases are described using a graphical notation called a User Interaction Diagram (UID) (Vila et al., 2000), which captures the flow of information and helps detail the information items and choices made by the user.

The specification of UIDs from use cases can be done following the guidelines described below. For illustration purposes, we detail the process of building the UID for the use case "Find a movie given its title," as described above.

1. Initially, the use case is analyzed to identify the information exchanged between the user and the application. Information provided by the user and information returned by the system are tagged accordingly. Next, the same information is identified and made evident in the use case.

2. Items that are exchanged during the interaction are shown in UID states. Information provided by the user and that provided by the system are always in separate states. Information that is produced from computations should be in separate states from the information used as input to this computation. The ordering of states depends on the dependencies between data provided by the user and returned by the application. In Figure 6.1, we show the first draft of the UID where parts of the use case are transcribed; information exchanged is shown in italics.

3. After identifying the data items exchanged, they must be clearly indicated in the UID. Data entered by the user (for example, the movie title) are specified using a rectangle; if it is mandatory, the border is a solid line; if it is optional, the border is a dashed line, as shown in Figure 6.2. Ellipsis (…) in front of a label indicates a list (e.g., …*Movie* indicates a list of *Movies*). The notation *Movie (Title, Actor(Name), Cover)* is called a *structure*. A shaded ellipsis represents a separate UID.

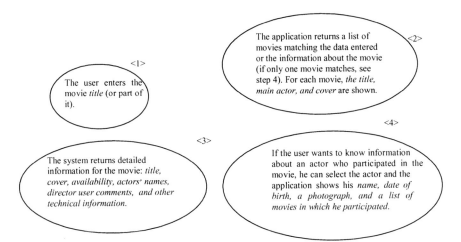

Figure 6.1. Defining the UID.

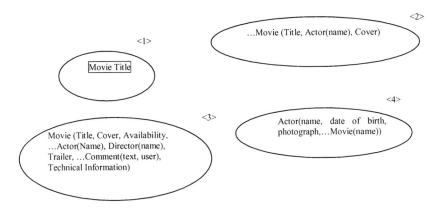

Figure 6.2. Refining interaction states in UIDs.

4. Transitions between interaction states must be indicated using arrows. Multiple paths as indicated in the use cases might arise as shown in Figure 6.3. Labels between brackets indicate conditions (e.g., [2..N] indicates more than one result); a label indicating cardinality represents a choice. (In the example, "1" indicates only one option may be chosen. For any choice, the source of the arrow is the list from which the option is selected, or the whole state if it is not ambiguous.)

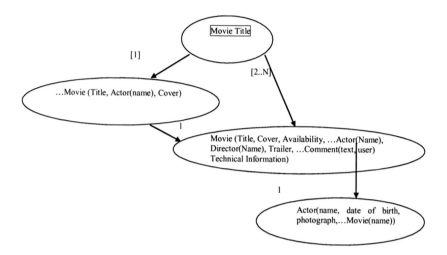

Figure 6.3. Transitions between interaction states in UIDs.

5.   Finally, operations executed by the user are represented using a line
     with a bullet connected to the specific information item to which it is
     applied, as shown in Figure 6.4. The name of the operation appears
     in parentheses.

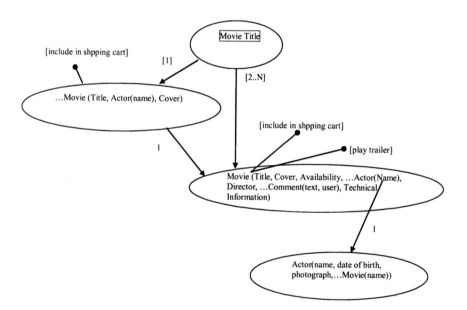

Figure 6.4. Complete specification of the UID for the use case "Find movie given its title
(including the buying operation)."

6.3 CONCEPTUAL MODELING

The conceptual model in OOHDM comprises a set of classes (their attributes and behaviors) and their relationships using UML. To develop a conceptual model, the information gathered from use cases and UIDs can help to identify core information classes that can later be refined. We next describe a set of guidelines to derive classes from UIDs, and we illustrate them using the UID in Figure 6.4 ("Find movie"). These guidelines are especially useful in aiding less experienced designers.

1. **Class definition.** For each data structure in the UID, we define a class. In the example: *Movie, Actor, Director.*
2. **Attribute definitions.** For each information item (provided by the user or returned by the system) appearing in the UID, an attribute is defined according to the following validations:
   (a) If, given an instance of the class X, it is possible to obtain the value of attribute A, then A can be an attribute of X (provided X is the only class fulfilling this condition).
   (b) If, given classes X and Y, it is possible to obtain the value of attribute A, then A will be an attribute of an association between X and Y.
   (c) If the attribute corresponding to a data item does not depend on an existing class, or combination of classes, this indicates the need to create a new one.
   The following attributes were identified from the information returned by the system as shown in the UID in Figure 6.4:
   > *Movie: title, cover, availability, trailer, user comments, technical information.*
   > *Actor: name, date of birth, photograph, list of movies*
   > *Director: name*
3. **Definition of associations.** For each UID, for attributes appearing in a structure that does not correspond to their class, include the association if there is a relationship between its class and the class representing the structure.
4. **Definition of associations.** For each UID, for each structure s1 containing another structure s2, create an association between the classes corresponding to structures s1 and s2.
5. **Definition of associations.** For each transition of interaction states in each UID, if different classes represent the source interaction state and the target interaction state, define an association between corresponding classes.

The following associations were identified by applying guidelines 3, 4, and 5 to the UID in Figure 6.4:

> *Movie-Actor*
>
> *Movie-Director*

6. **Operation definition.** For each option attached to a state transition in each UID, verify if there is an operation that must be created for any of the classes that correspond to the interaction states.

The following operations were identified from this last guideline:

> *Movie: includeInShoppingCart*
>
> *Movie: PlayTrailer*

In Figure 6.5, we show an initial conceptual model derived from the UID "Find movie given its title."

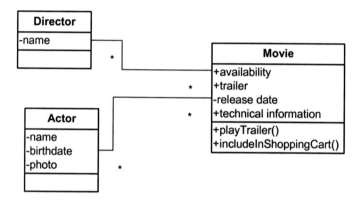

Figure 6.5. Initial conceptual model.

While the process and guidelines described above can help in defining a preliminary model, several refinements have to be made by hand, incorporating the designer's understanding of the domain. Among other concepts, the designer must identify

- Generalization and specialization hierarchies—for example, Actor and Director can be recognized as subclasses of Person.
- Association classes—for example, Role of an Actor in a Movie.
- Hidden classes—for example, Order. In fact, the Shopping Cart is not really a class by itself, but rather the set of Items that are part of an Order. Similarly, there is a User class, who is the buyer and also makes comments.
- Redundant classes.
- The arity of relations.

Besides these adjustments, it is worth noticing that this conceptual model might need further improvements as the application evolves, since these classes are "just" the ones we derive from the requirements gathering activity. However, this evolution belongs more to the general field of object-oriented design and is not as relevant for the current discussion.

After analyzing the complete set of UIDs and performing needed adjustments, we can obtain the conceptual model of Figure 6.6. Notice that we have included a Series class to stand for TV Series, and a generalization class Feature, abstracting both Series and Movies.

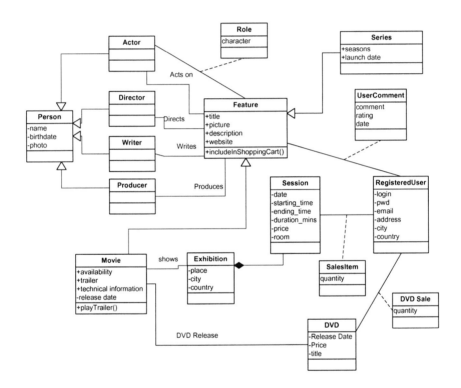

Figure 6.6. Conceptual model for the Movies Web site.

6.4 NAVIGATION DESIGN

To help understand the OOHDM approach to navigation design, we draw an analogy with supermarkets. Let's suppose you want to get some ground coffee, and you go to a supermarket you've never been to before. Not knowing where each type of merchandise is kept, you look up at the signs hanging from the ceiling, where the various categories of products are listed.

The signs establish a simple taxonomy of product types which is widely understandable, at least in Western society. Following the signs, you go to the aisle and section where ground coffee is kept.

However, looking at the shelves around the section, you notice that there are also coffee filters, jars, mugs, etc. Clearly, these items are not of the same category as ground coffee. The supermarket management put them here because they know that the user needs them to make coffee—just the grounds are not enough. One may regard the ground coffee, filters, jars, etc. as a "virtual" product, a "coffee making kit." What enables defining this kit is the knowledge that the user's task (or goal) in this case is to make coffee (there are no other obvious uses for ground coffee). Thus, if the management knows what the user is looking for, it may create "kits" containing the needed items; when management doesn't have prior knowledge, it provides a generic organization that is "task-neutral," based on a taxonomy of products that is culturally shared. In OOHDM, navigation nodes are equivalent to such "kits."

Continuing with the analogy, products must be organized in shelves, deployed along aisles that have a certain topology. Product placement in aisles is not random; for example, commonly bought items such as milk and bread are normally placed at the rear. The rationale is that since these are items that most people will buy, placing them at the rear of the store forces users to traverse several aisles, thus exposing users to more products and encouraging them to buy additional products, sometimes by impulse. A similar rationale justifies placing related product types near each other, such as beverages and snacks. The same can be said about placing children's products on the lower shelves, where children can easily see and reach them. Defining the application's navigation topology is analogous to establishing the aisles and product placement in the supermarket—the navigation paths should reflect the various goals and tasks of all stakeholders involved.

Thus, the goal of navigation design is to characterize the navigation objects and how they are organized into a navigation space. These are specified, respectively, through the navigation class schema and the navigation context schema. The latter indicates possible navigation sequences to help the user complete her task, and the former specifies the navigation objects (nodes and links) being processed. Whereas designers may create both schemas from different sources, User Interaction Diagrams, use cases, and the conceptual model are the natural sources from which to derive a sound navigational model. In addition to these, designers use their own experience or that from other designers, for example, using navigation patterns, as described in Section 6.7.

6.4.1 From Conceptual Modeling to Navigation Design

One of the cornerstones of the OOHDM approach is the fact that navigational objects—nodes and links—are explicitly defined as views on conceptual objects, according to each different user profile. These views are built using an object-oriented definition language that allows one to "copy and paste" or to filter attributes of different related conceptual classes into the same node class and to create link classes by selecting the appropriate relationships.

6.4.2 Navigational Schema

For each set of user profiles, we define a different navigational class schema and context schema. The navigational schema contains the nodes and links of the application. Nodes contain perceivable information (attributes) and anchors for links. Anchors are objects that allow triggering links. Links, meanwhile, are the hypermedia realization of conceptual relationships.

6.4.2.1 Nodes and Anchors

Nodes are derived from conceptual classes by selecting those classes we want that the user to perceive; attributes are defined in an opportunistic way according to usage needs. Sometimes it is necessary to combine attributes from different objects to describe a node.

In the example we may want nodes representing Movies to contain an attribute with the names of all the actors that participated in the movie, eventually using the names as anchors to each Actor's page.

As shown in the conceptual model of Figure 6.6, the name of the actor is an attribute of Class Actor and should not be included in Class Movie. Meanwhile, in a different application (for example, the application for administrators), we may want to filter out some attributes (such as detailed data of the movie) or include new relationships as links.

Node classes are defined using a query language similar to the one in Kim (1994). Nodes possess single-typed attributes, link anchors, and may be atomic or composite. Anchors are instances of Class Anchor (or one of its subclasses) and are parameterized with the type of link they host. In fact, since navigation always occurs within some context, as will be explained later, the Anchor specification must also include the destination context.

From an object-oriented point of view, nodes implement a variant of the Observer design pattern (Gamma et al., 1995) as they express a particular view on application objects. Changes in conceptual objects are broadcast to existing observers, while nodes may communicate with conceptual objects to forward events generated in the interface to them.

As an example we define the Node class Movie, including as one of its attributes the name of the director and an anchor for the link that connects both nodes. We say that the conceptual class Movie is the subject of Node class Movie. In OOHDM we defer the definition of how objects will be perceived until the interface design activity.

```
NODE Movie [FROM Movie:m]
director: String  [SELECT Name] [FROM Director:d WHERE D
          Directs m]
.... (other attributes "preserved" from the conceptual class Movie}
directedBy: Anchor [DirectedBy, Directors in Alphabetical order]
```

In the definition above, we express that attribute Director contains the name of the instance of the Director class corresponding to the director of the actual movie. Similarly, directedBy is a link to the Director node, in the context Directors in Alphabetical order. The notation above can be easily mapped into a query to a relational database of the implementation. We may combine both in case we want to have an anchor whose label is the Director's name, which would be expressed as

```
NODE Movie [FROM Movie:m]
directedBy: Anchor [DirectedBy, Director in Alphabetical order] label
          [SELECT Name]
               [FROM Director:d WHERE d Directs m]
.... (other attributes "preserved" from the conceptual class Movie}
```

Nodes may also possess attributes that are used to trigger operations in their object counterparts in the conceptual model.

6.4.2.2 Links

Links connect navigational objects. The result of traversing a link is expressed either by defining the navigational semantics procedurally as a result of the link's behavior or by using an object-oriented state-transition machine similar to Statecharts (Turine et al., 1997). Since Web applications usually implement simple navigation semantics (closing the source page and opening the target), we do not discuss this issue further.

The syntax for defining Link classes also allows one to express queries on relationships as shown in the example below in which, for the sake of simplicity, we omit link attributes.

```
LINK DirectedBy
SOURCE: Movie: M
TARGET: Director: D
WHERE S.D directs S.M
END
```

Notice that in a running implementation, links may not exist as full-fledged objects. For example, they may be just the result of selecting an anchor (that in fact might be simply a URL). However, expressing the navigational diagram considering nodes and links as object classes allows us to express the intended navigation semantics in a better way.

In Figure 6.7 we show the navigational class diagram of the Movie site, using a UML-like syntax. (Notice that the semantics of links are different from the semantics of UML associations.)

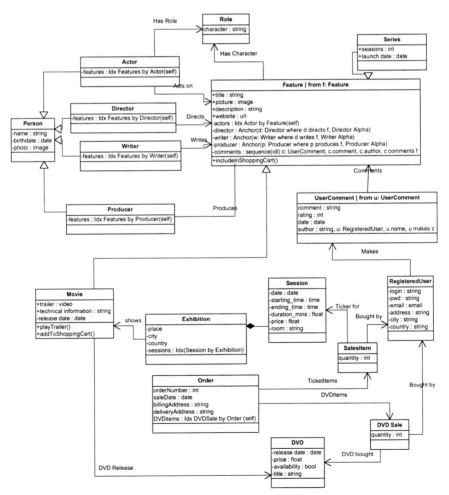

Figure 6.7. Navigational class diagram of the Movies Web site.

It is important to stress the similarities and differences among the conceptual and navigational schema. They are similar because both are abstract and implementation-independent and they represent concepts of the underlying application domain using objects. However, while the former should be neutral with respect to navigation, the latter expresses a particular user's view (in the navigation sense) that is strongly influenced by the tasks he is supposed to perform. OOHDM enforces a clear separation between the specification of navigation and other application behavior. However, in complex Web applications it may be necessary to integrate both kinds of behaviors, such as the process of buying the DVD of a movie.

This difference between navigation classes and conceptual classes can be seen in the diagram, where we can see that, while similar to the conceptual classes, navigation classes contain additional information. For instance, the navigation class Feature has several attributes that contain navigation information, such as "actors." This attribute contains an index to the Actors by Feature (for this Feature) context. Another example is the attribute "director," which is a link to this (indicated by the self parameter) Movie's Director in the Directors in Alphabetical Order context. The meaning of indexes and contexts will be explained next. Notice also that the UserComment has an attribute, "author," which is the name of the RegisteredUser who made the comment; this is an example of a mapped attribute from a different class.

6.4.2.3 Navigational Contexts

Most tasks supported by Web applications usually involve manipulating sets of objects that represent similar concepts, such as books by an author, CDs performed by a group, hotels in a city, movies of a genre, etc. These collections may be explored in different ways, according to the task the user is performing. For example, in an electronic bookstore a user may want to explore books by one author, books on a certain period of time or literary movement, etc. Sometimes it is also desirable to give the user different kinds of information or detail in different contexts, while allowing her to move easily from item to item. For example, it is not reasonable that if she wants to explore the set of all books written by Shakespeare, she has to backtrack to the index (the result of a keyword search, for example) to reach the next book in the set. In our example we might want to explore the set of movies in which an actor participated, the set of movies directed by a specific director, and so on.

As a result of organizing navigation objects into sets, several new navigation operations arise; these operations are called intraset navigation, such as "next," "previous," and "up." Therefore, we have to define links that allow such navigations; these links have no direct counterparts in the conceptual model. In other words, there is no conceptual relationship that directly translates into intraset navigation links.

Unfortunately, most modeling approaches (for example, the UML) ignore sets as first-class citizens, and therefore operations such as "next" and "previous" are not common while traversing sets. To complicate matters, the same node may appear in different sets: For instance, a movie directed by Spielberg may appear in the set of Comedies or in the set of movies acted by Tom Hanks. We may intend to include some comments about the movie in the corresponding context, such as when accessed as a comedy or some comments about comedies.

OOHDM structures the navigational space into sets, called navigational contexts, represented in a context schema. Each navigational context is a set of nodes, and it is described by specifying its elements, indicating its internal navigational structure (e.g., if it can be accessed sequentially) and associated indexes. Generally speaking, contexts are defined by properties of its elements, which may be based on their attributes or on their relations, or both. Navigational contexts usually induce associated access structures called indexes, which are collections of links pointing to each of the context's elements.

Another way to understand contexts is that they provide an abstraction mechanism that allows us to specify the navigation opportunities available to sets of objects all at the same time, without having to do so for each individual element within the context. In this respect, contexts play a role with respect to navigation that is analogous to the role classes play with respect to object structure and behavior—they allow us to specify navigation properties that are common to all its elements without requiring individual specification.

Consider a movie directed by Peter Jackson. While looking at its details, the user may want to see details of its actors or details of one of the songs in the soundtrack. In fact, these navigation alternatives are true not only for that particular movie, but also for the set of all movies directed by Peter Jackson. It is possible then to specify the navigation alternatives for any movie in the set in a more abstract way using navigational contexts. In this case, the navigational context would be "Movies by Peter Jackson." Additional reflection about this problem shows that one could generalize even further, since there is nothing particular about Peter Jackson in these alternatives — they are the same for any director. Therefore, we can define a group of navigational contexts as "Movies by director," where the particular director is a parameter, and all movies in any navigational context in this group share the alternatives of seeing the details of its actors or of songs in its soundtrack.

Figure 6.8 contains a portion of the navigational context diagram for our example; we will use it to explain the notation.

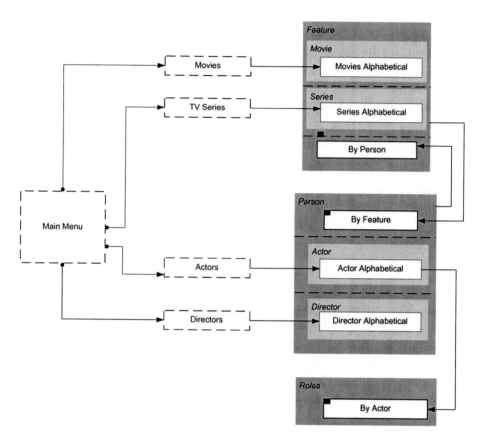

Figure 6.8. Partial navigation context diagram for the example.

The small black boxes within some contexts in Figure 6.8 indicate that these contexts have associated indexes. Instead of drawing them as dashed rectangles, this notation is used to prevent cluttering the diagram, making it graphically evident that these indexes are associated with the enclosed context.

The arrows with solid circles in the origin indicate landmarks, or places in the navigation space that are accessible from every other place. Typically, these landmarks are implemented as options included in a global navigation bar that is present on all pages of the application.

The details of each context and access structure are described by a context (respectively, access structure) specification card as shown in Figures 6.9 and 6.10.

Context: Feature by Person
Type: static
Parameters: p: Person
Elements: f: Feature WHERE a ActsIn m
In context Classes:
Ordering: by name, ascending
Internal navigation: by index (**Feature by Actor**)
Operations:
Users: Client   **Permissions:** read
Comments:

Figure 6.9. The context specification card.

Access structure : Feature by Actor
Type: simple
Parameters: a: Actor
Elements: m: Movie WHERE a *ActsIn* m
Attributes   **Target** title: m.name.................Ctx Feature by Artist (self) role: r.character, WHERE a Has Role r and m HasCharacter r cover: m.cover "Play Trailer"................ play_trailer() "Buy DVD"................. buy()
Ordering: by name, Ascending
Users: Client   **Permission:** read
Comments:

Figure 6.10. The access structure specification card.

Consider the access structure specification for Movie by Artist. Since this is an index induced by a context (Movies by Artist), it will contain one entry for each element in the context. Each entry has four attributes—the (movie) title, which is an anchor to the Movie by Artist context (for the movie corresponding to this entry); the artist's role in this movie; an activation that allows one to play the movie's trailer; and an activation that allows one to buy the movie's DVD. The former two attributes are calls to methods which will have to be mapped to active interface elements that can trigger the associated operations when activated by the user. This also illustrates how we separate application functionality from its interface rendering.

The reader will notice that both the context and the access structure specification cards also include information on access restrictions. Although we will not elaborate on this here, it is possible to restrict access to navigation objects by specifying the conditions in the corresponding specification cards.

6.4.3 Deriving Navigational Contexts

Navigation design is, to a large extent, the definition of the various navigational contexts that the user will be traversing while performing the various tasks the applications purports to support. Therefore, the natural place to look for them is in the task descriptions, as described in the UIDs.

For each task, we define a partial navigational context representing a possible navigational structure to support the task. As an example, we detail the derivation of the navigational contexts corresponding to the use case "Find Movie given its title," whose UID we repeat in Figure 6.11 for convenience.

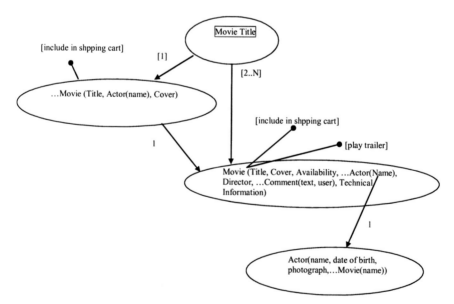

Figure 6.11. Complete specification of the UID for use case "Find Movie given its title (including the buying operation)."

First, each structure that has been represented in the UID (and the corresponding class in the conceptual model) is analyzed to determine the type of primitive that it will give raise to, e.g., an access structure, a navigational context, or a list. The following guidelines can be used to derive a navigational context:

1. When the task associated with the UID requires that the user inspects a set of elements to select one, we map the set of structures into an access structure. An access structure is a set of elements, each of which contains a link, and is represented by a rectangle with a dashed border. In Figure 6.12 we show the partial diagram for access structures Movies and Artists.

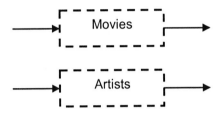

Figure 6.12. Access structures.

2. When the task does not require such inspection but requires the elements to be accessed simultaneously, map the set into a list, e.g., the list of Songs in the soundtrack of a DVD (see Figure 6.13).

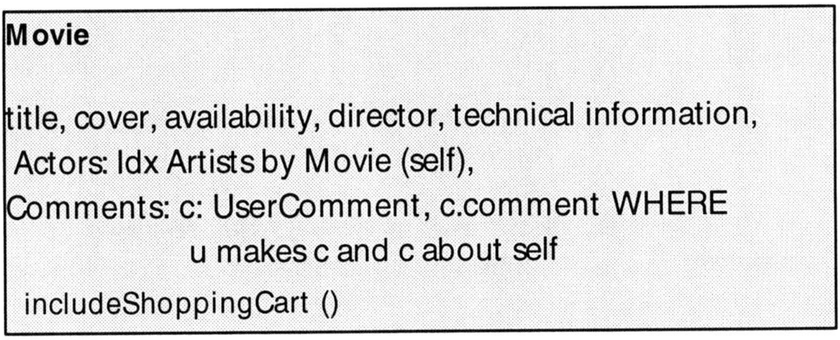

> **Movie**
>
> title, cover, availability, director, technical information,
> Actors: Idx Artists by Movie (self),
> Comments: c: UserComment, c.comment WHERE
>   u makes c and c about self
> includeShoppingCart ()

Figure 6.13. List for DVD soundtrack.

3. After mapping the different sets of structures, we analyze singular structures in the UID using the following guideline: When the task requires that the information about an element be accessed by the user, we map the structure into a navigational context, represented

by a rectangle with solid borders. In Figure 6.14 we show the partial context diagram from this example.

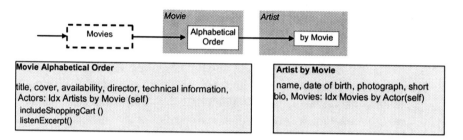

Figure 6.14. Partial context for the UID "Find Movie given its title."

In the example, both Movies in Alphabetical Order and Artist by Movie are contexts, which correspond to sets of elements. The elements and their attributes making up each set are described in the gray boxes.

Following an analogous reasoning, Figure 6.15 shows the navigation diagram for the task "Find Actor information (including movies) given the Actor name."

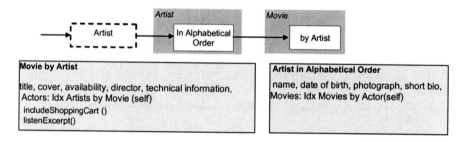

Figure 6.15. Partial context for the UID "Find Actor information (including movies) given the Artist name."

This process is repeated for each collected UID, resulting in a set of partial navigation diagrams supporting all intended tasks. The next step is to integrate these partial diagrams by unifying them, to arrive at a single diagram for the whole application. The unification process identifies contexts and indexes that are composed of either the same kind of elements or elements that could be substituted by elements of a more abstract (super) class. In addition, each time a partial diagram is integrated into the evolving final diagram, navigation between the various contexts in each partial diagram must also be considered and included when relevant.

Considering the diagrams in Figures 6.14 and 6.15, one would obtain the unified diagram shown in Figure 6.16.

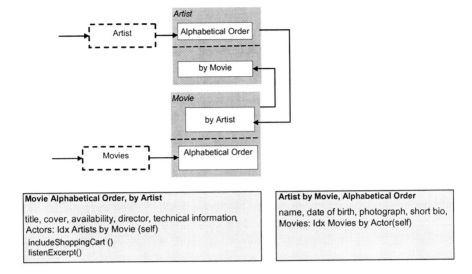

Figure 6.16. Unification of diagrams in Figures 6.14 and 6.15.

Notice that the navigation from the context "Artist in Alphabetical Order" to the "Movie by Artist" has been generalized to the "Artist by Movie" context—hence the arrow leaving the gray box "Artist," the Artist scope. The same reasoning applies to the contexts within the "Movies" scope.

The dashed lines within each scope in Figure 6.16 indicate that it is not possible to move freely between contexts separated by the lines. In other words, if one is looking at an Artist in the "Alphabetical Order" context, it is not possible to navigate to the next "Artist by Movie." If there was another context such as "Artist by Nationality," it could make sense to allow the user to navigate to the next artist of the same nationality, instead of the next artist in alphabetical order, so that these two contexts would not be separated by a dashed line in the corresponding diagram.

Another result from the unification process is the identification of generalizations. Consider the diagram in Figure 6.15. The reasoning that leads to the creation of the "Movie by Artist" context also applies to directors; similarly, for all contexts for TV series with respect to contexts with movies. The generalization becomes the "Feature by Person" context. Notice that scopes may be nested, as in Figure 6.8, to represent the subclass hierarchy of the classes for the corresponding elements (e.g., Movie and TV Series within Feature, and Artist and Director within Person).

6.4.4 InContext Classes

When the same node (e.g., Movie, Actor, etc.) may appear in more than one set (context), we need to express the peculiarities of this node within each particular context. We may take as a default that "next" and "previous" anchors and links are automatically defined for traversing each set; but we may also want that some context-sensitive information appears when accessing a Movie by genre context (for example, giving access to some comments on movies on that specific genre).

In OOHDM this is achieved with InContext classes; for each node class and each context in which it appears, we can define an InContext class that acts as a decorator (Gamma et al., 1995) for nodes when accessed in that particular context. Decorators provide a good alternative to subclassing and prevent us from defining multiple subclasses of the base node class. InContext classes are organized in hierarchies with some base classes already provided by the design framework; for example, InContext classes defined as subclasses of InContextSequential inherit anchors for sequential navigation and for backtracking to the context index. When we do not define InContext classes, a default one is assumed according to the type of context defined.

Notice that the navigational contexts schema complements the navigational schema by showing the way in which nodes are grouped into navigable sets. Additional nodes' behavior can be implemented in InContext classes; in amazon.com, for example, when we access a book in the context of a query, we have an option to move it to the shopping basket. When we access the same book in the context of the shopping basket, we should have other, different, operations to perform.

6.5 INTERFACE DESIGN

Any hypermedia (Web) application must exchange information with its environment in order to fulfill its tasks. The functions implemented by the application all receive some information, process it, and trigger changes in the interface, restarting the cycle. Very often the cycle is triggered by user actions at the interface, but sometimes the cycle is started by some other event, such as a timeout.

From this point of view, the role of the interface is to make the navigation objects and application functionality perceptible to the user, which is the goal of the interface design. From the application business logic's point of view, all that is needed regarding the interface is the definition of the information exchange between the application and the user, including activation of functionalities. In particular, from the standpoint of the interface, navigation is just another (albeit distinguished) application functionality.

Since the information exchange is driven by the tasks, it is reasonable to expect that it will be less sensitive to run-time environment aspects, such as particular standards and devices being used. The design of this task-related aspect of the interface can be carried out by interaction designers or software engineers and is almost totally independent of the particular hardware and software run-time environment. The concrete appearance of the interface, defining the actual look and feel of the application, including layout, font, color, and graphical appearance, is typically carried out by graphics designers. The result of this separation of concerns, specifying the information exchange at the interface separately from its look and feel, leads to isolating the essence of the interaction design from inevitable technological platform evolution, as well as from the need to support users in a multitude of hardware and software run-time environments.

The most abstract level is called the abstract interface and focuses on the various types of functionality that can be played by interface elements with respect to the information exchange between the user and the application. The vocabulary used to define the abstract interface is established by an abstract widget ontology (Moura and Schwabe, 1994), shown in Figure 6.17, which specifies that an abstract interface widget can be any of the following:

- SimpleActivator, a widget capable of reacting to external events, such as mouse clicks.
- ElementExhibitor, a widget able to exhibit some type of content, such as text or images.
- VariableCapturer, a widget able to receive (capture) the value of one or more variables. Examples are input text fields, selection widgets such as pull-down menus and checkboxes, etc. It generalizes two distinct (sub-) concepts.

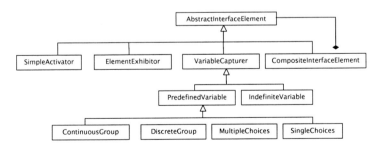

Figure 6.17. Abstract widget ontology.

- IndefiniteVariable, a widget allowing one to enter hitherto unknown values, such as a text string typed by the user.
- PredefinedVariable, a widget that allows the selection of a subset of values from a predefined set of possibilities; quite often this selection must be a singleton. Specializations of this concept are ContinousGroup, DiscreteGroup, MultipleChoices, and SingleChoice. The first allows one to select a single value from an infinite range of values; the second is analogous, but for a finite set; the remainder are self-evident.
- CompositeInterfaceElement, a widget composed of any of the above.

It becomes evident from this ontology the essential roles that interface elements play with respect to the interaction—they exhibit information, or they react to external events, or they accept information. Composite elements allow us to build more complex interfaces out of simpler building blocks. The abstract interface design should be carried out by the software designer, who understands the application logic and the kinds of information exchanges that must be supported to carry out the operations. This software designer does not have to worry about usability issues, or look and feel, which will be dealt with during the concrete interface design, typically carried out by a graphics (or "experience") designer.

Each element of the abstract interface must be mapped onto both a navigation element, which will provide or receive its contents, and a concrete interface widget, which will actually implement it in a given run-time environment. Figure 6.18 shows an example of an interface showing the information about an artist in the Artist in Alphabetical Order context, and Figure 6.19 shows an abstract representation of this interface as a composition of widgets from the vocabulary defined above.

Before proceeding to show how this is achieved, we must first define the concrete widget ontology, which characterizes the actual widgets available in concrete run-time environments.

The concrete interface is specified in terms of actual widgets commonly available in most graphical interface run-time environments. Examples of concrete widgets include text boxes, radio buttons, pull-down menus, check boxes, etc., as illustrated in Figure 6.18.

Actual abstract interface widget instances are mapped onto specific navigation elements (in the navigation model) and onto concrete interface

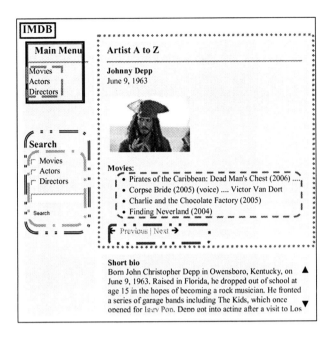

Figure 6.18. An example concrete interface.

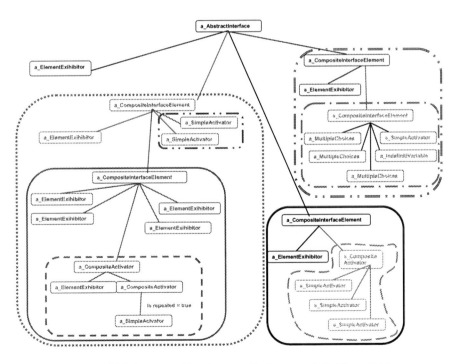

Figure 6.19. Abstract widget instance for the example in Figure 6.18.

widgets. Figure 6.20 shows an example illustrating how application functionality is integrated, giving the OWL (Smith et al., 2002) specification of the "Search" abstract interface element. It is composed of two abstract widgets, "ElementExhibitor" (lines 9–12) and "CompositeInterfaceElement" (lines 14–46). The first shows the "Search" string, using a "Label" concrete widget. The second aggregates the four elements used to specify the field in which the search may be performed, namely, three "MultipleChoices"— SearchMovies (lines 25–29), SearchArtists (31–35), and SearchDirectors (37–41)—and one "IndefiniteVariable"—"SearchTextField" (lines 43–45).

```
                              ...
1    <awo:CompositeInterfaceElement rdf:ID="Search">
2       <awo:fromIndex>idxSearch</awo:fromIndex>
3       <awo:mapsTo rdf:resource="&cwo;Composition"/>
4       <awo:isRepeated>false</awo:isRepeated>
5       <awo:hasInterfaceElement rdf:resource="#TitleSearch"/>
6       </awo:CompositeInterfaceElement>
8
9    <awo:ElementExihibitor rdf:ID="TitleSearch">
10      <awo:visualizationText>Search</awo:visualizationText>
11      <awo:mapsTo rdf:resource="&cwo;Label"/>
12   </awo:ElementExihibitor>
13
14   <awo:CompositeInterfaceElement rdf:ID="SearchElements">
15      <awo:fromIndex>idxSearch</awo:fromIndex>
16      <awo:abstractInterface>SearchResult</awo:abstractInterface>
17      <awo:mapsTo rdf:resource="&cwo;Form"/>
18      <awo:isRepeated>false</awo:isRepeated>
19      <awo:hasInterfaceElement rdf:resource="#SearchMovies"/>
20      <awo:hasInterfaceElement rdf:resource="#SearchArtists"/>
21      <awo:hasInterfaceElement rdf:resource="#SearchDirectors"/>
22      <awo:hasInterfaceElement rdf:resource="#SearchTextField"/>
23   </awo:CompositeInterfaceElement>
24
25   <awo:MultipleChoices rdf:ID="SearchMovies">
26      <awo:fromElement>SearchMovies</awo:fromElement>
27      <awo:fromAttribute>section</awo:fromAttribute>
28      <awo:mapsTo rdf:resource="&cwo;CheckBox"/>
29   </awo:MultipleChoices>
30
31   <awo:MultipleChoices rdf:ID="SearchArtists">
32      <awo:fromElement>SearchArtists</awo:fromElement>
33       <awo:fromAttribute>section</awo:fromAttribute>
34      <awo:mapsTo rdf:resource="&cwo;CheckBox"/>
35   </awo:MultipleChoices>
36
37   <awo:MultipleChoices rdf:ID="SearchDirectors">
38      <awo:fromElement>SearchDirectors</awo:fromElement>
39      <awo:fromAttribute>section</awo:fromAttribute>
40      <awo:mapsTo rdf:resource="&cwo;CheckBox"/>
41   </awo:MultipleChoices>
42
43   <awo:IndefiniteVariable rdf:ID="SearchTextField">
44      <awo:mapsTo rdf:resource="&cwo;TextBox"/>
45   </awo:IndefiniteVariable>
```

Figure 6.20. Example of the OWL specification of the "Search" part of Figure 6.19.

The *CompositeInterfaceElement* element, in this case, has the properties *fromIndex, isRepeated, mapsTo, abstractInterface,* and *hasInterfaceElement.* The *fromIndex* property in line 2 indicates to which navigational index this element belongs. This property is mandatory if no antecessor element of type *CompositeInterfaceElement* has declared it. The association with the "idxSearch" navigation element in line 2 enables the generation of the link to the actual code that will run the search. Even though this example shows an association with a navigation element, it could just as well be associated with a call to application functionality such as "buy."

The *isRepeated* property indicates if the components of this element are repetitions of a single type (false in this case). The *mapsTo* property indicates which concrete element corresponds to this abstract interface element. The *abtractInterface* property specifies the abstract interface that will be activated when this element is triggered. The *hasInterfaceElement* indicates which elements belong to this element.

The *ElementExhibitor* element has the *visualizationText* and *mapsTo* properties. The former represents the concrete object to be exhibited, in this case the string "Search."

The *MultipleChoices* element has the *fromElement, fromAttribute,* and *mapsTo* properties. The *fromElement* and *fromAttribute* properties indicate the corresponding element and navigational attribute in the navigational model, respectively. The *IndefiniteVariable* element has the *mapsTo* property.

6.6 FROM DESIGN TO IMPLEMENTATION

Mapping design documents into implementation artifacts is usually time-consuming, and, in spite of the general acceptance about the importance of software engineering approaches, implementers tend to overlook the advantages of good modeling practices.

A model here can be seen as a simplified, textual, or graphical description of the artifact being designed. Preferably, a model should have precise, non-ambiguous semantics that enables understanding of the artifact being modeled. Software development, according to the model-driven design approach (MDD), is a process whereby a high-level abstract model is successively translated into increasingly more detailed models, in such a way that eventually one of the models can be directly executed by some platform. The model that is directly executed by a platform that satisfies all the requirements, including the nonfunctional ones, is also called "code" and is usually the last model in the refinement chain.

Although this approach has been used for a number of years, its adoption is not completely widespread, at least not in its pure form. A major stumbling block has been the problem that the mapping between models, especially into actually executing code, has had little or no support from tools. Therefore, designers may use the models mostly as thinking tools, and at some stage they are forced to manually map these models into code. This process is error-prone, and once the code has been generated, changes or updates to the application are directly implemented in the code, instead of adjusting the models and re-generating the code.

On the other hand, several more recent proposals have attempted to alleviate this problem by having automated translations (or transformations) between models, supported by appropriate tools. Among the most prominent are MDA (Miller and Mukerji, 2003) and Software Factories (Greenfield and Short, 2004).

Following the MDD approach, we have developed the HyperDE environment (freely available at http://server2.tecweb.inf.puc-rio.br:8000/HyperDe), based on the MNVC framework, which extends the MVC framework with navigation primitives. It allows the designer to input OOHDM navigational models (the "model" in the MVC framework) and interface definitions (the "view" in the MVC framework), and it generates complete applications adherent to the specification. It also provides an interface to create and edit instance data, although, strictly speaking, this should actually be part of the generated application. Figure 6.21 shows the architecture of HyperDE. The actual version of OOHDM used in HyperDE is SHDM (Schwabe et al., 2002), which uses an object model derived from the RDF data model (Brickley and Guha, 2004) that has been proposed for describing data and meta-data on the Semantic Web.

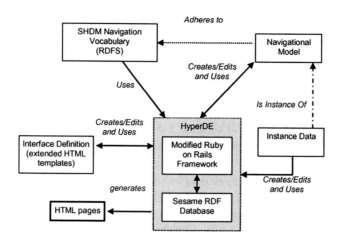

Figure 6.21. The architecture of the HyperDE environment.

HyperDE is implemented as a modification of the Ruby on Rails framework (http://www.rubyonrails.com), where the persistence layer (ActiveRecord) has been replaced by another one based on the Sesame RDF database. The SHDM meta-models, the user-defined navigation models, as well as the application instance data are all stored as RDF data.

Applying the MDD approach, designing a Web application using OOHDM (or SHDM) corresponds to instantiating its meta-model, which is supported by the HyperDE environment. Before giving an example, we briefly outline the meta-model used by HyperDE, so it will be clear from the example how it is being instantiated during a particular design.

6.6.1 SHDM Meta-Model

Figure 6.22 shows the SHDM meta-model, with the main classes highlighted. The class NavClass models the navigation nodes, and the class Link models the links between them. Each NavClass has NavAttributes, NavOperations, and links and can be a specialization of a BaseClass. Contexts are sets of objects belonging to a NavClass. This set is defined through a query whose expression is specified in one of the context attributes; this query may have a parameter. Indexes are made out of IndexEntries, which contain either anchors to other indexes or anchors to elements within a context. Landmarks are anchors to either Indexes or to Context elements. Views allow one to exhibit the contents of NavClass instances within some context or to exhibit Indexes.

All HyperDE functions can be accessed via Web interfaces. In addition, HyperDE also generates a domain-specific language (DSL) as an extension of Ruby, allowing direct manipulation within Ruby scripts of both the model and SHDM's meta-model.

To give an idea of HyperDE functionalities, we give a brief description of the example application. First, we show a couple of screen dumps of the generated application, and then we show how some of the model elements that generated this application are specified. It should be noted that HyperDE generates a default simple interface for models whose interface has not yet been fully specified; the examples below use this default interface. Evidently, the designer has all the freedom to override this default and define sophisticated interfaces with complex layouts.

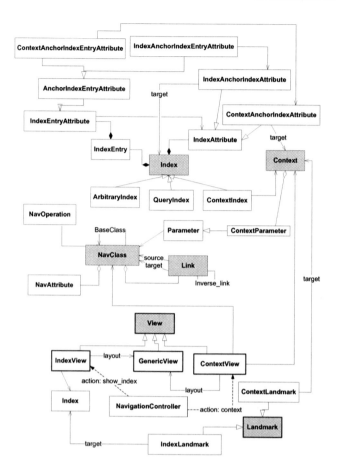

Figure 6.22. The SHDM meta-model.

Figure 6.23 shows the interface for a node "Movie" in the "Movies in Alphabetical Order" context. Notice the index for the context on the left and the contextual navigation (in this case, only the "previous" link, to "The Da Vinci Code," is defined, since it is the last node in the context). Suppose the user clicks on "Ian McKellen," leading to the interface shown in Figure 6.24. Notice that the link followed carries a parameter (the "Feature"), shown in the detail of the context, right beneath the Actor's name.

This particular actor has played roles in other movies, e.g., "The Da Vinci Code" (the "Sir Leigh Teabing" role). Following the link to this movie brings the user to the interface shown in Figure 6.25. Notice that this instance has more data defined than the one in Figure 6.23; HyperDE handles this because it is supported by the underlying RDF data model, which is more flexible than strict object-oriented models. Notice also that the context index that appears in the column on the left, automatically generated by HyperDE, is different in this case since the context is different.

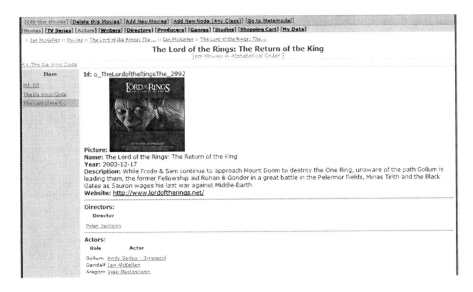

Figure 6.23. An interface showing a movie in the "Movies in Alphabetical Order" context.

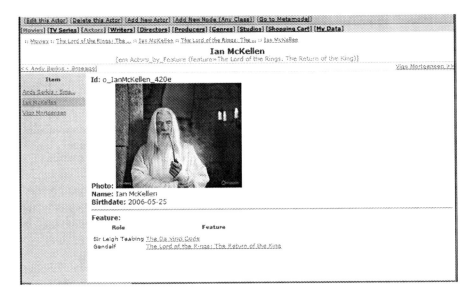

Figure 6.24. An interface for a node of type "Actor" in the "Actor by Feature" context.

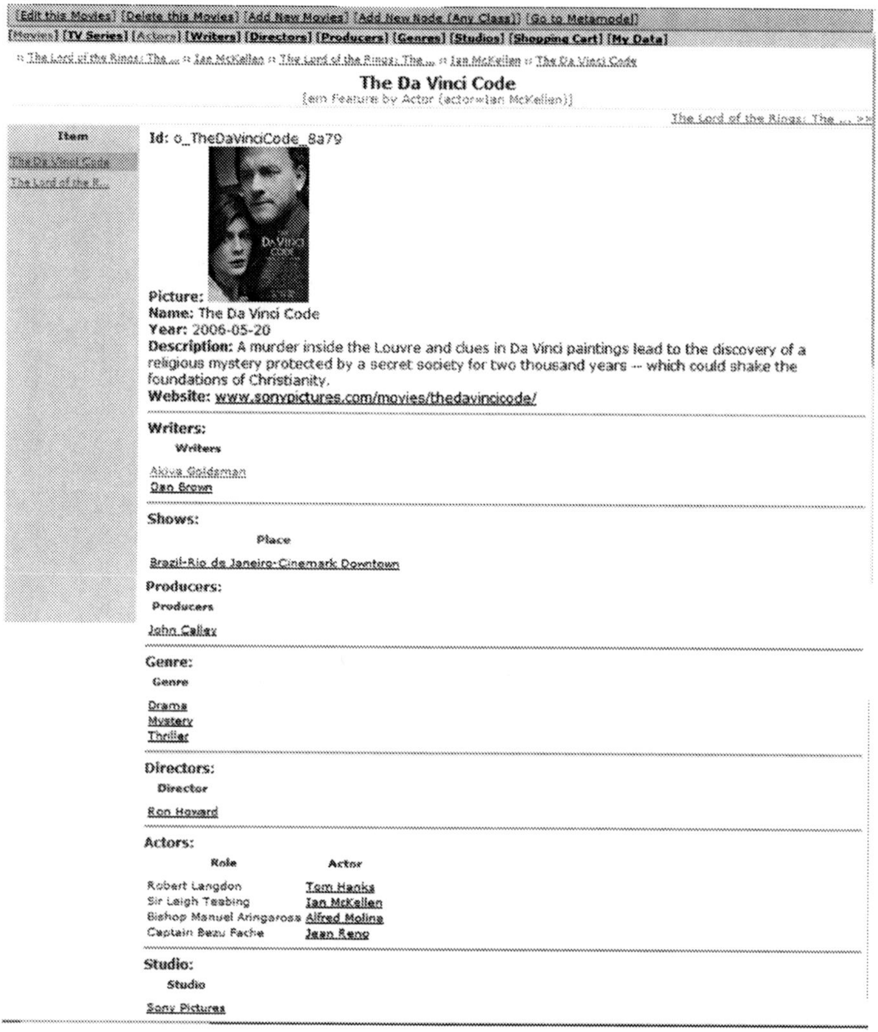

[Edit this Movies] [Delete this Movies] [Add New Movies] [Add New Node (Any Class)] [Go to Metamodel]
[Movies] [TV Series] [Actors] [Writers] [Directors] [Producers] [Genres] [Studios] [Shopping Cart] [My Data]

:: The Lord of the Rings: The ...   :: Ian McKellen   :: The Lord of the Rings: The ...   :: Ian McKellen   :: The Da Vinci Code

The Da Vinci Code
{am Feature by Actor (actor=Ian McKellen)}

The Lord of the Rings: The ... >>

Item
The Da Vinci Code
The Lord of the R...

Id: o_TheDaVinciCode_8a79

Picture:
Name: The Da Vinci Code
Year: 2006-05-20
Description: A murder inside the Louvre and clues in Da Vinci paintings lead to the discovery of a religious mystery protected by a secret society for two thousand years -- which could shake the foundations of Christianity.
Website: www.sonypictures.com/movies/thedavincicode/

Writers:

Writers

Akiva Goldsman
Dan Brown

Shows:

Place

Brazil-Rio de Janeiro-Cinemark Downtown

Producers:

Producers

John Calley

Genre:

Genre

Drama
Mystery
Thriller

Directors:

Director

Ron Howard

Actors:

Role	Actor
Robert Langdon	Tom Hanks
Sir Leigh Teabing	Ian McKellen
Bishop Manuel Aringarosa	Alfred Molina
Captain Bezu Fache	Jean Reno

Studio:

Studio

Sony Pictures

Figure 6.25. An interface for another "Feature" in the "Feature by Actor" context.

If we go into the meta-model editor of HyperDE and edit the "Actor" class, we get the interface shown in Figure 6.26. It allows us to specify the class name, its parent class if there is one ("Person" in this case), and its attributes and links. It also shows the inherited attributes.

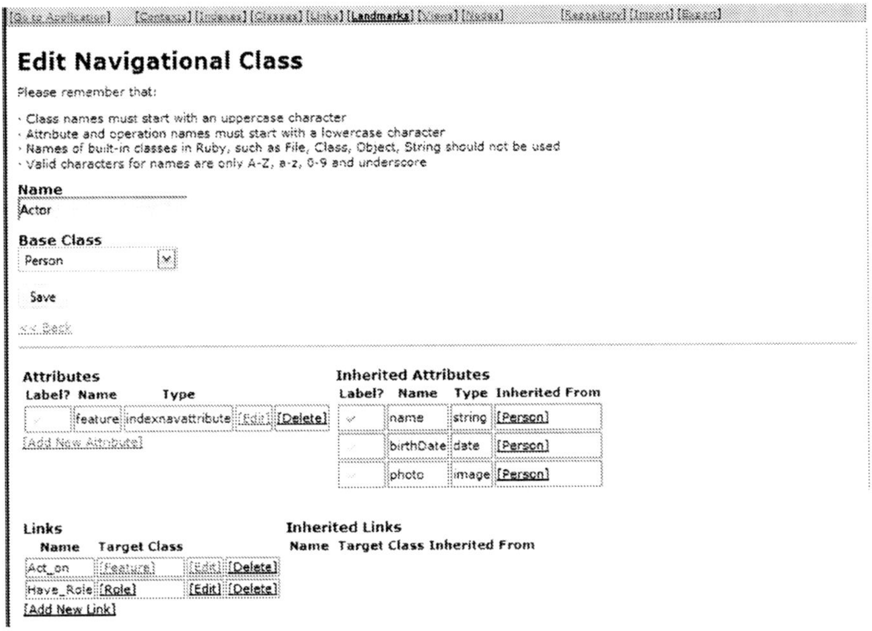

Figure 6.26. HyperDE interface to edit a navigational class.

As explained earlier, a navigational class may have attributes that are derived from other classes, and attributes that contain navigation information. An example here is the "feature" attribute of an actor, which is an index to the "Features by Actor" context (thus allowing navigation from an actor to one of the features he has acted in). Figure 6.27 shows the interface for defining the "Features by Actor" context.

There are two related aspects worth observing in this definition. The first is the use of a simplified query language to express the context selection. Since the vast majority of contexts found in practice fall into the "x by y" pattern—e.g., "Actor by Feature," "Feature by Director," etc., HyperDE uses a simple notation allowing the specification of the source class, the destination class, the relation (link) name, and the ordering. If desired, it is possible to specify a full query in the RQL query language, or to specify a Ruby expression using the generated domain-specific language that HyperDE provides. The second aspect to be noted is that this context is actually a group of contexts, since it is parameterized—there is one context for each actor, which is passed as a parameter.

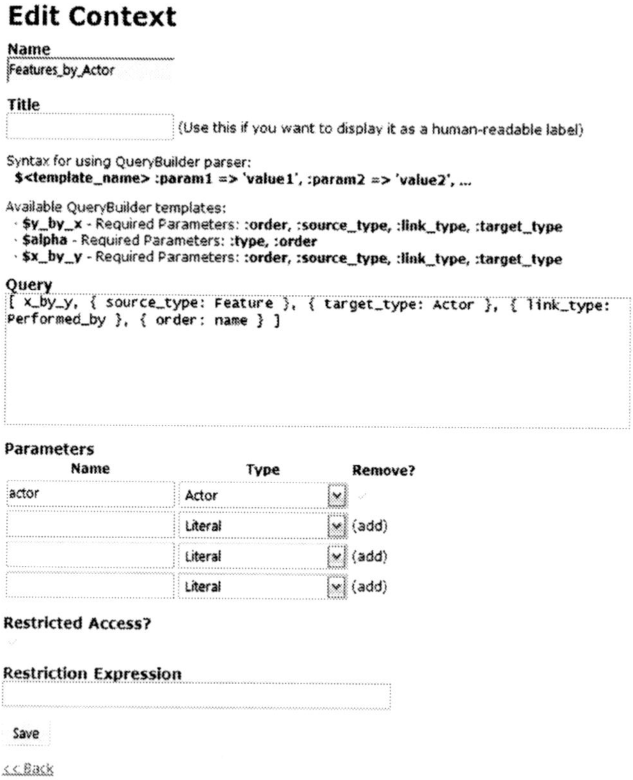

Edit Context

Name
Features_by_Actor

Title
_____ (Use this if you want to display it as a human-readable label)

Syntax for using QueryBuilder parser:
  $<template_name> :param1 => 'value1', :param2 => 'value2', ...

Available QueryBuilder templates:
  · $y_by_x - Required Parameters: :order, :source_type, :link_type, :target_type
  · $alpha - Required Parameters: :type, :order
  · $x_by_y - Required Parameters: :order, :source_type, :link_type, :target_type

Query
```
[ x_by_y, { source_type: Feature }, { target_type: Actor }, { link_type:
Performed_by }, { order: name } ]
```

Parameters
Name	Type	Remove?
actor	Actor ☑	
	Literal ☑	(add)
	Literal ☑	(add)
	Literal ☑	(add)

Restricted Access?

Restriction Expression
_____

Save

<< Back

Figure 6.27. HyperDE interface to edit a context definition.

It should be recalled that the "feature" attribute of an "actor" is an index into the context defined in Figure 6.27; entries in this index will have links to the actual nodes in the context.

Figure 6.28 shows the interface for defining the "Features by Actor" index.

The query definition for the index specified in this figure uses the generated DSL to compute the elements of the index. In this case, the expression first finds the Actor object whose id was passed as a parameter. Then it takes the list of features this actor has acted on ("aa.act_on"), and, for each feature in it, it generates a hash table of three keys: "feature," "role," and "actor." The value for the key "feature" is the feature itself; the value for the "role" key is the intersection between the list of roles the actor has played and the list of characters of the feature; and the value for the "actor" key is the actor that was passed as a parameter to the context. This hash table is used by HyperDE to generate the index entries, each of which will have two attributes: a role and a feature. This generates the list of "role, feature" pairs seen in the "Feature" attribute of an actor illustrated at the bottom of Figure 6.24. A similar definition is used to generate the list of "role, actor" pairs seen in the "Actors" attribute of a feature, illustrated in Figures 6.23 and 6.25.

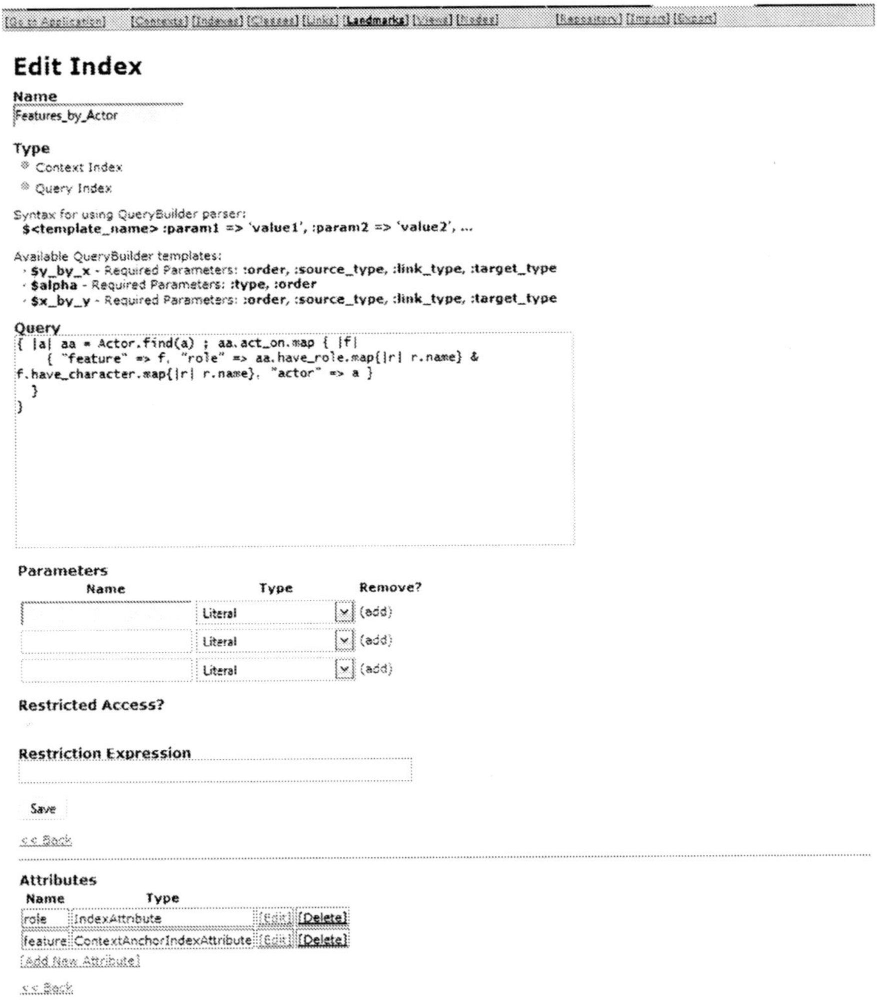

[Go to Application]   [Contexts] [Indexes] [Classes] [Links] [**Landmarks**] [Views] [Nodes]   [Repository] [Import] [Export]

Edit Index

Name
Features_by_Actor

Type
- Context Index
- Query Index

Syntax for using QueryBuilder parser:
$<template_name> :param1 => 'value1', :param2 => 'value2', ...

Available QueryBuilder templates:
- **$y_by_x** - Required Parameters: :order, :source_type, :link_type, :target_type
- **$alpha** - Required Parameters: :type, :order
- **$x_by_y** - Required Parameters: :order, :source_type, :link_type, :target_type

Query
```
{ |a| aa = Actor.find(a) ; aa.act_on.map { |f|
  { "feature" => f, "role" => aa.have_role.map{|r| r.name} &
f.have_character.map{|r| r.name}, "actor" => a }
  }
}
```

Parameters

Name	Type	Remove?
	Literal ⌄	(add)
	Literal ⌄	(add)
	Literal ⌄	(add)

Restricted Access?

Restriction Expression

Save

<< Back

Attributes

Name	Type		
role	IndexAttribute	[Edit]	[Delete]
feature	ContextAnchorIndexAttribute	[Edit]	[Delete]

[Add New Attribute]

<< Back

Figure 6.28. HyperDE interface to define an index.

HyperDE allows easy customization of interfaces. For example, it is possible to define a different layout to be used to exhibit nodes of a given class in a certain context, such as a movie in the Movies in Alphabetical Order context. Figure 6.29 shows an alternative layout for the interface shown in Figure 6.23.

Figure 6.29. An alternative interface to exhibit a movie in the Movies in Alphabetical order context. This is the same node as the one in Figure 6.23.

To define this interface, a new view is defined, as shown in Figure 6.30. This interface uses HTML interspersed with expressions in the generated DSL, which allows one to access the model elements to be exhibited. For instance, the expression @node.name retrieves the "name" attribute of the node being exhibited (a "Movie") in this case.

Application functionality is implemented through operations associated to the various navigational classes. The code for these operations also uses the generated DSL, which allows the data model to be updated as well as the values of existing instances of navigation objects to be created or altered.

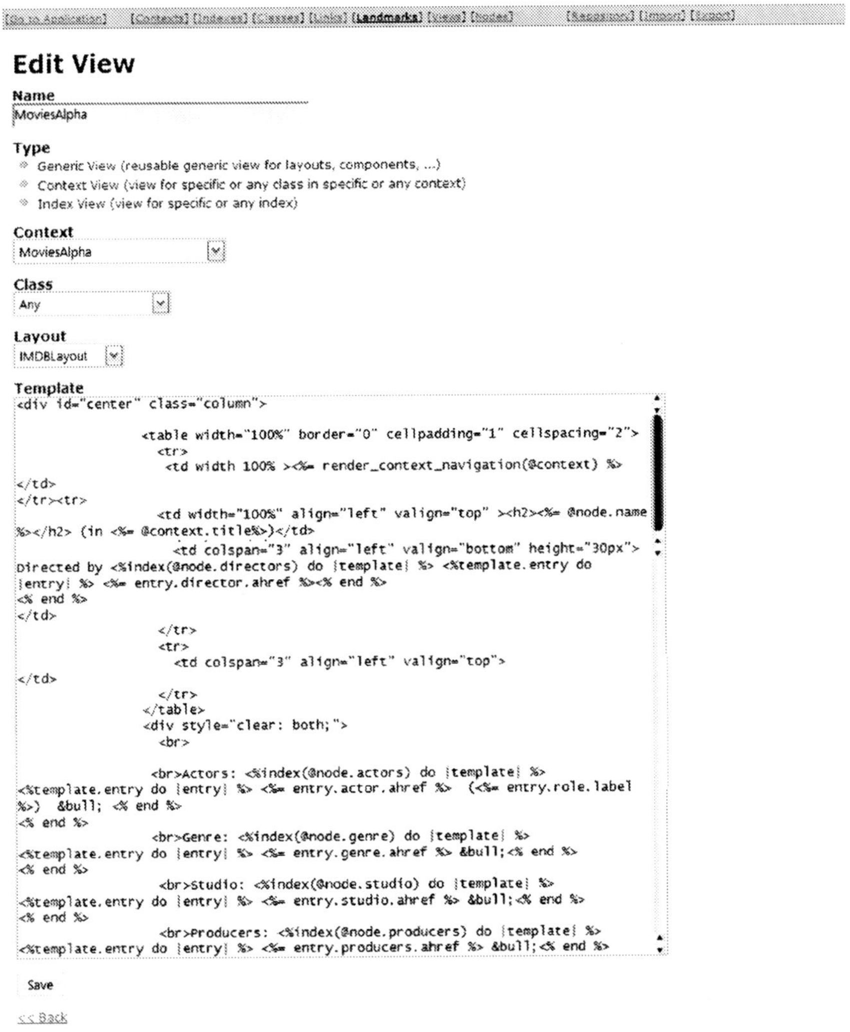

[Go to Application]   [Contexts] [Indexes] [Classes] [Links] [**Landmarks**] [Views] [Nodes]   [Sessions] [Import] [Export]

Edit View

Name

MoviesAlpha

Type

- Generic View (reusable generic view for layouts, components, ...)
- Context View (view for specific or any class in specific or any context)
- Index View (view for specific or any index)

Context

MoviesAlpha ▼

Class

Any ▼

Layout

IMDBLayout ▼

Template

```
<div id="center" class="column">
                <table width="100%" border="0" cellpadding="1" cellspacing="2">
                  <tr>
                   <td width 100% ><%= render_context_navigation(@context) %>
</td>
</tr><tr>
                    <td width="100%" align="left" valign="top" ><h2><%= @node.name
%></h2> (in <%= @context.title%>)</td>
                    <td colspan="3" align="left" valign="bottom" height="30px">
Directed by <%index(@node.directors) do |template| %> <%template.entry do
|entry| %> <%= entry.director.ahref %><% end %>
<% end %>
</td>
                 </tr>
                 <tr>
                   <td colspan="3" align="left" valign="top">
</td>
                 </tr>
               </table>
               <div style="clear: both;">
                 <br>

                 <br>Actors: <%index(@node.actors) do |template| %>
<%template.entry do |entry| %> <%= entry.actor.ahref %>  (<%= entry.role.label
%>)  &bull; <% end %>
<% end %>
                 <br>Genre: <%index(@node.genre) do |template| %>
<%template.entry do |entry| %> <%= entry.genre.ahref %> &bull;<% end %>
<% end %>
                 <br>studio: <%index(@node.studio) do |template| %>
<%template.entry do |entry| %> <%= entry.studio.ahref %> &bull;<% end %>
<% end %>
                 <br>Producers: <%index(@node.producers) do |template| %>
<%template.entry do |entry| %> <%= entry.producers.ahref %> &bull;<% end %>
```

Save

<< Back

Figure 6.30. The interface definition for the layout shown in Figure 6.29.

Let us briefly consider what happens when, while navigating in a "Movie" object, the user invokes the addToShoppingCart operation, which has the following (simplified) code:

```
1   o = Order.find_all.first
2   dvd = self.has_dvd.first
3   s = DVDSale.new
4   s.quantity = 1
5   s.orderNumber = o.number
6   s.dvd_bought << self
7   o.order_has_dvd_sale << s
```

In line 1, we obtain the latest Order placed—we assume this is the current open order, but this could be handled differently. Line 2 finds the DVD associated with the current Movie; lines 3–5 create a new DVDSale item; line 6 associates this DVDSale to the DVD (i.e., creates an instance of the DVD_Bought relation); and line 7 includes the DVDSale item in the (current) Order (i.e., creates a new instance of the Order_Has_DVD_Sale relation). Once this code has been executed, the Order data, as well as the DVD_Sale data, may be changed through operations made available at a suitable interface, oftentimes during the check-out process.

HyperDE has many additional features that cannot be detailed here, for reasons of space. The reader is encouraged to explore more details and download them from the site http://server2.tecweb.inf.puc-rio.br:8000/HyperDe.

We have also implemented another development environment, SHDM .Net (Ricci and Schwabe, 2006), which extends Microsoft Visual Studio 2005 to allow SHDM models to be created and edited and generates code running on the .Net environment.

6.7 IMPROVING DESIGN WITH PATTERNS

Web applications are usually built from scratch, which is not surprising given the relative youth of the Web Engineering discipline. However, the key reason why Web components are not systematically reused is that most design approaches are not completely effective in helping the designer to reason about the composition of existing structures. While reuse can be obtained at the application model level, less has been achieved in the domain of navigation structures. In this section we argue in favor of a high-level kind of reuse: the reuse of design experience.

Expert Web application designers typically do not solve every problem from scratch. Most of the time, they reuse solutions that they have used previously. It is common, however, that critical design decisions made while defining, for example, the interaction and navigational styles of an application usually remain hidden in code or are poorly documented. It is widely accepted that reusability of either design experience or design structures is the most valuable kind of reuse (Gamma et al., 1995). From the expert's point of view, it helps communicate the decisions made or discuss the different alternatives with the rest of the working team in a simple and accurate way.

Consider the question of how a Web designer can guarantee (in the context of our Movies site) that the user always knows that there are new films in the site. A good solution for this general problem would be to devote a space in the home page to inform users about novelties, including a link to new movies.

Note that in the simple example above we are not using any particular design notation though such a notation may be useful for expressing in a non-ambiguous way the relationships among objects in the solution. In this section we motivate the use of patterns to record design solutions in the Web applications domain. Reasoning about abstract design structures in terms of Web patterns is a key step toward reuse of Web applications design experience.

6.7.1 A Brief Summary of Design Patterns

Design patterns are being increasingly used in software design. They systematically name, explain, and evaluate important and recurrent designs in software systems. They describe problems that occur repeatedly, and describe the core of the solution to that problem, in such a way that we can use this solution many times in different contexts and applications.

A design pattern is described by stating the context in which the pattern may be applied, the problem and interacting forces that bring it to life, and the collaborating elements that make up the reusable solution. These elements are described in an abstract way because patterns are like templates that can be applied in many different situations. Patterns allow communication to be improved within and across software development teams, by providing a shared vocabulary. They help to capture explicitly the knowledge that designers use implicitly.

The patterns movement began in the area of architectural design 30 years ago with the work of Christopher Alexander (Alexander et al., 1977). In the 1990s, the object-oriented community started using patterns to capture and convey object-oriented micro-architectures. Hypermedia patterns were introduced in Rossi et al. (1997), and an interesting corpus of hypermedia (The Hypermedia Patterns, 2002) and Web patterns (van Duyne et al., 2002) already exists.

There is no fixed format to describe patterns, although the essential elements must always appear: name, problem, solution, consequences. We next give a framework to describe and discuss patterns, and then we present some examples of Web patterns, exemplifying them in the context of our exemplary application.

6.7.2 A Pattern Taxonomy

In our research we have identified different categories in which patterns can be classified and organized. As a direct consequence of the activities in the OOHDM design space (similar to other methods), we can classify patterns in

- Conceptual or design patterns. These patterns appear during conceptual design and, as a consequence, are similar to traditional design patterns such as those in Gamma et al. (1995) or Fowler (2004).
- Navigation patterns. These patterns address the problem of organizing the navigational space of an application.
- User interface patterns. These deal with recurrent decisions in the layout and interaction styles of Web software. See, for example, Rossi et al. (2000).
- Implementation patterns. These patterns tend to be specific to a concrete run-time environment, such as J2EE, Struts, .Net, Ajax, XML, etc. See, for example, Ajax Patterns (2004) and XML Patterns (2004).

Patterns can be general or domain-specific. General-purpose patterns can be used in any application, while domain-specific patterns arise in a particular domain and are usual in that domain, such as e-commerce [see Lyardet et al. (2000)]. In other specific domains such as e-learning, other patterns may arise.

6.7.3 Examples

To illustrate the subject, we will next describe some of the patterns we discovered in the past, by mining design structures in successful Web applications. For each one, we indicate the kind of pattern and the intended domain. Patterns are described using a simple template that indicates the intent of the pattern, the problem being addressed, and the solution including examples. Complete descriptions of these patterns can be found in Rossi et al. (1999).

Landmark (Navigational, Generic)
  Intent:
  Provide easy access to different though unrelated items or sets of items in a hypermedia or Web application.

Problem:

Suppose we are building a Web Information System for a complex electronic shopping store such as www.amazon.com. By entering the site, we can build many different products such as videos, books, or CDs. We can explore the products and provide links to recommendations, comments on the products, news, etc. When we build the navigational schema, we try to follow closely those relationships existing in the underlying object model; for example, we can navigate from an author to his books, from a DVD to the list of songs it includes. We can go from a book to some comments previous readers made, read about related books, etc. However, we may want the reader to be able, at any moment, to jump to the music or book (sub-) stores or to her shopping basket.

Solution:

Define a set of landmarks and make them accessible from every node in the network. Make the interface of links to a landmark look uniform, so that users have a consistent visual cue about the landmark. We may have different levels of landmarking according to the hypertext area we are visiting. In Figure 6.31 we can see an example of landmarks in www.imdb.com, where we have landmarks to Showtime and tickets, DVD/Video, TV Movies, etc.

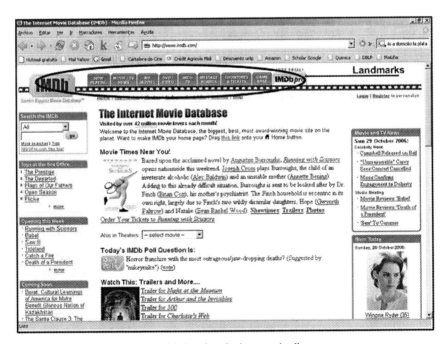

Figure 6.31. Landmarks in www.imdb.com.

News (Navigational, Generic)
  Intent:

Given a large and dynamic Web application, provide the users with information about new items that have been added.

  Problem:

Most large Web sites are tree-structured, which, though not perfect, offers a simple mechanism to organize considerable amounts of information. These information spaces tend to be large and are hardly ever completely navigated by a single user. In our example, each new movie is added in the corresponding branch of a huge tree (according, for example, to film genre taxonomies). However, the user has no way to know that there is a novelty. In e-commerce sites, for example, there is a need to make the user aware of the addition of new products. This problem poses a design challenge for Web designers, who must balance between a well-structured Web site where information is organized in items with subitems, etc. and a structure-less, star-shaped navigational structure where all information is reachable from the home page. The latter approach is clearly not desirable because the site's usability is greatly reduced and it may become unmanageable as it grows. Therefore, how is the user provided with instant feedback of any recent changes or additions to the information available while maintaining a well-structured Web site?

  Solution:

Structure the home page in such a way that space is devoted to the newest additions, presenting descriptive "headlines" regarding them. Use those headlines as anchors to link them with their related pages. This approach allows the designer to preserve good organization of the information while giving users feedback of the changes that take place within the Web site. Implement shortcuts to information that may be located in the leaves of a tree-structured site, without compromising the underlying structure. Notice that the navigational structure of the application is slightly affected by the addition of (temporary) links from one node to others. In Figure 6.32 we show an example of news in www.imdb.com.

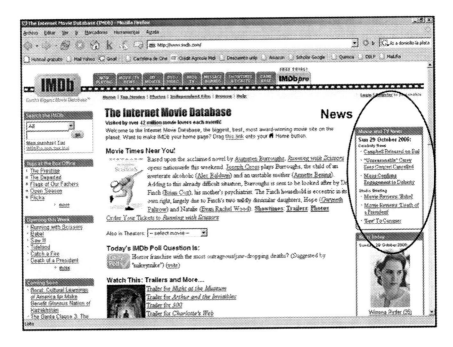

Figure 6.32. News pattern in www.imdb.com.

6.8 CONCLUSIONS

Work on OOHDM and SHDM has been taking place since 1995. OOHDM was one of the first methods to identify the currently common separation of concerns into contents, navigation, presentation, and (business) functionality. It has been extensively used in industry and academia, in applications that are running to this day.

Based on this continuous experimentation and evaluation in practice, it is an evolving method, and several new aspects are being constantly added, and improvements and refinements of earlier versions are being made.

One of the first improvements of OOHDM was in the area of personalization (see Schwabe et al., 2002). More recent work has generalized these concepts, extending SHDM to include user modeling and adaptivity, and HyperDE has also been extended accordingly (Assis et al., 2006).

This work also integrates with the original OOHDM primitives in allowing specification of access restrictions to navigation objects and contexts.

Another important aspect dealing with reuse is the study of design rationale, which allows one to capture entire reasoning structures behind a given design. Once this rationale has been recorded, it is possible to reapply it to similar problems encountered in new designs, thus achieving an even higher level of reuse. More details can be found in Medeiros et al. (2005). A more recent trend in Web applications is the so-called Web 2.0, where applications have rich interfaces (closer in interaction power to desktop applications) and can make use of "mash-ups," i.e., integrating APIs of various services to provide new application functionality. SHDM and HyperDE are being extended once again to be able to easily model such applications.

ACKNOWLEDGEMENTS

The authors wish to thank Adriana Pereira de Medeiros for her invaluable assistance in reviewing, revising, and improving this chapter. Daniel Schwabe has been partially supported by grants from CNPq–Brazil, UOL, and Microsoft Research. Gustavo Rossi has been partially supported by Secyt under project PICT 13623.

REFERENCES

Ajax Patterns, 2004. http://www.ajaxpatterns.org.
Alexander, C., Ishikawa, S., Silverstein, M., Jacobson, M., Fiksdahl-King, I., and Angel, S., 1977, *A Pattern Language,* Oxford University Press, New York.
Assis, P.A., Schwabe, D., and Nunes, D.A., 2006, ASHDM—Model-driven adaptation and meta-adaptation. *Proceedings Fourth International Conference on Adaptive Hypermedia and Adaptive Web-Based Systems*, Dublin, Ireland, June 21-23, pp. 213-222.
Brickley, D., and Guha, R.V., 2004, RDF Vocabulary Description Language 1.0, RDF Schema, W3C Recommendation, February 10. http://www.w3.org/TR/2004/REC-rdf-schema-20040210/.
Ceri, S., Fraternali, P., Bongio, A., Brambilla, M., Comai, S., and Matera, M., 2002, *Designing Data-Intensive Web Applications,* Morgan Kaufmann, San Francisco.
Fowler, M., 1997, *UML Distilled,* Addison-Wesley, Reading, MA.
Fowler, M., 2006, Analysis Patterns. http://www.martinfowler.com/articles.html.
Gamma, E., Helm, R., Johnson, R., and Vlissides, J., 1995, *Design Patterns, Elements of Reusable Object-Oriented Software,* Addison-Wesley, Reading, MA.
Greenfield, J., and Short, K. 2004, *Software Factories, Assembling Applications with Patterns, Frameworks, Models & Tools,* Wiley, New York.
Hypermedia patterns repository. http://www.designpattern.lu.unisi.ch/.
Kim, W., 1994, *Advanced Database Systems,* ACM Press, New York.
Koch, N., and Kraus, A., 2002, The expressive power of UMLbased Web engineering. *Proceedings Second International Workshop on Web-Oriented Software Technology* (IWWOST02), Málaga, Spain, June.
Lyardet, F., Rossi, G., and Schwabe, D., 2000, Patterns for E-commerce applications. *Proceedings of EuroPLoP.*
Medeiros, A.P., Schwabe, D., and Feijó, B., 2005, Kuaba ontology, design rationale representation and reuse in model-based designs. *Proceedings 24th International Conference on Conceptual Modeling* (ER 2005), Klagenfurt, Austria, pp. 241-255.

Miller, J., and Mukerji, J., 2003, The MDA Guide. Draft version 2, OMG doc. ab/2003-01-03.

Moura, S.S., and Schwabe, D., 2004, Interface development for hypermedia applications in the Semantic Web. *Proceedings LA Web 2004*, Ribeirão Preto, Brazil, pp. 106–113.

Nunes, D.A., and Schwabe, D., 2006, Rapid prototyping of Web applications combining domain-specific languages and model-driven design. *Proceedings Sixth International Conference on Web Engineering* (ICWE'06), pp. 153–160.

Ricci, L., and Schwabe, D., 2006, An authoring environment for model-driven Web applications. XII Simpósio Brasileiro de Sistemas Multimídia e Web—Webmedia 2006, Sociedade Brasileira de Computação, pp. 11–19.

Rossi, G., Schwabe, D., and Garrido, A., 1997, Design reuse in hypermedia applications development. *Proceedings of Hypertext 1997*, pp. 57–66.

Rossi, G., Schwabe, D., and Lyardet, F., 1999, Patterns for designing navigable information spaces. In *Pattern Languages of Programs IV*, Addison-Wesley, Reading, MA.

Rossi, G., Schwabe, D., and Lyardet, F., 2000, User interface patterns for hypermedia applications. *Proceedings of AVI00, Advanced Visual Interfaces*, Palermo, Italy.

Schmid, H., and Rossi, G., 2004, Modeling and designing processes in e-commerce applications. *IEEE Internet Computing*, January–February.

Schwabe, D., and Rossi, G., 1998, *An Object Oriented Approach to Web-Based Application Design. Theory and Practice of Object Systems*, **4**(4). Wiley and Sons, New York.

Schwabe, D., Guimarães, R., and Rossi, G., 2002, Cohesive design of personalized Web applications. *IEEE Internet Computing*, March.

Schwabe, D., Szundy, G., de Moura, S.S., and Lima, F., 2004, Design and implementation of Semantic Web applications. *Proceedings of the Workshop on Application Design, Development and Implementation Issues in the Semantic Web* (WWW 2004), CEUR Workshop Proceedings, **105**, May.

Smith, M., McGuiness, D., Volz, R., and Welty, C., 2002, Web Ontology Language (OWL) Guide Version 1.0. W3C working draft, November 4. http://www.w3.org/TR/owl-guide/.

Turine, M.A.S., de Oliveira, M.C.F., and Masiero. P.C., 1997, A navigation-oriented hypertext model based on statecharts. *Proceedings Eighth ACM International Hypertext Conference*, Southampton, UK.

van Duyne, D.K., Landay, J.A., and Hong, J.I., 2002, *The Design of Sites, Patterns, Principles, and Processes for Crafting a Customer-Centered Web Experience,* Addison-Wesley, Reading, MA.

Vilain, P., Schwabe, D., and de Souza, C.S., 2000, A diagrammatic tool for representing user interaction in UML. *Proceedings UML 2000.* York, UK, pp. 133–147.

XML Patterns Web page, 2004. www.xmlpatterns.com.

Chapter 7

UML-BASED WEB ENGINEERING
An Approach Based on Standards

Nora Koch,[1,2] Alexander Knapp,[1] Gefei Zhang,[1] Hubert Baumeister[3]

[1]*Institut für Informatik, Ludwig-Maximilians-Universität München, Germany,*
`{kochn, knapp, zhangg}@pst.ifi.lmu.de`

[2]*F.A.S.T. GmbH, Germany,* `koch@fast.de`

[3]*Informatik og Matematisk Modellering, Danmarks Tekniske Universitet, Lyngby, Denmark,*
`hub@imm.dtu.dk`

7.1 OVERVIEW

UML-based Web Engineering (UWE; `www.pst.ifi.lmu.de/projekte/uwe`) came up at the end of the 1990s (Baumeister et al., 1999; Wirsing et al., 1999) with the idea to find a standard way for building analysis and design models of Web systems based on the then-current methods of OOHDM (Schwabe and Rossi, 1995), RMM (Isakowitz et al., 1995), and WSDM (de Troyer and Leune, 1998). The aim, which is still being pursued, was to use a common language or at least to define meta-model-based mappings among the existing approaches (Koch and Kraus, 2003; Escalona and Koch, 2006).

At that time the Unified Modeling Language (UML), which evolved from the integration of the three different modeling techniques of Booch, OOSE, and OMT, seemed to be a promising approach for system modeling. Since those early integration efforts, UML became the "lingua franca" of (object-oriented) software engineering (Object Management Group, 2005). A prominent feature of UML is that it provides a set of aids for the definition of domain-specific modeling languages (DSL)—so-called extension mechanisms. Moreover, the newly defined DSLs remain UML-compliant, which allows the use of all UML features supplemented, e.g., with Web-specific extensions.

Both the acceptance of the UML as a standard in the development of software systems and the flexibility provided by the extension mechanisms are the reasons for the choice of the Unified Modeling Language instead of the use of proprietary modeling techniques. The idea followed by UWE to adhere to standards is not limited to UML. UWE also uses XMI as a model exchange format (in the hopes of future tool interoperability enabled by a truly portable XMI), MOF for meta-modeling, the model-driven principles given by OMG's Model-Driven Architecture (MDA) approach, the transformation language QVT, and XML.

UWE is continuously adapting, on the one hand, to new features of Web systems, such as more transaction-based, personalized, context-dependent, and asynchronous applications. On the other hand, UWE evolves to incorporate the state of the art of software engineering techniques, such as aspect-oriented modeling, integration of model checking using Hugo/RT (Knapp et al., 2002; `www.pst.ifi.lmu.de/projekte/hugo`), and new model transformation languages to improve design quality.

The remainder of this chapter is structured as follows: The features distinguishing UWE's development process, visual notation, and tool support are briefly outlined below. UWE's modeling techniques are discussed step by step in Section 7.2 by means of the online movie database case study. The UWE extensions of the UML meta-model are outlined in Section 7.3. UWE's model-driven process and, in particular, the model transformations integrated into the process are described in Section 7.4. The CASE tool ArgoUWE, which supports the UWE notation and method, is described in Section 7.5. Finally, we give an outlook on future steps in the development of UWE.

7.1.1 Characteristics of the Process

The development of Web systems is subject to continuous changes in user and technology requirements. Models built so far in any stage of the development process have to be easily adaptable to these changes. To cope efficiently with the required flexibility, UWE advocates a strict separation of concerns in the early phases of the development and implements a model-driven development process, i.e., a process based on the construction of models and model transformations. The ultimate challenge is to support a development process that allows fully automated generation of Web systems.

7.1.1.1 Separation of Concerns

Similarly to other Web Engineering methods, the UWE process is driven by the separate modeling of concerns describing a Web system. Models are built at the different stages of requirements engineering, analysis, design, and implementation of the development process and are used to represent different views of the same Web application corresponding to the different concerns (content, navigation structure, and presentation). The content model is used to specify the concepts that are relevant to the application domain and the relationships between these concepts. The hypertext or navigation structure is modeled separately from the content, although it is derived from the content model. The navigation model represents the navigation paths of the Web system being modeled. The presentation model takes into account representation and user–machine communication tasks.

UWE proposes at least one type of UML diagram for the visualization of each model to represent the structural aspects of the different views. However, in addition, very often UML interaction diagrams or state machines are used to represent behavioral aspects of the Web system. Figure 7.1 shows how the scope of modeling spans these three orthogonal dimensions: development stages, systems' views, and aspects.

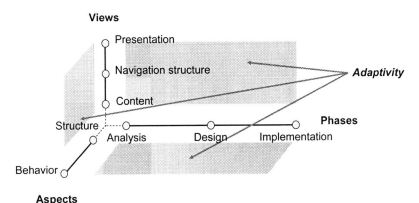

Figure 7.1. Modeling aspects in UWE (from Schwinger and Koch, 2006).

Another concern also handled separately is adaptivity. Personalized and context-dependent Web systems provide the user with more appropriate information, links, or pages by being aware of user or contextual features. We propose to view adaptivity as a cross-cutting concern and thus use aspect-oriented techniques to model adaptive Web systems. It can be seen as a fourth dimension influencing all other Web modeling dimensions: views, aspects, and phases. Requirements models and architecture models focusing on specific Web aspects complete the specification of the Web system. Separation of concerns offers advantages in the maintenance and re-engineering of a Web system as well as for the generation of Web systems for different contexts and platforms.

7.1.1.2 Development Driven by Models

The model-driven development (MDD) approach not only advocates the use of models (as those described above) for the development of software, but also emphasizes the need of transformations in all phases of the development, from requirements specification to designs and from design models to implementations. Transformations between models provide a chain that enables the automated implementation of a system in successive steps from the different models.

The development of Web systems is a field that lends itself to applying MDD due to the Web-specific separation of concerns and continuous changes in technologies in the Web domain.

Meta-model-based methods such as OO-H (Gómez et al., 2001) and UWE constitute a good basis for the implementation of a model-driven process for the development of Web systems. They included semiautomated model-based transformations even before MDD concepts became well-known. For the first guidelines for a systematic and stepwise construction of models for UWE, we refer to Hennicker and Koch (2001) and Koch (2001).

UWE emphasizes the relevance of requirements engineering starting with modeling activities in this early development phase (Escalona and Koch, 2006). Therefore, the UWE meta-model includes a set of modeling primitives that allows for simpler and more specific specification of the requirements of Web systems.

7.1.2 Characteristics of the Notation

As the saying goes, a picture is worth a thousand words. Visual models are naturally used not only for documentation purposes but also as the crucial chain link in the software development process. The trend is the production of domain-specific visual models. Conversely, the importance of the selection of the modeling language is not self-evident.

From our point of view, a modeling language has to

1. provide powerful primitives to construct expressive, yet intuitive models
2. offer wide CASE tool support
3. facilitate extension
4. provide a formal or at least a semiformal semantics
5. be easy to learn

Although UML fulfills only the first three requirements, it seems that UML is currently the best approach. UML and various UML extensions are successfully used in many different application domains. However, there is no formal semantics covering the whole UML, and the fifth requirement can only be satisfied if we restrict ourselves to a subset of the modeling constructs of UML.

7.1.2.1 Modeling with UML

The distinguishing feature of UWE is its UML compliance since the model elements of UWE are defined in terms of a UML profile and as an extension of the UML meta-model (Koch and Kraus, 2002, 2003).

Although the UML is expressive enough to model all requirements that arise in modeling Web systems, it does not offer Web domain-specific elements. To ease the modeling of special aspects of Web applications, we define in UWE special views—using UML's extension mechanisms—graphically represented by UML diagrams, such as the navigation model and the presentation model (Koch, 2001; Koch et al., 2001).

UML modeling techniques comprise the construction of static and dynamic views of software systems by object and class diagrams, component and deployment diagrams, use case diagrams, state and activity diagrams, sequence and communication diagrams. The UML extension mechanisms are used to define stereotypes that we utilize for the representation of Web constructs, such as nodes and links. In addition, tag definitions and constraints written in OCL (Object Constraint Language) can be used. This way we obtain a UML-compliant notation—a so-called UML lightweight extension or better known as a UML profile. UWE notation is defined as such a UML profile.

The advantage of using UML diagrams is the common understanding of these diagrams. Furthermore, the notation and the semantics of the modeling elements of "pure" UML, i.e., those modeling elements that comprise the UML meta-model, are widely described in the OMG documentation (Object Management Group, 2005). For any software designer with a UML background, it is easy to understand a model based on a UML profile, such as the extension that UWE suggests. We observe that UML extensions "inherit" the problems of UML, e.g., the lack of a complete formal semantics covering all modeling elements.

UWE focuses on visual modeling together with systematic design and automatic generation. The aim is to cover the entire development life cycle of Web systems, providing techniques and notations to start with requirements models, moving through design models, as well as including architecture and aspect models. All these models are visualized using UML diagrammatic techniques.

7.1.2.2 Meta-Modeling

Meta-modeling plays a fundamental role in CASE tool construction and is as well the core of the model-driven process. A meta-model is a precise definition of the elements of a modeling language, their relationships, and the well-formedness rules needed for creating syntactically correct models.

Tool-supported design and model-based system generation are becoming essential in the development process of Web systems due to the need for rapid production of new Web presences and Web applications. CASE tools have to be built on a precisely specified meta-model of the modeling constructs used in the design activities, providing more flexibility if modeling requirements change. Meta-models are essential for the definition of model transformations and automatic code generation.

The UWE meta-model is defined as a conservative extension of the UML meta-model (Koch and Kraus, 2003). It is the basis for the UWE notation and UWE tool support. "Conservative" means that the modeling elements of the UML meta-model are not modified, e.g., by adding additional features or associations to the UML modeling element Class. OCL constraints are used to specify additional static semantics (analogous to the well-formedness rules in the UML specification). By staying thereby compatible with the MOF interchange meta-model, we can take advantage of meta-modeling tools based on the corresponding XML interchange format (XMI).

In addition, the UWE meta-model is "profileable" (Baresi et al., 2002), which means that it is possible to map the meta-model to a UML profile. A UML profile consists of a hierarchy of stereotypes and a set of constraints. Stereotypes are used for representing instances of metaclasses and are written in guillemets, like «menu» or «anchor». The definition of a UML profile has the advantage that it is supported by nearly every UML CASE tool either automatically, by a tool plug-in, or passively when the model is saved and then checked by an external tool. The UWE meta-model could also be used as the basis for building a common meta-model (or ontology) of the concepts needed for the design in the Web domain (cf. Koch and Kraus, 2003; Escalona and Koch, 2006). Using for this purpose the standardized OMG meta-modeling architecture would facilitate the construction of meta-CASE tools.

7.1.3 Characteristics of the Tool Environment

The UML compliance of UWE has an important advantage: All CASE tools that support the Unified Modeling Language can be used to build UWE models. For this purpose it is sufficient to name stereotypes after the names of the UWE modeling concepts. Many tools offer additional support with an import functionality of predefined UML profiles. In such a case, the profile model elements can be used in the same way as the built-in UML model elements.

7.1.3.1 CASE Tool Support

A wider developer support is achieved by the open source plug-in ArgoUWE (`www.pst.ifi.lmu.de/projekte/uwe`) for the open source CASE tool ArgoUML (`www.argouml.org`). In addition to providing an editor for the UWE notation, ArgoUWE checks the consistency of models and supports the systematic transformation techniques of the UWE method. Using the UWE profile, models designed with other UML CASE tools can be exchanged with ArgoUWE. The use of tools that support not only the modeling itself but also a model-driven approach shortens development cycles and facilitates re-engineering of Web systems.

7.1.3.2 Model Consistency Check

ArgoUWE also checks the consistency of models according to the OCL constraints specified for the UWE meta-model. Consistency checking is embedded into the cognitive design critiques feature of ArgoUML and runs in a background thread. Thus, model deficiencies and inconsistencies are gathered during the modeling process, but the designer is not interrupted. The designer obtains feedback at any time by taking a look at this continuously updated list of design critiques, which is shown in the to-do pane of the tool.

In the following, we exemplify how UWE's model-driven process, notation, and tool support are used to develop Web applications.

7.2 METHOD BY CASE STUDY

We use a simple online movie database example that allows users to explore information about movies and persons related to the production of the movies. This example is inspired by `www.imdb.org` and named the "Movie UWE Case Study" (MUC). Movies are characterized, among other things, by their genre, the cast, memorable quotes, trailers, and a soundtrack. Persons related to the movie production include the director, producer, composer, and the actors. The user interested in watching a movie can access information on theaters that show the movie. Registered users—identified by an email address and a password—can provide comments, rate comments, vote movies, manage "their movies," and buy tickets in theaters of their preference. The MUC online movie database personalizes the application, giving some recommendations about movies and providing personalized news to the user.

The focus in the following is on the models built for the different views of the analysis and design phases (see Figure 7.1). Model transformations are described as part of the model-driven process in Section 7.4.

7.2.1 Starting with Requirements Specification

The first step toward developing a Web system is the identification of the requirements for such an application that are specified in UWE with a *requirements model*. Requirements can be documented at different levels of detail. UWE proposes two levels of granularity when modeling Web system requirements. First, a rough description of the functionalities is produced, which are modeled with UML use cases. In a second step, a more detailed description of the use cases is developed, e.g., by UML activity diagrams that depict the responsibilities and actions of the stakeholders.

7.2.1.1 Overview of Use Cases

Use case diagrams are built with the UML elements Actor and UseCase. Actors are used to model the users of the Web system. Typical users of Web systems are the anonymous user (called User) in the MUC case study, the registered user (RegisteredUser), and the Web system administrator. Use cases are used to visualize the functionalities that the system will provide. The use case diagram depicts use cases, actors, and associations among them, showing the roles the actors play in the interaction with the system, e.g., triggering some use cases.

In addition to the UML features, UWE distinguishes among three types of use cases: navigation, process, and personalized use cases. Navigation use cases are used to model typical user behavior when interacting with a Web application, such as browsing through the Web application content or searching information by keywords. The use case model of Figure 7.2, for example, includes the «navigation» (□) use cases ViewMovie, Search, and GoToExternalSite. Process use cases are used to describe business tasks that end users will perform with the system; they are modeled in the same way as it is done for traditional software. These business tasks normally imply transactional actions on the underlying database. We use "pure" UML notation for their graphical representation. Typical examples for business use cases are Register, CommentMovie, and BuyTicket. A third group of use cases are those that imply personalization of a Web system, such as ViewRecommendations and ViewLatestNews. They are denoted by a stereotype «personalized» (✩). Personalization is triggered by user behavior.

All UML elements for modeling use case diagrams are available, such as system boundary box, package, generalization relationship, stereotyped dependencies «extend» and «include» among use cases. Figure 7.2 illustrates the use case diagram for the MUC case study restricted to the functional requirements from the User and RegisteredUser viewpoint.

7.2.1.2 Detailed View of Use Cases

The level of detail and formality of requirements specifications depends on project risks and the complexity of the Web application to be built. But very often a specification based only on use cases is not enough (Vilain et al., 2000). Analysts use different kinds of refinement techniques to obtain a more detailed specification of the functional requirements, such as workflows, formatted specifications, or prototypes. These representations usually include actors, pre- and postconditions, a workflow description, exceptions and error situations, information sources, sample results, and references to other documents. In particular, for the development of Web

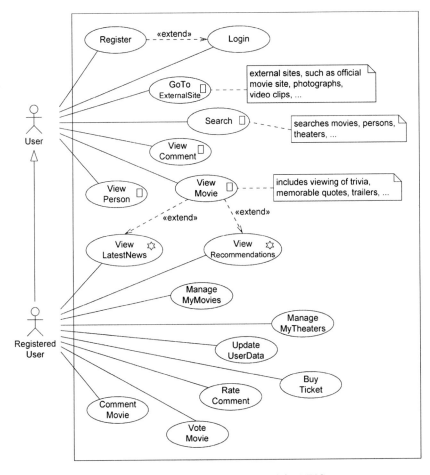

Figure 7.2. UWE use case model for MUC.

systems, the informational, navigational, and process goals have to be gathered and specified. Informational goals indicate content requirements. Navigational goals point toward the kind of access to content, and process goals specify the ability of the user to perform some tasks within the Web system (Pressman, 2005).

Following the principle of using UML whenever possible for the specification, we refine requirements with UML activity diagrams. For each nontrivial business use case, we build at least one activity diagram for the main stream of tasks to be performed in order to provide the functionality indicated by the corresponding use case. Optionally, additional diagrams can be depicted for exceptions and variants. Activity diagrams include activities, shareholders responsible for these activities (optional), and control flow elements. They can be enriched with object flows showing relevant objects for the input or output of those activities.

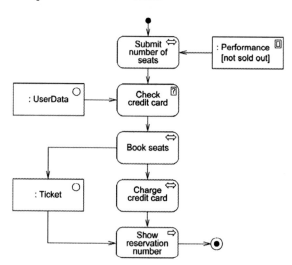

Figure 7.3. MUC case study: UWE activity diagram detailing the buy-ticket use case.

Figure 7.3 illustrates the activity diagram for the use case BuyTicket of our MUC case study. The UWE profile includes a set of stereotypes adding Web-specific semantics to UML activity and object nodes. For example, a distinction is made between the objects that define content, nodes of the application, and presentation elements. Visualization is improved by the use of the corresponding icons: O for «content», □ for «node», and ▣ for Web user interface («WebUI»). Stereotypes of activities are used to distinguish possible actions of the user in the Web environment: browse, search, and transactional activities that comprise changes in at least one database. To this category of stereotypes belong ⇨ for «browse», ▤ for «query», and ⇔ for transactional actions.

7.2.2 Defining the Content

Analysis models provide the basis for the design models, in particular the *content model* of a Web system. The aim of the content model is to provide a visual specification of the domain-relevant information for the Web system that mainly comprises the content of the Web application. However, very often it also includes entities of the domain required for customized Web applications. These entities constitute the so-called user profile or user model.

Customization deals not only with adaptation to the properties of users or user groups, but also with adaptation to features of the environment. A so-called context profile or context model is built in such a case. The objects occurring in the detailed view of the use cases provide natural candidates of domain entities for the content and user model.

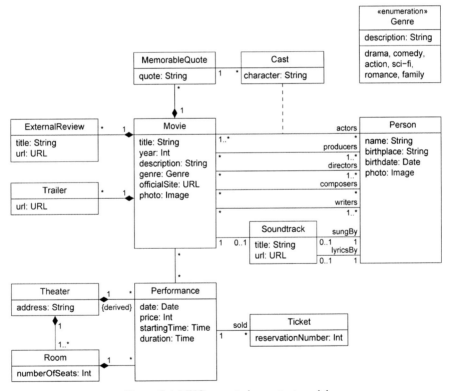

Figure 7.4. MUC case study: content model.

The separation of content and user model (or context model) has proven its value in practice. Both are graphically represented as UML class diagrams. The content model of MUC is depicted in Figure 7.4; the user model is shown in Figure 7.5. The entities representing content and user or context properties respectively, are modeled by classes, i.e., instances of the UML metaclass Class. Relationships between content and user properties are modeled by UML associations. In particular, movies are modeled by a class Movie with a set of properties, such as title and genre forming the attributes of the class Movie, or as classes associated to Movie

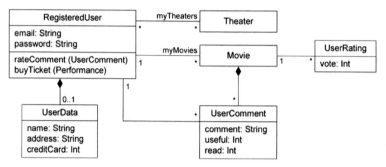

Figure 7.5. MUC case study: user model.

like Trailer and ExternalReview. Stakeholders of the film production, e.g., a movie's producer, composer, and cast, are modeled as roles of associations to the class Person. Note that Performance and Ticket were inferred from the activity diagram in Figure 7.3.

The user model contains the user data (again see Figure 7.3) needed for the login of the user and the comments and rating of the movies. All these data are provided by the users themselves during registration or use of the Web application. In addition, the system collects information on users by observing their behavior. The collected data are used for adaptation and are modeled as a cross-cutting aspect and woven into the user model and other parts of the system (see Section 7.2.6 on aspect-oriented modeling of adaptivity).

There is no need for the definition of additional elements as there is no distinction to modeling of non-Web applications. We use "pure" UML notation and semantics. All the features provided by the UML specification for constructing class diagrams can be used, in particular, packages, enumerations (e.g., Genre in Figure 7.4), generalizations, compositions, and association classes (e.g., Cast in Figure 7.4).

7.2.3 Laying Down the Navigation Structure

Based on the requirements analysis and the content modeling, the *navigation structure* of a Web application is modeled. Navigation classes (visualized as ☐) represent navigable nodes of the hypertext structure; navigation links show direct links between navigation classes. Alternative navigation paths are handled by «menu» (▤). Access primitives are used to reach multiple instances of a navigation class («index» ☰, or «guided tour» ⇻) or to select items («query» ▣). In Web applications that contain business logic, the business processes must be integrated into the navigation structure. The entry and exit points of the business processes are modeled by process classes (⊵) in the navigation model, the linkage between each other and to the navigation classes is modeled by process links. Each process class is associated with a use case that models a business process. Navigation

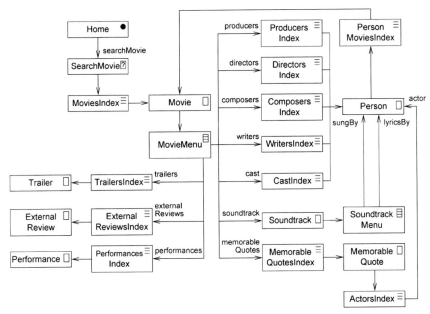

Figure 7.6. MUC case study: navigation from Movie (fragment).

structures are laid down in stereotyped UML class diagrams with navigation and process classes, menus, and access primitives extending the UML metaclass Class, and navigation and process links extending the UML metaclass Association.

7.2.3.1 Initial Navigation Structure

UWE provides methodological guidelines for developing an initial sketch of the navigation structure from the content model of a Web application (see also Koch and Kraus, 2002; Knapp et al., 2003): Content classes deemed to be relevant for navigation are selected from the content model, and these classes as well as their associations are put into a navigation model as navigation classes and navigation links, respectively. Navigation links represent possible steps to be followed by the user, and thus these links have to be directed; if navigation back and forth between two navigation classes is desired, an association is split into two. Menus are added to every navigation class that has more than one outgoing association. Finally, access primitives (index, guided tours, and queries) allow for selecting a single information entity, as represented by a navigation class. An index, a guided tour, or a query should be added between two navigation classes whenever the multiplicity of the end target of their linking association is greater than 1. The properties of the content class corresponding to the navigation class over which the index or the query runs are added as navigation attributes to the navigation class.

The result of applying these steps of the UWE method to the content model of the MUC case study in Figure 7.4 is shown in Figure 7.6.

From the home page Home the user can, by means of a query SearchMovie, search for movies of his interest by criteria like movie name, actors, or directors, etc. Soundtrack is directly reachable through MovieMenu as there may be at most one soundtrack for each movie whereas there may be several directors among which to select from DirectorsIndex. As an example for a bidirectional linkage between navigation classes, the actors of a movie can be selected from CastIndex reaching a Person, where, conversely, one can choose from all movies this person has contributed to. The navigation structure has been refined by adding a home node (●) as the initial node of the MUC Web application, as well as a main menu.

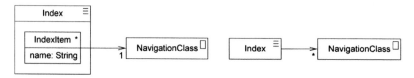

Figure 7.7. "Pure" UML (left) and shorthand notation (right) for index.

The UWE profile notation for menus and access primitives provides a compact representation of patterns frequently used in the Web domain. Figure 7.7 (right) shows the shorthand notation for indexes. Using "pure" UML for modeling an index would instead require an additional model element: an index item as depicted in Figure 7.7 (left). The result would be an overloaded model if it contains many such indexes.

7.2.3.2 Adding Business Processes

In a next step, the navigation structure can now be extended by process classes that represent the entry and exit points to business processes. These process classes are derived from the nonnavigational use cases. In Figure 7.8 the business processes Register (linked to the use case Register) and Login (linked to the use case Login) have been added. The integration of these classes in the navigation model requires an additional menu (MainMenu), which provides links to Register, Login, and SearchMovies. A user may only manage her movies if she has logged in previously. Finally, a user can buy tickets for a selected movie and a selected performance by navigating to BuyTicket.

A single navigation structure diagram for a whole Web application would inevitably lead to cognitive overload. Different views to the navigation structure should be produced from the content model focusing on different aspects of the application, like navigation to particular content or integration of related business processes.

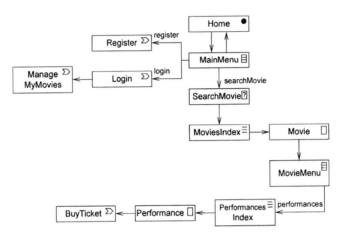

Figure 7.8. MUC case study: integration of business processes into navigation (fragment).

7.2.4 Refining the Processes

Each process class included in the navigation model is refined into a process model consisting of a process flow model and optionally of a process structure model. The control and data flow is modeled in the process flow model in the form of a UML activity diagram. It is the result of a refinement process that starts from the workflow in the requirements model.

Figure 7.9 illustrates the result of the refinement process applied to Figure 7.3. This process mainly consists of the integration of the main stream of the actions with alternatives, such as Enter new credit card info in case of invalid card numbers or exception handling (not included in this example). Control elements are added with the purpose of providing the business logic. Activities and objects can be added to the activity diagram. A process structure model has the form of a class diagram and describes the relationship between a process class and other classes whose instances are used to support the business process.

7.2.5 Sketching the Presentation

The presentation model provides an abstract view of the user interface (UI) of a Web application. It is based on the navigation model and abstracts from concrete aspects of the UI, like the use of colors, fonts, and the location of UI elements on the Web page; instead, the presentation model describes the basic structure of the user interface, i.e., which UI elements (e.g., text, images, anchors, forms) are used to present the navigation nodes. The advantage of the presentation model is that it is independent of the actual techniques used to implement the Web site, thus allowing the stakeholders to discuss the appropriateness of the presentation before actually implementing it.

The basic elements of a presentation model are the presentation classes, which are directly based on nodes from the navigation model, i.e., navigation classes, menus, access primitives, and process classes. A presentation class (⊡) is composed of UI elements, like text («text» ≈), anchor («anchor» ─), button («button» ●), image («image» ▣), form («form» 吕), and anchored collection («anchored collection» ≔).

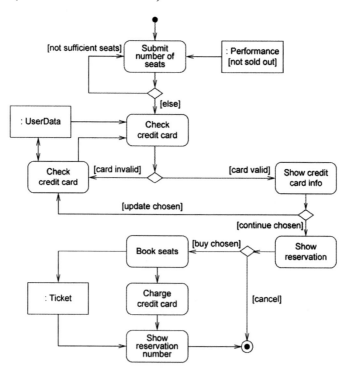

Figure 7.9. MUC case study: UWE process flow model for the buy-ticket process.

Figure 7.10 shows an example of a presentation class for the navigation class Movie. Note that to ease the identification of which navigation node is presented by a presentation class, the presentation class uses by default the same name as the corresponding navigation node. Each attribute of a navigation class is presented with an appropriate UI element. For example, a text element is used for the title attribute, and an image element is used for the photo attribute. The relationship between presentation classes and UI elements is that of composition. For presentation models, composition is pictured by drawing the component, i.e., the UI element, inside the composite, i.e., the presentation class; note, however, that this notation is not supported by all CASE tools.

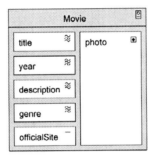

Figure 7.10. MUC case study: presentation class Movie.

Usually, the information from several navigation nodes is presented on one Web page, which is modeled by pages («page») in UWE. Pages can contain, among other things, presentation classes and presentation groups («presentation group»). A presentation group can itself contain presentation groups and presentation classes. An excerpt of the presentation model of the movie page is shown in Figure 7.11. It contains a presentation class for the main menu, which in turn contains a link (represented by the anchor UI element) to home, a presentation class for the SearchMovie query, and button UI elements to start the login and registration processes. The SearchMovie query also provides an example of the form UI element to enter the movie name to search for. The presentation class for MovieMenu contains links to the presentation classes of the corresponding indexes— based on the navigation model in Figure 7.6—providing additional information on the movie.

The presentation classes of these indexes plus the presentation classes for movie are assembled in a presentation group. The use of the stereotypes «default» and «alternative» for the associations from Movie, ProducersIndex, etc. to MovieMenu indicates that the elements of the presentation groups are alternatives, i.e., only one of them is shown depending on which link was followed from the movie menu, with the presentation class Movie being shown by default. For example, when the user follows the producers link in the MovieMenu, the ProducersIndex is shown, containing the list of the producers of that film.

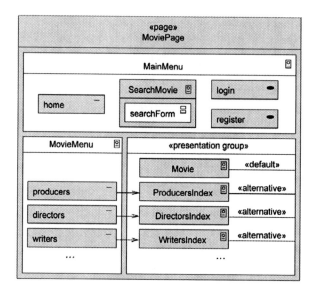

Figure 7.11. MUC case study: the presentation model of the movie page.

7.2.6 Aspect-Oriented Modeling of Adaptivity

Adaptivity is an increasingly important feature of Web applications. Adaptive Web applications provide more appropriate pages to the user by being aware of user or context properties. An example of adaptivity is recommendations based on user behavior, like movie of favorite actors in our MUC case study. In general, adaptivity is orthogonal to three views: content, navigation structure, and presentation (see Figure 7.1). In order to model adaptive features of Web applications non-invasively, we use techniques of aspect-oriented modeling (AOM; cf. Filman et al., 2004) in UWE.

We introduce a new model element named *aspect*. An aspect is composed of a *pointcut* part and an *advice* part. It is a (graphical) statement expressing that, in addition to the features specified in the principal model, each model element selected by the pointcut also has features specified by the advice. In other words, a complete description, including both general system functionality and additional, cross-cutting features of the quantified model elements, is given by the composition of the principal model and the aspect. The process of composition is called *weaving*.

UWE defines several kinds of aspects for modeling different static and run-time adaptivity (Baumeister et al., 2005). In order to model the recommendation feature modularly, we use on the one hand a model aspect and a run-time aspect for keeping track of the number of visits to movie pages. On the other hand, another run-time aspect integrates the recommendation feature into the login process: A list of movies is presented ranked according to the appearing actors, who in turn are ranked according to their relevance in the visited movies.

The static model aspect for extending the user model (see Figure 7.5) by an operation that returns the number of visits of a registered user to a movie page is shown in Figure 7.12 (left). The pointcut is a pattern containing a special element, the *formal parameter*, which is annotated by a question mark. The pointcut selects all model elements in the base model that match the pattern, thereby instantiating the formal parameter. In our case the formal parameter is a class in which only the name RegisteredUser is specified. The pointcut therefore selects all classes (actually, there is exactly one such class) in the navigation model with the name RegisteredUser. The advice defines the change to the selected model elements. After weaving, our RegisteredUser class is thus extended by the operation visited (see Figure 7.12, right); no other elements are affected by this aspect.

Model aspects are a special case of aspect-oriented class diagrams (AOCDs), which are also defined in a lightweight UML extension and are therefore UML-compatible; see Zhang (2005). Since a model aspect specifies a static modification of the base model, other, standardized model transformation languages such as the Atlas Transformation Language (ATL; Jouault and Kurtev, 2005), QVT-P (QVT-Partners, 2003), or QVT (QVT-Merge Group, 2004) may also be used. The advantage of AOCD compared with these languages is, however, that it does not require the modeler to have expert knowledge of the UML meta-model, which may make AOCD easier to use (cf. Section 7.4).

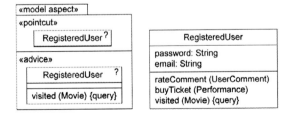

Figure 7.12. MUC case study: model aspect (left) and the weaving result (right).

The dynamic behavior of our MUC system is extended by two run-time aspects. Figure 7.13 shows a link traversal aspect, used to ensure that visited returns the correct result: The pointcut selects all links from any object—note that neither the name nor the type of the object to the left is specified and thus it matches any object—to some Movie object. The advice defines with an OCL constraint the result of the action fired when such a link is visited: If the current user is logged in, the system increases his respective record by 1. After weaving, the system's behavior is thus enriched by counting user visits to the movie pages.

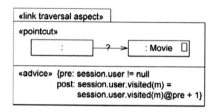

Figure 7.13. MUC case study: link traversal aspect for counting movie visits.

Figure 7.14 shows how the business process Login is extended by a flow aspect. The base model depicted in Figure 7.14 (top) defines the normal workflow without considering adaptivity: The user is asked to input her email address and password, and then the system verifies the input and responds accordingly.

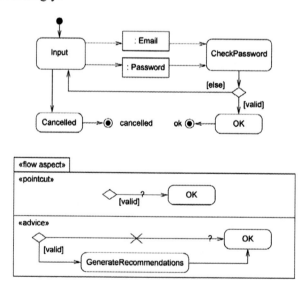

Figure 7.14. MUC case study: flow aspect (bottom) extending business process Login (top).

The adaptive feature of generating recommendations for the user is added by the aspect shown in Figure 7.14 (bottom). The pointcut selects every (in this concrete example, exactly one) control flow edge from a decision point to the OK action, which is guarded by the condition valid. The advice deletes this edge by crossing it out and adds an action for recommendation generation and two new control flow edges to bind it into the process.

7.3 UWE META-MODEL

The UWE meta-model is defined as a conservative extension of the UML 2.0 meta-model. "Conservative" means that the model elements of the UML meta-model are not modified. Instead, all new model elements of the UWE meta-model are related by inheritance to at least one model element of the UML meta-model. We define additional features and relationships for the new elements. Analogous to the well-formedness rules in the UML specification, we use OCL constraints to specify the additional static semantics of these new elements. The resulting UWE meta-model is profileable, which means that it is possible to map the meta-model to a UML profile (Koch and Kraus, 2003). In particular, UWE stays compatible with the MOF interchange meta-model and therefore with tools that are based on the corresponding XML interchange format XMI. The advantage is that all standard UML CASE tools that support UML profiles or UML extension mechanisms can be used to create UWE models of Web applications. If technically possible, these CASE tools can further be extended to support the UWE method. ArgoUWE (see Section 7.5) presents an instance of such CASE tool support for UWE based on the UWE meta-model.

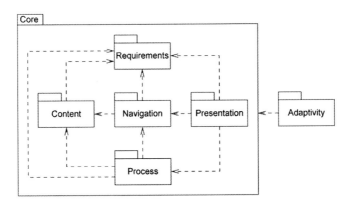

Figure 7.15. Overview of the UWE meta-model.

The UWE extension of the UML meta-model consists of adding two top-level packages, Core and Adaptivity, to the UML (cf. Figure 7.15). The separation of concerns of Web applications is reflected by the package structure of Core and the cross-cutting of adaptation by the dependency of Adaptivity on Core (see Figure 7.1). The package Requirements comprises the UWE extensions on UseCase for discerning navigational from business process and personalized use cases and the different markings for ActivityNode («browse», «query», and «transaction») and ObjectNode («content», «node», and «WebUI») (see Escalona and Koch, 2006).

The navigation and presentation packages bundle UWE's extensions for the corresponding models. Figure 7.16 details a part of the meta-model for Navigation with the connection between Node and Link and their various subclasses. NavigationClass and ProcessClass with the related NavigationLink and ProcessLink as well as Menu and the access primitives Index, GuidedTour, and Query provide the Web domain-specific metaclasses for building the navigation model. The packages Contents and Process are currently only used as a stub, reflecting the fact that UWE allows the designer to develop content and process models using all UML features. Finally, Adaptation contains UWE's aspect facilities by representing Aspect as a UML Package with two subpackages, Pointcut and Advice.

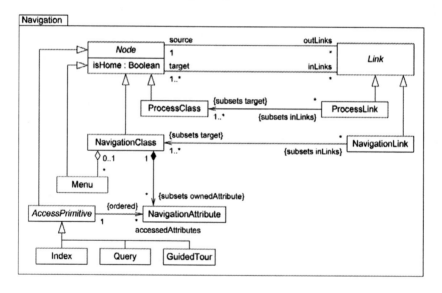

Figure 7.16. UWE navigation meta-model.

In order to transfer the UWE meta-model into a UML profile, we use UML's extension mechanisms (see Section 7.1). Figure 7.17 shows how the metaclasses of the UWE navigation meta-model are rendered as a stereotype hierarchy, forming the UWE navigation profile: Node becomes a stereotype of Class, NavigationAttribute a stereotype of Property, and Link a stereotype of Association.

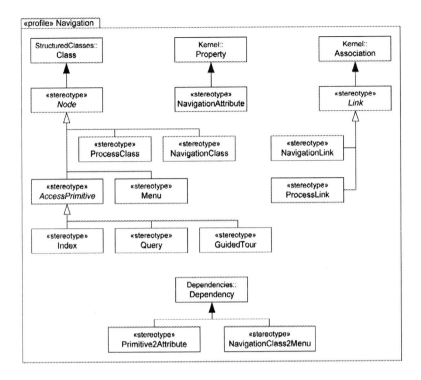

Figure 7.17. UWE navigation profile.

The associations of the UWE navigation meta-model, e.g., connecting Link to Node, cannot be represented by meta-associations (see Object Management Group, 2005) and have to be added either by stereotyping the UML metaclass Dependency or by using the association from the UML meta-model from which the association is derived. The latter approach is used for representing the composition between NavigationClass and NavigationAttribute using the association ownedAttributes; for the association between AccessPrimitive and NavigationAttribute and the association between NavigationClass and Menu, we stereotype Dependency, leading, e.g., to the following constraint:

```
context Dependency
inv: self.stereotypes->
            includes("Primitive2Attribute") implies
        (self.client.stereotypes->
              includes("AccessPrimitive") and
      self.supplier.stereotypes->
            includes("NavigationAttribute"))
```

where client and supplier denote the ends of the Dependency relationship.

7.3.1 Consistency Rules

Following the UML, we use OCL to state more precisely the static semantics of UWE's new meta-model elements as well as the dependencies of meta-model elements both inside a single meta-model package and between packages. As an example, the following constraint states that every use case that is neither a navigation nor a personalized use case needs a process class and that the converse direction holds as well (cf. Figure 7.18):

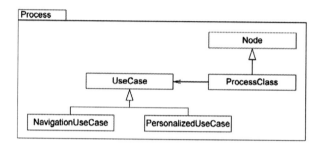

Figure 7.18. UWE process meta-model.

```
context ProcessClass
inv: not self.useCase.oclIsKindOf(NavigationUseCase) and
        not self.useCase.oclIsKindOf(PersonalizedUseCase)


context UseCase
inv: (not self.oclIsKindOf(NavigationUseCase) and
        not self.oclIsKindOf(PersonalizedUseCase)) implies
      ProcessClass.allInstances()->
        exists(pn | pn.useCase = self)
```

7.4 MODEL-DRIVEN DEVELOPMENT IN UWE

The UWE approach includes the specification of a process for the development of Web systems in addition to the UML profile and the UWE meta-model. The UWE process is model-driven following the MDA principles and using several other OMG standards, like MOF, UML, OCL, and XMI, and forthcoming standards, like QVT (QVT-Merge Group, 2004). The process relies on modeling and model transformations, and its main characteristic is the systematic and semiautomatic development of Web systems, as detailed in Chapter 12 by Moreno et al. on model-driven Web Engineering. The aim of such an MDD process is automatic model transformation, which, in each step, is based on transformation rules.

Focusing on model transformations, the UWE process is depicted in Figure 7.19 as a stereotyped UML activity diagram (Meliá et al., 2005). Models are shown as objects, and transformations are represented with stereotyped activities (special circular icon).

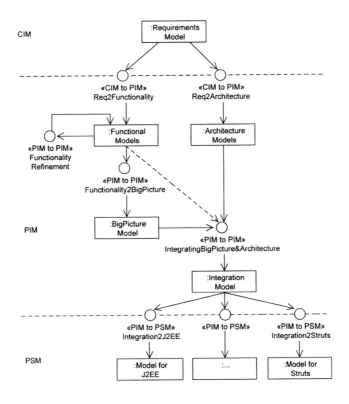

Figure 7.19. Overview of model transformations in the UWE process.

The process starts with the business model, which MDA calls the computational independent model (CIM), used to specify the requirements. Platform-independent models (PIMs) are derived from these requirement models. The set of design models represents the different concerns of the Web applications, comprising the content, the navigation, the business processes, the presentation, and the adaptation of the Web system (summarized as FunctionalModels in Figure 7.19). In a next step, the different views are integrated into a "big picture" model of the Web systems, which can be used for validation (Knapp and Zhang, 2006) and also for generation of platform-dependent models (see below). A merge with architectural modeling features, either of the "big picture model" or of the design models directly, results in an integrated PIM covering functional and architectural aspects. Finally, the platform-specific models (PSMs) derived from the integration model are the starting point for code generation.

7.4.1 Transformations from Requirements to Functional Models

The overall objective of modeling the requirements is the specification of the system as a CIM and providing input for the construction of models in the other development phases (see Figure 7.1, Schwinger and Koch, 2006, and Section 7.2). In particular, specific objectives for Web systems are the specification of content requirements, the specification of the functional requirements in terms of navigation needs and business processes, the definition of interaction scenarios for different groups of Web users, and, if required, the specification of personalization and context adaptation. The first model transformation step of the UWE process consists of mapping these Web system requirements models to the UWE functional models. Transformation rules are defined therefore as mappings from the requirements meta-model package to the content, navigation, presentation, process, and adaptivity packages of the meta-model. How these packages depend on each other is shown in Figure 7.15.

For example, UWE distinguishes in the requirements model between different types of navigation functionality: browsing, searching, and transactional activities. Browse actions can be used to enforce the existence of a navigation path between a source node and a target node. An action of type search indicates the need for a query in the navigation model in order to allow for user input of a term, and the system responds with a resulting set matching this term (see Section 7.2.1).

Figure 7.20 shows the Search2Query transformation rule specified in QVT's graphical notation (QVT-Merge Group, 2004). The source and target of the transformation are the UWE meta-model defined as *checkonly* and *enforce*, respectively (identified with a "c" and "e" in Figure 7.20). For each search with content p2 in the requirements model, a query in the navigation model is generated with an associated navigation attribute p2. For the associated node object in the requirements model, an index and objects of a navigation class, as well as corresponding links, will be generated.

For more details about the UWE meta-model for Web requirements, we refer the reader to Escalona and Koch (2006). A detailed description of the transformation rules between CIMs and PIMs for the functional aspects of Web applications has been presented in Koch et al. (2006). A meta-model of the nonfunctional requirements for Web applications and mappings of nonfunctional requirements to architectural model elements are subject to future work.

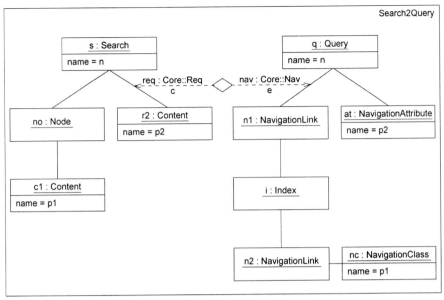

Figure 7.20. Transformation rule Search2Query.

7.4.2 Refinement of Functional Models

The transformations for refining the functional models comprise mappings from content to navigation model, refinements of the navigation model, and from the navigation into the presentation model. In UWE, an initial navigation model is generated based on classes of the content model marked as navigation-relevant (see Section 7.2.3). This generation step can be rendered as a transformation Content2Navigation. From a single content model, different navigation views can be obtained, e.g., for different stakeholders of the Web system like anonymous user, registered user, and administrator. The generation of each navigation view requires a set of marks on elements of the content model that form a so-called marking model kept separately from the content model. The development process cannot be completed in an entirely automatic way, as the designer has to make the decision about the "navigation relevance" marks; the Content2Navigation transformation is applied once the marks have been set.

Conversely, the remaining transformation steps for navigation models mentioned in Section 7.2.3 are turned into transformation rules that can be applied fully automatically. These rules include, for example, the insertion of indexes and menus. Presentation elements are generated from navigation elements. For example, for each link in the navigation model, an appropriate anchor is required in the presentation model. The main difficulty is the introduction of the "look and feel" aspects.

All these transformations are defined as OCL constraints (by preconditions and postconditions) in UWE and are implemented in Java in the CASE tool ArgoUWE.

7.4.3 Creation of Validation and Integration Models

The UWE MDD process comprises two main integration steps: the integration of all functional models and the integration of functional and nonfunctional aspects; the latter integration step is related to architectural design decisions.

The aim of the first step is the creation of a single model for validating the correctness of the different functional models and that allows seamless creation of PSMs. This "big picture" model is a UML state machine, representing the content, navigation structure, and business processes of the Web application as a whole (presentation aspects will be added in the future). The state machine can be checked by the tool Hugo/RT (Knapp et al., 2002)—a UML model translator for model checking, theorem proving, and code generation.

The transformation rules Functional2BigPicture are defined based on a meta-model graph transformation system. For the implementation of the graph transformation rules, any (non-Web-specific) tool for graph transformations can be used. An example of the graph transformation of a navigation node to a state of the validation model is sketched in Figure 7.21. The aim of the second step is the merge of the validation model elements with information on architectural styles. Following the WebSA approach (Meliá et al., 2005), we propose merging functional design models and architecture models at the PIM level. For example, the elements of the WebSA models provide a layer view and a component view of the architecture, which are also specified as PIMs. Transformation rules are defined based on the UWE and WebSA meta-models.

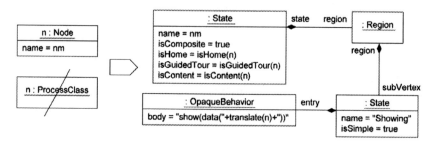

Figure 7.21. Transformation rule Node2State.

7.4.4 Generation of Models and Code for Specific Platforms

In order to transform PIMs into PSMs, additional information about the platform is required. It can be provided as an additional model or it can be implicitly contained in the transformations. For mappings from UWE design models (PIMs) to PSMs for Web applications, we tested different model transformation languages. The query-view-transformation languages we use are ATL (Jouault and Kurtev, 2005), QVT-P (QVT-Partners, 2003), and QVT (QVT-Merge Group, 2004). For example, the following QVT-P transformation tackles the generation of J2EE elements from Java server pages of the integration model:

```
relation ServerPage2J2EE {
  domain { (IM.IntegrationModel)
            [(ServerPage)
              [name = nc,
                services = { (WebService) [name = on,
                                            type = ot] },
                views = { (View) [name = vn] }]] }
  domain { (JM.J2EEModel)
            [(JavaServerPage)
              [name = nc,
                forms = { (Form) [name = on,
                                   type = ot] },
                beans = { (JavaClass) [name = vn] }]] }
  when { services->forAll(s |
              WebService2Form(s, F1set.toChoice()))
           views->forAll(v |
            View2Bean(v, J1set.toChoice())) }
}
```

The ATL code below exemplifies a transformation rule that maps the element Anchor of the UWE presentation model to a JSP element. Note that the transformation rule also involves elements of the navigation model (NavigationLink).

```
rule Anchor2JSP {
  from
    uie : UWE!Anchor
          (not uie.presentationClass.oclIsUndefined() and
           not uie.navigationLink.oclIsUndefined())
  to
    jsp : JSP!Element
          (name <- 'a',
           children <- Sequence { hrefAttribute,
                                  contentNode }),
    hrefAttribute : JSP!Attribute
      (name <- 'href',
      value <- thisModule.createJSTLURLExpr
        (uie.navigationLink.target.name,'objID')),
    contentNode : JSP!TextNode
                (value <- uie.name)
}
```

7.5 CASE TOOL ARGOUWE

We have extended the CASE tool ArgoUML into a tool for UWE-based Web application development, called ArgoUWE (Knapp et al., 2003; www.pst.ifi.lmu.de/projekte/argouwe). We decided to extend ArgoUML as it is a feature-rich, open source tool and offers a plug-in architecture. The drawback of this decision is that the UWE meta-model cannot be used directly since ArgoUML is based on UML 1.3/4. However, a UML 1.x-compatible profile can easily be derived from the UWE meta-model along the same lines as sketched in Section 7.3.

ArgoUML provides support for designing Web applications in the phases of requirements elicitation and content, navigation, business process, as well as presentation modeling. It provides not only tailored editors for UWE diagrams, but also semiautomatic model transformations defined in the UWE development process. As these model transformations are based on the UWE meta-model, the tool ensures both consistency between the different models and integrity of the overall Web application model with respect to UWE's OCL constraints. ArgoUWE fully integrates the UWE meta-model (Koch and Kraus, 2003), provides XMI export, and thus facilitates data transfer with other UML-compliant tools. Design deficiencies, such as violations of the OCL constraints, are reported by an extension of the cognitive design critiques of ArgoUML and can also be checked upon request (see Section 7.5.2).

Working with ArgoUWE is intuitive for ArgoUML users, as ArgoUWE makes use of ArgoUML's graphical interface. In particular, the UML model

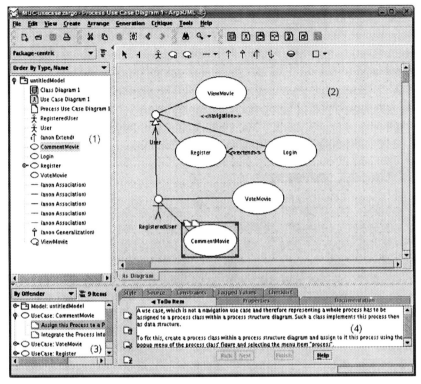

Figure 7.22. MUC case study: ArgoUWE screenshot of a fragment of the use case model.

elements and diagrams are structured in a tree view in the *explorer* [(1) in Figure 7.22]; the diagrams are edited in the *editor pane* (2); to-do items of the designer are listed in the *to-do pane* (3); tagged values, constraints, and documentation of the currently selected model as well as automatically generated code skeletons are shown in the *details pane* (4).

7.5.1 Model Transformations

ArgoUWE implements some of the aforementioned model transformations as semiautomatic procedures.

- In the content model, the designer may mark classes as navigation-relevant. ArgoUWE can then generate an initial navigation model by creating for each navigation-relevant class a navigation class and for each association between navigation-relevant classes a link between the corresponding navigation classes.

- In the navigation model, ArgoUWE can add indexes and menus automatically. The designer may add queries and guided tours between navigation nodes manually or, alternatively, by selecting a generated index and changing it into a query or a guided tour.
- From the navigation model, ArgoUWE can generate a first draft of a presentation model. For each navigation class and each of its attributes, a presentation class is created. The presentation classes of attributes are associated to those of the navigation classes by composition.

The generation of Web applications from the presentation model is out of scope for ArgoUWE. This is done either by hand by the Web designer or semiautomatically by using frameworks for the implementation of Web applications, such as Struts (`struts.apache.org`).

7.5.2 Model Consistency

An important requirement of any CASE tool is to support the modeler to keep his models consistent. Upon model inconsistency, the tool may either interrupt the modeler and force him first to correct it before continuing modeling or simply give a warning. We implemented ArgoUWE to do the latter since we believe that the usability of the modeler being warned yet not interrupted outweighs the drawback of the model being inconsistent for a short time. Moreover, the ArgoUML feature of design critiques provides an excellent starting point for the implementation of the non-interruptive warnings for UWE models.

The "cognitive design critiques" of ArgoUML is one of its distinguishing features compared to other modeling tools (cf. Robbins, 1999). During run time, a thread running in the background keeps checking if the current model shows deficiencies. For each deficiency found, a design critique item is created and added to the to-do pane. Design critiques not only warn the user that her design may be improved but can also, by means of a wizard, lead to a better design. The design critique items range from incompleteness, such as unnamed model elements, to inconsistency, such as name collisions of different attributes or operations in a class. Furthermore, design critiques also suggest the use of certain design patterns (Gamma et al., 1995). The issues of design critiques can be sorted by several criteria like priority or the model element causing the design critique. Design critiques are only warnings and do not interrupt the designer.

ArgoUWE inherits the feature of design critiques from ArgoUML. In fact, all well-formedness constraints of UWE have been fully integrated and are continuously checked by ArgoUWE in the background at run time. In Figure 7.22 the highlighted design critique indicates that the use case CommentMovie does not show a corresponding process class yet; this critique corresponds to the meta-model constraints shown in Section 7.3.

7.6 OUTLOOK

The UML-based Web Engineering (UWE) approach is continuously evolving. Evolution is due to improvement of existing features, such as personalization of Web systems; adaptation to new technologies, e.g. asynchronous client-server communication; and introduction of new software engineering techniques, like aspect orientation and model-driven principles. The challenge in all these cases is to provide a more intuitive and useful tool for the methodological development of Web systems, to increase Web systems quality, and to reduce development time.

The evolution we can currently observe is driven by a set of improvements that are being addressed and a set of extensions we are planning for UWE. The most important are

- specification of the transformations (at the meta-model level) of (nonfunctional) requirements to architecture models
- implementation of the "weaving" process for the integration of the aspect-oriented features in UWE models
- engineering of Rich Internet Applications (RIAs), e.g., Web applications based on asynchronous communication such as using AJAX (Garrett, 2005)
- tool support for transformations from CIM models to PIM models and for the UML 2.0 features in UWE
- integration of a QVT engine (when available) in the tool environment
- extension of UWE with test models

Our higher-level goal is the convergence of Web design/development methods. It is the only way to obtain a powerful domain-specific modeling and a development language that benefits from the advantages of the different methods. Obviously, there is a trend toward using UML as the common notation language. Some methods are moving from their proprietary notation to a UML-compliant one and introduce a UML profile; others define an MOF-based meta-model. It is currently hard to predict how far this converging trend will go and whether it will eventually lead to a "Unified Web Modeling Language."

ACKNOWLEDGEMENTS

Thanks go to Andreas Kraus for providing the ATL transformation rule and fruitful discussions. This work has been partially supported by the MAEWA project, "Model Driven Development of Web Applications" (WI841/7-1) of the Deutsche Forschungsgemeinschaft (DFG), Germany, and the EC 6th Framework SENSORIA project, "Software Engineering for Service-Oriented Overlay Computers" (FET-IST 016004).

REFERENCES

Baresi, L., Garzotto, F., Mainetti, L., and Paolini, P., 2002, Meta-modeling techniques meet Web application design tools. In R.-D. Kutsche and H. Weber, eds., *Proceedings Fifth International Conference on Fundamental Approaches to Software Engineering* (FASE'02), pp. 294–307.

Baumeister, H., Knapp, A., Koch, N., and Zhang, G., 2005, Modelling adaptivity with aspects. In D. Lowe and M Gaedke, eds., *Proceedings Fifth International Conference on Web Engineering* (ICWE'05), pp. 406–416.

Baumeister, H., Koch, N., and Mandel, L., 1999, Towards a UML extension for hypermedia design. In R. France and B. Rumpe, eds., *Proceedings Second International Conference on Unified Modeling Language* (UML'99), pp. 614–629. .

de Troyer, O., and Leune, C.J., 1998, WSDM: A user centered design method for Web sites. *Computer Networks*, **30**(1–7): 85–94.

Escalona, M.J., and Koch, N., 2006, Metamodeling the requirements of Web systems. *Proceedings Second International Conference on Web Information Systems and Technologies* (WebIST'06), Setubal, Portugal.

Filman, R.E., Elrad, T., Clarke, S., and Aksit, M., eds., 2004, *Aspect-Oriented Software Development*, Addison-Wesley, Reading, MA.

Gamma, E., Helm, R., Johnson, R., and Vlissides, J., 1995, *Design Patterns*, Addison-Wesley, Reading, MA.

Garrett, J.J., 2005, Ajax: A New Approach to Web Applications. http://www. adaptivepath.com/publications/essays/archives/000385.php.

Gómez, J., Cachero, C., and Pastor, O., 2001, Conceptual modeling of device-independent Web applications. *IEEE Multimedia*, **8**(2): 26–39.

Hennicker, R., and Koch, N., 2001, Systematic design of Web applications with UML. In K. Siau and T.A. Halpin, eds., *Unified Modeling Language: Systems Analysis, Design and Development Issues*, Idea Group, Hershey, PA, pp. 1–20.

Isakowitz, T., Stohr, E.A., and Balasubramanian, P., 1995, MM: A methodology for structuring hypermedia design. *Communications of the ACM*, **38**(8): 34–44.

Jouault, F., and Kurtev, I., 2005, Transforming models with ATL. In J.-M. Bruel, ed., *Revised Selection of Papers on Satellite Events at the MoDELS 2005 Conference*, pp. 128–138.

Knapp, A., Koch, N., Moser, F., and Zhang, G., 2003, ArgoUWE: A CASE tool for Web applications. *Proceedings First International Workshop on Engineering Methods to Support Information Systems Evolution* (EMSISE'03), Geneva.

Knapp, A., Merz, S., and Rauh, C., 2002, Model checking timed UML state machines and collaborations. In W. Damm Werner and E.R. Olderog, eds., *Proceedings Seventh International Symposium on Formal Techniques in Real-Time and Fault Tolerant Systems*, pp. 395–416.

Knapp, A., and Zhang, G., 2006, Model transformations for integrating and validating Web application models. In H.C. Mayr and R. Breu, eds., *Proceedings Modellierung 2006* (MOD'06), pp. 115–128.

Koch, N., 2001, Software engineering for adaptive hypermedia systems: Reference model, modeling techniques and development process. PhD thesis, Ludwig-Maximilians-Universität, München.

Koch, N., and Kraus, A., 2002, The expressive power of UML-based Web engineering. In D. Schwabe, O. Pastor, G. Rossi, and L. Olsina, eds., *Proceedings Second Internatioanl Workshop on Web-Oriented Software Technology* (IWWOST'02), pp. 105–119.

Koch, N., and Kraus, A., 2003, Towards a common metamodel for the development of Web applications. In J.M.C. Lovelle, B.M.G. Rodríguez, L.J. Aguilar, J.E.L. Gayo, and M. del

Puerto Paule Ruiz, eds., *Proceedings Third International Conference on Web Engineering* (ICWE'03), pp. 495–506.

Koch, N., Kraus, A., and Hennicker, R., 2001, The authoring process of the UML-based Web engineering approach. In D. Schwabe, ed., *Proceedings First International Workshop on Web-Oriented Software Technology* (IWWOST'01). `http://www.dsic.upv.es/ ~west2001/iwwost01/`.

Koch, N., Zhang, G., and Escalona, M.J., 2006, Model transformations from requirements to Web system design. In D. Wolber, N. Calder, C. Brooks, and A. Ginige, eds., *Proceedings Sixth International Conference on Web Engineering* (ICWE'06), pp. 281–288.

Lowe, D., and Gaedke, M., eds., 2005, *Proceedings Fifth International Conference on Web Engineering* (ICWE'05).

Meliá, S., Kraus, A., and Koch, N., 2005, MDA transformations applied to Web application development. In D. Lowe and M. Gaedke, eds., *Proceedings Fifth International Conference on Web Engineering* (ICWE'05), pp. 465–471.

Object Management Group (2005). Unified Modeling Language. www.uml.org.

Object Management Group (2005). Unified Modeling Language: Superstructure, version 2.0. Specification, OMG. `http://www.omg.org/cgi-bin/doc?formal/05-07-04`.

Pressman, R., 2005, *Software Engineering—A Practitioner's Approach,* 6th edition, McGraw-Hill, Boston.

QVT-Merge Group (2004). Revised Submission for MOF 2.0 Query/Views/Transformations RFP (ad/2002-04-10). Submission, OMG. `http://www.omg.org/cgi-bin/doc?ad/ 04-04-01.pdf`.

QVT-Partners (2003). Revised Submission for MOF 2.0 Query/Views/Transformations RFP, version 1.1. `http://qvtp.org/downloads/1.1/qvtpartners1.1.pdf`.

Robbins, J.E., 1999, Cognitive support features for software development tools. PhD thesis, University of California, Irvine.

Schwabe, D., and Rossi, G., 1995, The object-oriented hypermedia design model. *Communications of the ACM,* **38**(8): 45–46.

Schwinger, W., and Koch, N., 2006, Modeling Web applications. In G. Kappel, B. Pröll, S. Reich, and W. Retschitzegger, eds., *Web Engineering: Systematic Development of Web Applications*, John Wiley, Hoboken, NJ, pp. 39–64.

Vilain, P., Schwabe, D., and de Souza, C.S., 2000, A diagrammatic tool for representing user interaction in UML. In A. Evans, S. Kent, and B. Selic, eds., *Proceedings Third International Conference on Unified Modeling Language* (UML'00), pp. 133–147.

Wirsing, M., Koch, N., Rossi, G., Garrido, A., Mandel, L., Helmerich, A., and Olsina, L., 1999, Hyper-UML: Specification and modeling of multimedia and hypermedia applications in distributed systems. In *Proceedings Second Workshop on German-Argentinian Bilateral Programme for Scientific and Technological Cooperation*, Königswinter, Germany.

Zhang, G., 2005, Towards aspect-oriented class diagrams. In *Proceedings 12th Asia Pacific Software Engineering Conference* (APSEC'05), pp. 763–768.

Chapter 8

DESIGNING MULTICHANNEL WEB APPLICATIONS AS "DIALOGUE SYSTEMS": THE IDM MODEL

Davide Bolchini[1] and Franca Garzotto[2]

[1]*TEC-Lab, Faculty of Communication Sciences, University of Lugano, Via G. Buffi, 13 6900 Lugano, Switzerland*
[2]*HOC (Hypermedia Open Centre), Department of Information and Electronics, Politecnico di Milano, Milan, Italy*

8.1 BACKGROUND

IDM, the design method discussed in this chapter, is the distillation of a long experience of building, using, and teaching models for hypermedia design. At the beginning of the 1990s, we started with HDM (Hypertext Design Model), (Garzotto el al., 1991; Garzotto and Paolini, 1993) which was the first model for the conceptual design of this class of applications that appeared in the literature. HDM was relatively simple and, in some respects, naïve. Still, it proposed some core concepts that inspired many subsequent models for (Web-based) hypermedia that we and other researchers proposed: the distinction among different conceptual design "dimensions" (content, navigation/interaction, presentation) and the proposal, for complex applications, of a "schema-based" design process, as opposed to "design-by-page" (or "design-by-instance"), which was the common practice at the time.

HDM progressively evolved into models (named HDM+, HDM2, and W2000) (Garzotto et al., 1994, 1995, 1999; Baresi et al., 2001a) that, to address the increasing complexity of hypermedia applications, were significantly richer and more sophisticated than their ancestor. These models provided a rich set of primitives that enabled designers to specify a wide spectrum of design solutions, at both a general level and a very detailed level. Unfortunately, the increase in expressive power had some drawbacks. In many graduate courses in different faculties (computer engineering, industrial design, and communication sciences), the difficulty of learning the theory and practice of our models did not completely pay off in terms of the increased design quality delivered by students' designs. Building design documentation in industrial projects became more and more time-consuming (since design specifications were more and more detailed), while its power as a communication medium among project stakeholders dramatically decreased (especially among persons who had no formal training in modeling). An empirical survey we carried on in the industrial arena confirmed that usability in general, and learnability and effectiveness in particular, are crucial factors for the acceptability and adoption of the design models and methods in the real world (Garzotto and Perrone, 2003).

Thus, after moving from simplicity (HDM) to complexity (W2000), we progressively moved back to simplicity, as oftentimes occurs in scientific research (in art, too). IDM (Bolchini and Paolini, 2006) is the "end" of this "parabola." It focuses on design concepts that are truly fundamental for making a design process cost-effective. It makes the "deep" meaning of design concepts more intuitive. It does not simply offer a specification tool for designers to render their creative design solutions: It helps them to create abstract, minimal, but expressive representations and, above all, to understand how they may think when they do design.

We like to quote the following sentence, attributed to Albert Einstein: "… A complex 'phenomenon' … cannot be modeled as simple, but we (scientists) should try at least to give it a representation that is as simple as possible." Designing a complex hypermedia application is not simple. Our hope is that IDM makes it as simple as possible.

8.2 THE DIALOGICAL APPROACH OF IDM

"Design" (from the Latin *designare* = to mark out) is the process of developing plans or schemes; more particularly, a design may be a developed plan or scheme, …, set forth as a drawing or model. … A design is ordinarily conceived with a number of limiting factors in mind: the capacities of the material employed; ….; the effect of the end result on those who may see it, use it, or become involved in it.

The above quotation, from the *Encyclopaedia Britannica*, captures some essential aspects of the concept of "design"(which different authors defined in so many different ways) and provides us with a reference definition to better explain IDM.

Next, we should define the scope for design in the specific domain of hypermedia. Unfortunately, also in this restricted domain, the definition of the design scope is not obvious, being strongly related to the profile of who is making a design, to the goal of a design artifact, and to its users.

For a graphic designer, the scope of hypermedia design is the appearance of "pages." The goal of a design artifact is to convey a brand and identity "image," for discussing it with the customer: "Design" means defining (a schema for) the visual, directly perceivable properties of a hypermedia interface. For an interaction designer, the design scope is the definition of the interaction modalities available to the user to interact with the "pages" (e.g., form filling, menu selection, icons and direct manipulation capability, etc.); the goals of a design artifact are to render the tangible experience of the user with the application and to provide both the interaction requirements for the implementers and a preliminary "prototype" to be evaluated by usability experts. For an information architect, the scope is the organizational structures for the content delivered by the application; the goal is to provide both the content requirements for authors and the data requirements for implementors. For a computer engineer, the design scope is the definition of both the data structures for the contents and the functions provided by the systems. And so on.

For IDM, the "designer" is anyone who is translating the problem space represented by users' and stakeholders' requirements into a solution space represented by a design artifact. The goals of design are to reify requirements in terms of general properties of the application, to support early brainstorming among the different profiles of designers listed above (who must later add details to the design specs), as well as to discuss general solutions among them and among other stakeholders (customers and users).

To achieve these goals, we use a dialogue metaphor: We conceive user interactions with a hypermedia as a sort of dialogue, namely, as a sequence of question-answering "acts": The selection of a link is the operational counterpart to a question that the user "asks" herself and turns to "the system" (e.g., "who is the director of this movie?"). The effect of link selection, i.e., the display of the link destination page, is the answer is the system materially offers, according to the designers, on how to respond to the user's question. The scope of hypermedia design is therefore to shape the possible dialogues between the users and the system, and the design is the process concerning the construction of a dialogue plan. The different design activities are progressive steps in forming this plan, from a more general level of abstraction, to a more concrete level where the various limiting (or contextual) factors for the execution of the plan are progressively taken into account (including, among others, the characteristics of the delivery device, the actual context of use, the specific user's characteristics).

In general, we can say that a dialogue-based design offers a number of advantages:

- It is conceptually simple even for people who are not used to design (e.g., content experts and newcomer designers). We have experienced (as we will discuss in the conclusions) that a dialogue-metaphor is far more intuitive and natural (especially for the above profiles) than an information-navigation metaphor.
- It is very close to the way requirements are specified and therefore allows for better traceability, i.e., keeping track of how the different requirements were taken into account during the definition of the various design solutions.
- It captures the "essence" of the dialogues that the user can establish, easily avoiding all the details connected to technology and implementation.
- As a special case of the last point, it is suitable for paving the ground for specific versions of the dialogue aiming at users with special needs (e.g., aural interaction for visually impaired users).

8.3 IDM ACTIVITIES

The design process envisioned by IDM comprises three main activities: conceptual design, logical design, and page design. Each addresses different aspects of the application under design, at different levels of abstractions. For each activity, IDM provides a set of concepts and notations, as discussed and exemplified in the rest of this section.

8.3.1 Conceptual IDM (or C-IDM)

Assuming a dialogue-oriented perspective, the first set of issues that the designer should try to address can be summarized by the following questions:

1. What are the *dialogue subjects*, i.e., what can (should) the application say to the user?
2. What are the relevant *shifts of subjects* to be supported during the user/application dialogue?
3. What are the possible different ways to organize the dialogue, i.e., to group the different subjects through which the user may start the actual flow of conversation?

Precise and detailed answers to the above questions can be provided only when a specific channel of delivery has been chosen (determining factors like screen size, pointing mechanisms, available media, performances, etc.). Still, important decisions can be made in advance, in what we call "conceptual design."

In this initial phase, a *conceptual schema* of the interactive application must be defined to convey all the necessary "dialogue strategies," without (and before) digging into details that may depend on technical issues of the actual delivery device (and should be addressed in the following design activities).

At this stage, a conceptual schema has multiple uses:

1. to support brainstorming among designers
2. to allow traceability and comparison with requirements (e.g., needs and goals of the stakeholders) and therefore to support discussion with stakeholders (are we making the most appropriate design decisions?)
3. to provide a firm suggestion to the technical designers, who must add details to it

C-IDM (Conceptual IDM) is a model for the definition of conceptual schemas. It is simple to grasp and effective in representing the most relevant features of the application in terms of content of the dialogue and dialogue moves. Indeed, three basic design elements characterize C-IDM: "topic," "relationship," and "group of topics."

An interactive application may "talk about" a "topic" (e.g., a "movie" or an "actor"), or it may allow the user to switch the dialogue focus to a "related topic" (e.g., switching from the "actor" to the "movies" in which he starred), or it may allow the user to start from a "group of topics" (e.g., "the top at the box office movies" or "movies of 2006") and then lead the dialogue among the different topics within the group.

The "informative" quality of the dialogue comes from the choice of the topics and the "objective ways" of relating and grouping topics; the "argumentative" quality of the dialogues is based upon the choice of the specific content associated to each topic, upon the "subjective ways" of relating topics and grouping them.

More precisely, the above simple ideas have been translated into the following C-IDM design primitives:

- **Topic:** something that can be the subject of conversation between the user and the interactive application. "Mission: Impossible III," "Tom Cruise," and "Paramount Pictures" are examples of topics, i.e., possible subjects of a dialogue between the user and the application.

- **Kind of topic:** the category of possible subjects of conversation. "Movie," "Actor," and "Company" are kinds of topics. "Tom Cruise" is an example of "Actor."
- **Change of subject (or relevant relation):** it determines how the dialogue can switch from one kind of topic to another one. "Produced by" is a possible change of subject relating any Movie to one Company.
- **Group of topics:** it determines a specific group of topics, possible subjects of conversation. Announced Movies is a specific group of Movies, while All 2006 movies is another, larger, group.
- **Multiple group of topic:** it determines a family of group of topics. It could be nice, for example, to group the Movies according to genres. All the movies of the same genre are a group of topics; "Movies by Genre," overall, is a family of groups of topics (as many as there are Genres). Each multiple group of topics has a corresponding "higher-level" group of topics (e.g., "all genres"), which allows one to select the specific group of topics of interest (e.g., "Movies of the genre Comedy").

The above list of terms and concepts has a number of advantages over most of the current design models and methods:

1. The number of concepts is short and therefore easy to teach (and to learn).
2. Despite their limited number, the concepts are expressive enough for describing the content of most (information-intensive) applications.
3. The concepts (and terms) relate to the "human" dialogue experience, rather than to informatics; therefore, they can be more effectively conveyed to people without a computer science or engineering background.

The concepts are of the proper "level" to allow an in-depth comparison between requirements and design decisions (if requirements have been explicitly stated, of course).

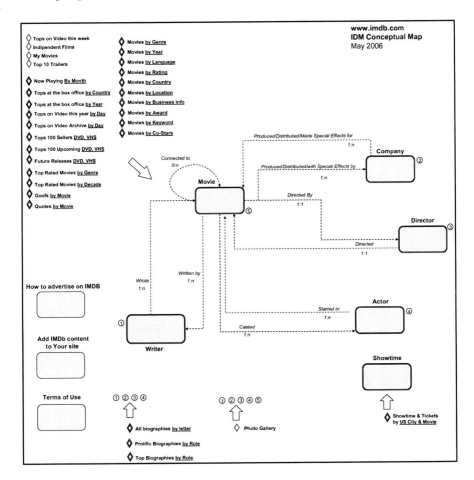

Figure 8.1. Conceptual IDM modeling of www.imdb.com.

Figure 8.1 describes a potential conceptual design for the IMDB (Internet Movie Database) Web site (www.imdb.com), presenting it as a possible modeling result through C-IDM. The graphical primitives of C-IDM are illustrated in Figure 8.2.

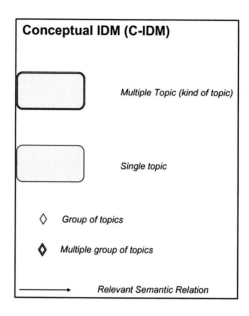

Figure 8.2. IDM conceptual design: key.

The reader should notice how the schema simply and effectively communicates the basic dialogue strategies underlying the application. Some of the information conveyed, for example, includes the following: The dialogue can be about "movies," "actors," "writers," etc. In addition, the dialogue can concern the "terms of use," "how to add content to your site," etc. If a "movie" is the subject, the dialogue can move to the corresponding "actor," to the "director," or to the "writer," and so on. The dialogue about a movie can start in various ways: "Independent Films," "My Movies," or selecting movies by rating, by country, by genre, the "now playing" movie, and so on. Guessing the rest is left to the reader as a simple exercise.

This schema, however, is not fully sufficient: Additional information needs to be provided for a fully satisfactory design document. Here is an outline of suggested additional information:

- *Topic*: description of the motivations (i.e., why has it been considered?; what's its purpose?); description of the content (i.e., what can be said when the topic is "selected" as subject of the dialogue?)
- *Kind of topic*: description of the motivations (see above); description of the content (see above); cardinality (i.e., an indication of the expected number of topics instances or exemplars: e.g., how many movies do we expect to have?)
- *Change of subject (relevant relation)*: description of the semantics (i.e., what is the actual meaning of the relations?) and motivations (i.e., why is

it considered important?); cardinality (i.e., an indication of the expected numbers; e.g., changing subject from a writer to the movie, how many movies should we expect to have—on average—for a given writer?)

- *Group of topics*: description of the motivations (i.e., why is this group of topics useful or interesting and to whom?); cardinality (i.e., expected number of topics to be part of the group)

Design documents do not always need to be complete. Designers often want to negotiate strategic decisions with stakeholders and to document those decisions, without being forced to commit on premature details early in the development. Nor do all the different choices need an adequate explanation: They may be obvious in a given context. In many situations design documents can be left "unfinished," still fulfilling their role of conveying most of the "crucial" ideas about the application. Even with the above enrichments indicated, a conceptual design document can be kept very simple, easy to write, and effective for the reader.

In synthesis, the main advantages of the dialogue map shown in Figure 8.1 may be summarized as follows:

1. The schema is quite simple, and it does not take too much time to write it down (any common editor tool may fit).
2. The schema expresses all the most relevant aspects of a "real-life" interactive application.
3. The schema conveys the basic interaction ideas, without commitment to a specific "channel" of delivery (whether it is the Web technology, a PDA, a Car Navigator System).
4. The schema can be used to brainstorm, debate alternatives, and discuss preliminary decisions.

As we will see in the next section, the conceptual schema can be translated into one or more logical schemas, according to the choices made for a specific channel of communication.

8.3.2 L-IDM Logical Design

Unlike conceptual design, logical design starts by making decisions that are typically dependent on a specific fruition channel through which the application may be conveyed (be it the traditional Web, an oral channel, an interactive TV, or a mobile channel).

Whereas a C-IDM conceptual design schema defines the overall interaction strategy to be supported during the dialogue of the application with the user, designers can develop one or more "logical" designs, one for each specific channel they want to design the application for. IDM "logical" design can be seen as a detailed version of the conceptual design, where details are decided on the basis of a variety of channel-dependent factors, such as the constraints imposed by the type of device available on a given channel (e.g., screen size), the pointing devices (e.g., keyboard, smart pen, mouse, scroller, audio input, touch pointers, eye-tracking pointers), the media that can be used (e.g., audio, visual text, images, graphics, or video), the expected performance, and—of utmost importance—the typical scenarios of use (e.g., home or office desktop use, walking or standing contexts, mobile use on car, etc.).

All these "technicalities" may influence key decisions for the user experience, which concern at the logical level the ways detailed pieces of content are split and structured and how and when navigation possibilities are made available and may be traversed.

Starting from C-IDM, logical design (called L-IDM) for a specific channel may be defined by answering two basic questions: What are the units of dialogue? How can units of dialogue be combined in a user experience? A unit of dialogue is an atomic object, in the sense that it will be delivered to the user in its totality.

These two basic questions, in order to be addressed, need a number of technical steps:

1. Organize each (kind of) topic into dialogue units, and organize the possible dialogue flows across them.
2. Organize the needed dialogue units that allow the shift of subjects.
3. Organize the dialogue units that allow the exploration of a group of topics

In order to provide all the answers, we have developed the design primitives of L-IDM, explained below.

- **Dialogue act:** a unit of the dialogue within a topic. The content of a topic is represented by either a single dialogue act or several of them. Decisions are based both on technical considerations (the relevant features of the channel) and on user profiles and/or needs.
- **Structural strategy:** the possible development of a dialogue for exploring a topic with more than one dialogue act. What must be specified are the initial dialogue act and the possibilities for changing the dialogue from one act to another one.
- **Transition act:** when changing the subject from a (kind of) topic (e.g., "movie") to another (kind of) topic (e.g., "director"), no additional dialogue is need, since the dialogue can immediately switch, upon request. When the new subject is multiple (e.g., switching from "movie" to its "actors"), an additional part of dialogue is needed, which we call

the *transition act*. A transition act is, in essence, a list of possible new topics (e.g., a list of actors who starred in that movie).

- **Transition strategy:** the existence of the transition act, as explained above, does not entirely solve all the problems. A dialogue substrategy must be developed to explain the way a user can explore all the new topics (all the "actors" starring in the movie, in the example).
- **Introductory act:** a piece of dialogue that allows the application (and the user) to consider the group of topics as a whole. It consists, in general, of an introduction followed by a list of the topics belonging to the group. Introductory acts are the unique *starting points* for the dialogue, in the sense that any dialogue starts with an introductory act. For example, the list of "Top of the Box Office Movies" may be introduced by some engaging text and a representative picture.
- **Subject strategy:** as was the case for transitions, creating introductory acts does not solve the problem of "engaging a conversation" about the group of topics. There must be a dialogue strategy coordinating how the conversation can involve the introductory act and support the exploration of all the topics belonging to the group.
- **Multiple introductory acts:** an introductory act corresponding to a "Multiple Group of Topics." It is a strange technicality, not difficult to explain: If there is a group of "movies" for each "genre," we need an introductory act for each genre (listing all the movies belonging to that genre), but we also need another introductory act listing all the genres (to let the user choose one genre), possibly with an introduction and/or an explanation accompanying that list. In other words, for a multiple group of topics we need a family of introductory acts (one for each theme, in the example) and a further introductory act (the list of genres in the example), holding the family together.

On the basis of the same C-IDM schema, Figure 8.3 provides the L-IDM graphical primitives, while Figure 8.4 illustrates L-IDM design for the IMDB Web site.

Whereas the C-IDM conceptual schema represents the utmost degree of interactivity potential (resembling the richest channel of the ones available, such as the Web, for example), the L-IDM design defines a subset of interactions that are sound and suitable for the channel at issue.

On the basis of our project experience, the common activities that can be undertaken to specialize the conceptual schema into a "channel-dependent" version are the following:

- Dialogue acts or entire topics may be removed.
- Relevant relations may be removed.
- Groups of topics may be removed or simplified.
- … Other adaptations are possible.

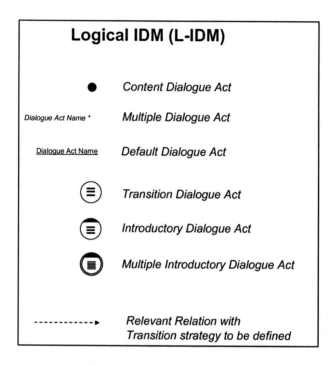

Figure 8.3. IDM logical design: key.

Based on the results of these decisions, the design should be refined without totally changing the overall dialogue pattern. In fact, the user should perceive that she is dealing with the same application across different channels. Design decisions made at this stage should cope with the trade-off between a unifying user experience and the constraints imposed by each specific channel.

As a demonstrative example, let us now assume to design a palm-held version of IMDB to support the following scenarios:

- A person waiting for the movie to start (outside the theater or not yet in the projection room) wants detailed information, anticipation, and trivia about the movie he is going to watch.
- A person wants to go to the movies tonight. She does not know yet which movie to watch. She would like to get an idea about the latest releases, browse the movies, and then see the showtimes in her town.
- A person has decided which movie to watch and wants to know the showtimes in his town.

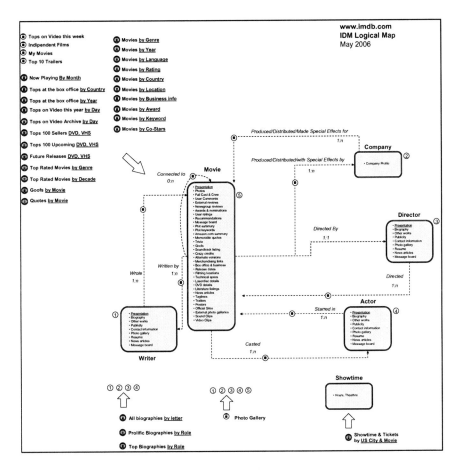

Figure 8.4. IDM logical modeling of www.imdb.com.

Figure 8.5 shows the IDM logical schema for a PDA-version IMDB application that we have designed to support the scenarios described above.

With respect to the conceptual design, the logical schema for the PDA shows that there have been changes "in-the-large" concerning the simplification of the content and the navigation possibilities, with the aim of supporting the above-described scenarios and focusing on those that are potentially the most "appealing" and useful for the situations of use envisioned. In particular, two multiple topics have been removed (company and writer) along with the attached relevant relations. The set of groups of topics has been dramatically reduced, decreasing from more than 20 to 5, thus offering few relevant options to browse the movies.

In comparison with the logical design for the Web, the logical schema for the PDA have been simplified in the perspective of offering a more usable, straightforward access to content and fewer but more relevant details about a movie and the correlated topics. Namely, the many dialogue acts for the

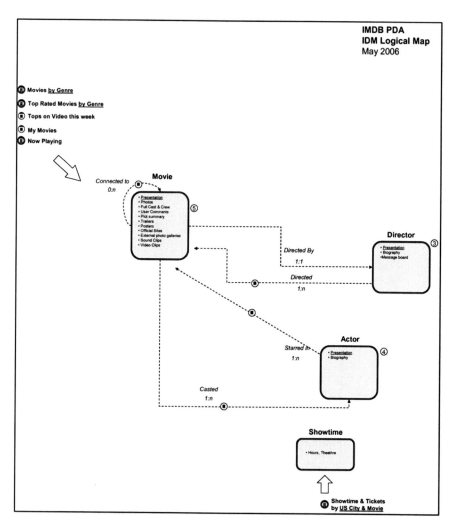

Figure 8.5. IDM logical schema for the PDA version of the IMDB application.

multiple topic "Movie" have been left out (e.g., soundtrack listing, crazy credits, alternate versions, etc.) with the aim of offering the user a selection of suggested content to browse. This design choice has also taken into account the fact that managing a huge set of dialogue acts (more than 25 in the Web version) would have made navigation within the topic very cumbersome in the PDA version, thus negatively affecting the usability of the application. Similarly, the decision to reduce the number of introductory acts for the PDA will have a positive effect on the page's design, which will have to provide access to fewer options.

8.3.3 P-IDM: From Logical Design to Pages

IDM page design (P-IDM) means defining the elements to be communicated to the user in a single dialogue act. With respect to previous decisions (see the L-IDM schema), designers now have to craft the actual pages containing the necessary elements to sustain the dialogue.

Note that page design should not yet go into wireframe design (defining the visual page grid) or into layout design (how elements are physically arranged in the grid) or into graphic design (actual rendering of the visual elements in the page). Whereas all these aspects contribute to define the visual communication strategy of the application, page design should provide the proper input to these activities just by specifying the important elements to be presented in the page.

In this view, there are simple guidelines for transitioning from L-IDM (channel design) to P-IDM (page design):

- Each dialogue act becomes a page type.
- Each introductory act becomes a page type.
- Each transition act becomes a page type.
- Relevant topics become landmarks [i.e., links present in (almost) any page]. Landmarks are usually either single topics or important groups of topics that are always accessible.
- Relevant groups of topics become landmarks.

Different page types can be easily derived from dialogue acts, introductory acts, and transition acts. We have a set of specific guidelines for page derivation. Let us consider the following excerpt of the guidelines, namely those specific for the page design of the dialogue acts. A page for a dialogue act (e.g., Presentation) for a kind of topic (e.g., Movie) should basically contain the elements listed in Table 8.1.

Table 8.1 Page Elements for a Dialogue Act

Page Element	Description
Content	The actual content of the dialogue act (e.g., text, graphics, voice, video, audio, or any combination of these)
Structural links (if any)	To pages of the other dialogue acts of the same topic
Transition links (if any)	To pages of related topic (1:1) or to pages of transition acts (1:n)
Group of topic links	Next-previous (in case of guided tour) or to pages of introductory acts/introductory act I came from
Orientation info (if any)	Messages communication "where I am"
Landmarks	To relevant sections of the site (pages of single topics) or a group of topics

These hints serve as a reminder for the designer about the elements to consider when building a page. Visual communication designers can then make layout and graphic decisions on the basis of this input to create mock-up prototypes or the final rendered page.

Figures 8.6 and 8.7 describe two Web pages of the IMDB Web site, displaying, respectively, a Dialogue Act ("Presentation," of the multiple topic Movie) and an Introductory Act. Figure 8.8 shows the same dialogue act as it is rendered in the PDA version of the application.

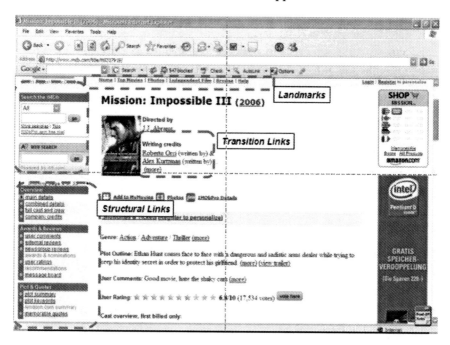

Figure 8.6. IDM page design elements on an instance of the multiple topic "Movie"—Dialogue Act "Presentation" (www.imdb.com—accessed June 2006).

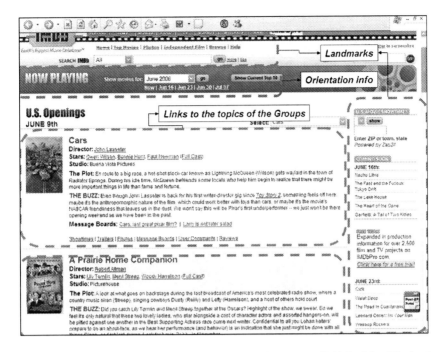

Figure 8.7. IDM page design elements for the Introductory Act "Movies Now Playing" (www.imdb.com—accessed June 2006).

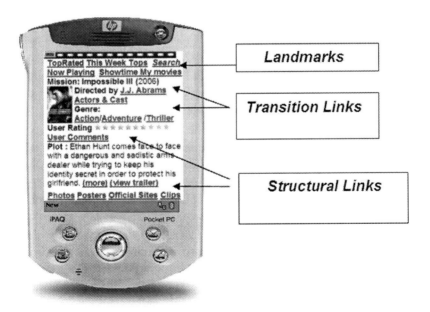

Figure 8.8. IDM page design elements on an instance of the multiple topic "Movie"—Dialogue Act "Presentation"—PDA version.

8.4 IDM IMPLEMENTATION TOOLS

By their very nature, IDM design specifications are "abstract" and semiformal: The main purpose of IDM is to act as a communication and brainstorming tool among the project stakeholders involved in the design process, and a number of details, especially those related to layout, are omitted. Therefore, generating running applications from IDM specifications cannot be performed in a totally automatic way. Still, we have built a number of tools that support the development of IDM applications and exploit some key concepts of the model. The last version of these tools is called CHEF, which stands for Cultural Heritage Enterprise Framework since it was originally built for a specific class of applications, in the cultural heritage domain, as described in Garzotto and Megale, 2006.

CHEF can be regarded as an IDM application framework. It provides a reusable implementation architecture for content-intensive multichannel hypermedia that are designed using IDM, and it supports an IDM-based design and development process. CHEF can be regarded as an application "skeleton" that can be customized to produce a specific application.

The main originality of CHEF stems from its "philosophy," which makes it rather different from most of the existing hypermedia application frameworks and development tools. The latter are traditionally designed by software professionals and are conceived as tools for programmers. In contrast, CHEF applies the concept of end-user development, which is "about taking control" by non-computer professionals, "not only of personalizing computer applications and writing programs, but of designing new computer based applications without ever seeing the underlying program code" (Wulf, 2004). In other words, CHEF shifts the perspective from hypermedia application programmers to application domain experts: professionals who lack technological expertise and usually remain in the background of the development process, but are obviously crucial players.

Domain experts know the requirements of the end users of the product under development, and they plan, select, structure, edit, and revise the actual contents. Indeed, they can be considered among the "owners of problems" for hypermedia frameworks and, therefore, the main target users for this class of systems.

CHEF's ultimate goal is therefore to empower application domain experts to create and maintain the hypermedia artifacts built to communicate their domain know-how, without the need for shoulder-by-shoulder trained programmers. As such, CHEF is a particularly appropriate tool for companies or institutions that cannot rely upon in-house programmers or IT departments; it helps them to avoid expensive outsourcing aid so that they can focus their financial resources on design and on high-quality content, rather than on code production.

CHEF has been conceived for and with domain specialists in different knowledge-intensive fields (e.g., cultural heritage, tourism, e-learning, e-commerce), during a requirements elicitation process that has tried to understand the (domain-independent) aspects of their process of information production, communication, and management. CHEF provides a user-friendly, easy-to-use, visual environment where domain experts can design "by reuse" their applications, instantiate the resulting design schemas with the proper multimedia contents (built using conventional multimedia authoring tools), and generate high-quality multidevice hypermedia applications without learning any specific implementation technology.

A simple interface guides the design process, which is carried on through the customization of a general design space. The systematic instantiation of the customized design is performed by a data entry interface that is automatically customized to become consistent with the actual schemas, without any implementation effort by the framework users. The paradigms of learning-by-examples and immediate visual feedback are supported by CHEF to facilitate the creation of a shared understanding within the development team of what is achievable and of the effects of the different design choices, leading to new insights, new ideas, and new artifacts.

More precisely, CHEF provides the following set of tools.

8.4.1 Customization Design Tool

This allows the domain expert to define IDM information, navigation, or presentation schemas. This work can be regarded as a *customization process* and comprises various activities.

During the definition of the information and navigation schemas, the designer can specialize a set of general design data structures, which are defined in the CHEF *meta-model*. This meta-model captures the general IDM abstractions needed to specify the actual information and navigation properties of the application under development. Information and navigation design involves various tasks:

- the definition of (kinds of) topics by selecting, in the corresponding meta-structure, the proper combination of attributes and cardinalities for the (kind of) topics under definition; definition of relevant associations, by specifying the association name and the kind of topics involved in the relationship.
- the definition of (multiple) groups of topics, by selecting the kinds of topic involved in each group under definition.

- the definition of the various categories of acts (Dialogue, Introductory, and Transition Acts), by mapping the attributes of the different kinds of topics (Topics) into the different acts.
- the definition of the various strategies, by mapping each (kind of) topic, (multiple) group, and relevant association to the proper *navigation pattern* (Garzotto et al., 1999). For this task, CHEF provides a *pattern library* that includes the most popular navigation design patterns (*Index, GuidedTour, Index+GuidedTour, All-to-all*), i.e., generic topologies that are acknowledged as successful solutions to allow users to navigate across groups of hypermedia "objects."

For page design, CHEF provides a library of *Presentation Meta Templates*—basically abstract layout "grids" such as the ones adopted by graphic designers during the very early stage of design. CHEF users can map acts and patterns to the different Meta Template components, also specifying landmarks elements and orientation information. The "concrete" layout can be defined by *decorating* the so-instantiated meta-template with specific visual or typographical properties (color, shape, size, etc.) and application-specific elements (e.g., logos) to meet the "corporate image" requirements of the application under development.

8.4.2 Instantiation Tool

This is a *schema-driven data entry tool* that supports the instantiation of the various types of information and navigation structures defined as conceptual and logical design in the different delivery devices.

For each instantiation task, the tools provide the editorial author with the proper data entry "form" that is *consistent* with the current C-IDM and L-IDM schemas of the application under development (and the proper delivery channel). These forms are automatically generated by CHEF according to the current design specifications (i.e., the parameters provided by the customization tool).

8.4.3 Feedback Tools

Two original tools are offered in CHEF to meet the need for continuous feedback during the design and instantiation activities process: the Mockupper and the Previewer.

The *Mockupper* is used at design time. It exploits a *fictitious* set of multimedia contents and links (prestored in CHEF) to *automatically instantiate* the schemas of the current design and, by means of the generation tool (discussed below), produces a fictitious application after a design schema has been defined. The result can be regarded as a running demo that allows the designer to experiment with the user interaction that results from his design choices, helping him to decide how to adjust or improve them.

The *Previewer* is used during the instantiation activity. When a new instance is created or updated, the Previewer allows developers to inspect the effects of their work. The developer can see and navigate across the pages for the instances created or updated *with the same layout and navigation capability that appears in the end-user application.*

8.4.4 Generation Tool

CHEF supports both the dynamic generation of the online application pages and the "batch" generation of "static" pages, which can be exploited for offline use of the application, e.g., when the application is delivered on CD-ROM or, more generally, when it cannot rely upon a client-server Web architecture.

Dynamic generation is triggered by HTTP requests when a page is needed during Web-based use of the application. In contrast, the generation tool creates a static version of the entire application, by repeatedly simulating a link activation and the corresponding page requests, invoking the dynamic generation capability of the framework, and storing all pages of the applications as they are generated.

The software architecture that implements CHEF tools is sketched in Figure 8.9. In this figure we highlight different user profiles for the CHEF framework:

- the *editorial designer*, i.e., the domain expert who shapes the general properties of the application and takes the main design choices (for the different channels)
- the *editorial author*, i.e., the domain expert who is responsible for identifying the proper "cultural objects" of the domain and for instantiating the design with the proper multimedia contents; the *end users* of the final application, who may use it on different technological contexts—Web-enabled or offline stationary workstation, and online or offline PDA

Indeed, the CHEF software environment is the same for all these profiles, since it serves both the execution of the customization and instantiation operations and the dynamic generation of the final application on the different technological contexts.

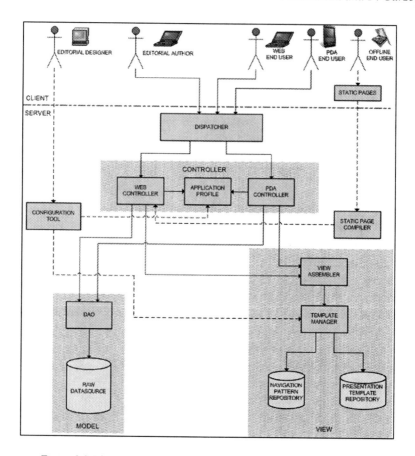

Figure 8.9. The architecture of CHEF—an IDM application framework.

As highlighted in Figure 8.9, the framework architecture is modeled according to the Model-View-Controller (MVC) design pattern. The MVC pattern divides an application into three logical categories of objects: model, view, and controller.

Model objects (collectively referred to as "Model") represent application domain data and the business rules that govern access and updates to this data. *View* objects are responsible for rendering the contents of the Model and forwarding user commands to the Controller.

Controller objects (collectively referred to as Controller) are responsible *for mapping user requests to operations* on the Model, for executing them, for building the proper View, and for returning them to the client. In Web applications, user "commands" appear as HTTP page requests.

View objects typically correspond to HTML pages. Based on the page request, the results of the operations on the Model, and the state of, the Model, the Controller generates the next HTML page.

The main logical components of CHEF comprise

- a module for the *configuration tool*. This component creates the configuration parameters for the customized design schemas and data entry forms (stored in the Application Profile component) and selects the proper navigation and presentation templates that will be used by the customized instantiation tools and by the final application.
- a *static compiler* that implements the functionalities of the static pages generation tool.
- a set of components for the *dynamic generation* of the pages requested by the editorial manager, during the instantiation activities, and by the end users of the final application. The dynamic generation approach exploits a well-known approach in Web Engineering, separating the application business logic from its presentation and control logic. The presentation logic, delegated to the client side, manages user interaction and data (dis)play. The control logic, delegated to the server side, interprets the requests from the presentation level, manages the functionality defined by the business logic (e.g., data retrieval or update, composition of the required HTML page), and returns an HTML page to the presentation level via the network infrastructure using the HTTP protocol.

So far, CHEF has been successfully implemented in three large projects, where, in most cases, the framework users had limited or no programming know-how:

- the EC project *MEDINA* #314 (MEDiterranean by INternet Access), which is developing the "Portal on Mediterranean Cultural Heritage" for Web-based stationary PCs (www.medinataproject.net) and PDAs, with the contribution of Ministries of Tourism and Culture, Cultural Tourism Associations, National Tourism Agencies, Museums and Cultural Institutions, of 9 countries in the Mediterranean basin (Morocco, Tunisia, Algeria, Cyprus, Malta, Lebanon, Palestinian Authority, Syria, Jordan)
- the *Bramantino* project, which produced hypermedia about the current exhibition on Bramantino's Adorations held in December 2005 at the Biblioteca Ambrosiana Museum in Milan, available on the Web (www.bramantino.it) and on CD-ROM for exhibition visitors
- *SYRIA DGAM*, which is developing the new Web site for the General Directorate of Syrian Antiquities and Musuem, sponsored by the Syrian Ministry of Tourism and the Syrian Ministry of Cultural Heritage, with the partial contribution of the European Union.

8.5 DISCUSSION AND CONCLUSIONS

Lightweight design processes and usability are being recognized, more and more, as relevant for all the design methodologies, and for the design of interactive applications in particular. Different factors are being implied here:

- It should be easy to teach the design methodology (and the design model) to anyone (from students to practitioners). Professionals, especially, do not have the time and resources to invest in learning new methodologies; one of the success factors of the "entity relationship" (probably the most successful design model, ever) stems from the fact that it was very easy to transmit its basic concepts, both in academia and in a professional environment.
- It must be possible to use the design model for brainstorming, i.e., for generating and discussing ideas among developers, with stakeholders, and with potential users. It is of little use to have a design model capable of representing only fully developed solutions.
- It must take little time to write down design ideas: Developers do not like to spend too many resources on preliminary activities.
- It must be possible to move, smoothly, from a general design to a more detailed design, without the need for excessive reworking and for completeness; in other words, even an incomplete design document must be useful and understandable.

IDM may appear to be an oversimplified model, with respect to other models discussed in this book. Still, its simplicity has been gained not at the expense of expressiveness, but at the expense of "technical details."

IDM is mainly intended as a model for *brainstorming design*, where people with different backgrounds (content experts, communication experts, computer scientists, graphic designers, marketing people, etc.) throw in ideas, which they then evaluate and discuss. A number of experiences (both in academia and in industry environments) have proved that IDM, by eliminating technical details and encouraging the expression of more semantic features, works beautifully for this purpose: It can be used from the very early stage of design (when decisions are still in the clouds) down to the moment when details start to surface.

Other, more technical models (e.g., W2000 and WEBML, for example) do not allow semantic annotation, but rather require the expression of a number of details that cannot be known at the brainstorming phase: They can be used to record decisions already made, rather than helping to make decisions.

A second point is that the *simplicity* and the dialogue-oriented terminology of IDM do not intimidate anyone and allow everybody around the table to discuss design issues. A more tech-oriented model, in the best case, may be used to "communicate" a design to nontechnical people, but nontechnical people cannot use it to freely discuss ideas.

A third, crucial, point is about the *usability* of a design model, which entails at least two key performance indicators: the amount of time required for teaching the model and the amount of time necessary to sketch the design of an application. The reduction in the time spent teaching the model has been astonishing: In an engineering environment the time has been cut down to 25% (moving from either W2000 or WEBML), with no loss at all in understanding the issues. The reduction of time required to sketch the design of an application (by several groups of students) can be estimated at approximately 50% (with a similar reduction in the amount of paper documentation being produced). Also, a few experiments in the "transfer" to industry have shown that a half-day is enough to convey effectively all important ideas in details, compared with the 1.5 or 2 days usually required for training on our previous models.

The fourth, and perhaps most important, issue of all is about the *quality of design*. We have verified something that was initially only a hypothesis: Simplifying the technique and encouraging brainstorming (besides being less "expensive" in terms of time) generally produce better design, in the sense of requirements and goals satisfaction. Designers can focus on and discuss the possible choices and their trade-offs, which leads to better solutions.

Currently, IDM is being used in seven different courses at Politecnico di Milano (three undergraduate and four graduate ones) and five different courses at the University of Lugano (two undergraduate and three graduate ones): It has shown to be tremendously effective, significantly reducing the teaching-learning effort and dramatically improving the quality of design.

We will discuss one example, to give an idea of what happened. TEC-CH (Technology-Enhanced Communication for Cultural Heritage) is an international master's program (in English) awarded by the University of Lugano (first edition: October 2004). We have enrolled 11 students (from Switzerland, Italy, Romania, Sri Lanka, Ghana, Nigeria, and the United States), 8 of whom have never designed an interactive application and only 1 of whom has experience in computer programming. An 8-hour lecture on IDM was sufficient to convey the technique; in a 3-week-long intensive class, these students were able to produce 3 complete projects (for real-life problems) that were technically correct and, above all, superb in terms of design solutions.

As far as non-academic environments are concerned, we had a number of episodes of transferring the methodology to industries (in the area of Milan, Rome, and Southern Italy): In all situations IDM was highly appreciated for its simplicity, expressiveness, and "efficiency." In these contexts we also used IDM for "reverse engineering," i.e., conceptualizing what existing applications do. Industry people were pleased by the possibility of easily visualizing a complex application and, through the IDM notation, discussing how their applications worked. As far as we know, those companies have plans for extensive internal use of IDM, outside the groups that initially cooperated with us.

APPENDIX: ONLINE APPLICATIONS DESIGNED USING IDM

IDM has been validated in both the academic and industry environments, in the design of a large number of content-intensive Web applications. The most recent and relevant are listed below:

- MEDINA: a multichannel transnational portal for cultural tourism in the Mediterranean, connecting the national Web sites for cultural tourisms of nine Mediterranean countries; see an example at http://www.medinaproject.net/tunisia/pages/
- MUNCH: a multichannel Web application for the Munch's Prints exhibition (State Museums of Berlin, April 2003); Web version: http://www.munchundberlin.org; PDA version: http://munchpda.sytes.net/simulatore.html (user id: 1)
- TEC-Lab: the Web site of the Technology-Enhanced Communication Laboratory at the University of Lugano (Faculty of Communication Sciences); http://www.tec-lab.ch
- SeRiAC: Web site for promoting accessibility research results and initiatives for the Public Administration in Italy; http://www.seriac.net
- BRAMANTINO: a multichannel Web application for the exhibition on Bramantino's Adorations (Museo Ambrosiano di Milano, Dec. 2005– Feb. 2006); http://hoc.elet.polimi.it/bramantino
- SYRIA TOURISM: official Web site of the Syrian Ministry of Tourism (under redesign); http://www.syriatourism.org
- UNIVERSITY OF LUGANO: Web site for the Faculty of Communication Sciences at the University of Lugano; http://www.com.unisi.ch

REFERENCES

Baresi, L., Garzotto, F., and Paolini, P. 2001a, Extending UML for modeling Web applications. In *Proceedings IEEE 34th International Conference on System Sciences,* Maui, January.

Baresi, L., Garzotto, F., and Paolini, P., 2001b, Supporting reusable Web design with HDM-Edit. In *Proceedings IEEE 34th International Conference on System Sciences,* Maui, January.

Bolchini, D., and Paolini, P., 2006, Interactive dialogue model: A design technique for multi-channel applications. *IEEE Transactions on Multimedia,* **8**(3).

Garzotto, F., Mainetti, L., and Paolini, P., 1994, HDM2: Extending the E-R approach to hypermedia application design. In *Proceedings ER'04—International Conference on the Entity Relationship Approach,* R.A.-E. Vram Kouramajian and B. Thalheim, eds.

Garzotto, F., Mainetti, L., and Paolini, P., 1995, Hypermedia design, analysis, and evaluation issues. *Communications of the ACM,* **38**(8).

Garzotto, F., and Megale, L., 2006, CHEF: A user-centered perspective for cultural heritage enterprise frameworks. In *Proceedings ACM AVI'06,* Venice, Italy, May.

Garzotto, F., and Paolini, P., 1993, A model-based approach to hypertext application design. *ACM Transactions on Information Systems,* **11**(1): 1–26.

Garzotto, F., Paolini, P., Bolchini, D., and Valenti S., 1999, "Modeling-by-patterns" of Web applications. In *Proceedings WWWCM'99—World-Wide Web and Conceptual Modeling,* ER'99 Workshop, Paris.

Garzotto, F., Paolini, P., and Schwabe, D., 1991, HDM—A model for the design of hypertext applications. In *Proceedings ACM Hypertext '91,* San Antonio, TX.

Garzotto, F., and Perrone, V., 2003, On the acceptability of conceptual design models for Web applications. In *Conceptual Modeling for Novel Application Domains—ER'03 Workshops Proceedings,* M. A. Jeusfeld and Ó. Pastor, eds., Chicago, October.

Wulf, V., Jarke, M., 2004, The Economics of End-User Development, *Communication of the ACM,* 47(49): P.31

Chapter 9

DESIGNING WEB APPLICATIONS WITH WEBML AND WEBRATIO

Marco Brambilla, Sara Comai, Piero Fraternali, Maristella Matera
Dipartimento di Elettronica e Informazione, Politecnico di Milano, Pizza L. da Vinci 32, 20133, Milan, Italy

9.1 INTRODUCTION

The Web Modeling Language (WebML) is a third-generation Web design methodology, conceived in 1998 in the wake of the early hypermedia models and the pioneering works on hypermedia and Web design, like HDM (Garzotto et al., 1993) and RMM (Isakowitz et al., 1995). The original goal of WebML was to support the design and implementation of so-called data-intensive Web applications (Ceri et al., 2002), defined as Web sites for accessing and maintaining large amounts of structured data, typically stored as records in a database management system, like online trading and e-commerce applications, institutional Web sites of private and public organizations, digital libraries, corporate portals, and community sites.

To achieve this goal, WebML reused existing conceptual data models and proposed an original notation for expressing the navigation and composition features of hypertext interfaces. WebML's hypertext model took an approach quite different from previous proposals: Instead of offering a high number of primitives for representing all the possible ways to organize a hypertext interface that may occur in data-intensive Web applications, the focus was on inventing a minimal number of concepts, which could be composed in well-defined ways to obtain an arbitrary number of application configurations.

This initial design choice deeply influenced the definition of the language and its evolution toward more complex classes of applications. Four major versions of WebML characterize the progression of the language:

- **WebML 1**: The original version comprised only a fixed set of primitives for representing read-only data-intensive Web sites; the focus was on the modular organization of the interface, navigation definition, and content extraction and publication in the interface.
- **WebML 2**: It added support for representing business actions (called operations) triggered by the navigation of the user; in this way, the expressive power was extended to support features like content management, authentication, and authorization.
- **WebML 3**: The introduction of the concept of model plug-ins transformed WebML into an open language, extensible by designers with their own conceptual-level primitives, as to widen the expressive power to cover the requirements of new application domains. This transition emphasized the role of component-based modeling and was the base of all subsequent extensions.
- **WebML 4**: The notion of a model plug-in was exploited to add orthogonal extensions to the core of WebML, covering sectors and applications not previously associated with model-driven development. For example, Web service interaction and workflow modeling primitives were added as plug-in components, to enable the modeling and implementation of distributed applications for multi-actor workflow enactment (Manolescu et al., 2005; Brambilla et al., 2006); other extensions pointed in the direction of multichannel and context-aware Web applications (Ceri et al., 2007).

A distinctive trait of the WebML experience is the presence of an industrial line of development running in parallel to the academic research. One of the original design principles of WebML was implementability, with the ultimate goal of bringing model-driven development (MDD) to the community of "real" developers. To achieve this objective, Politecnico di Milano spun off a company (called Web Models) in 2001, with the mission of implementing and commercializing methods and tools for model-driven development of Web applications, based on WebML. Even before then, WebML had been used for modeling and automatically implementing an industrial project, the Acer-Euro system (http://www. acer-euro.com), comprising the multilingual B2B and B2E content publishing and management applications of Acer, the number 4 PC vendor in the world.

The major result of the industrial R&D is WebRatio (WebModels, 2006), an integrated development environment supporting the modeling of applications with WebML and their implementation with model-driven code generators. Today WebRatio is a consolidated industrial reality: More than 100 applications have been developed by WebModels' customers, over 4,000 trial copies are downloaded per year, and many universities and institutions worldwide use the tool in their Web Engineering courses. In retrospect, the most fruitful and challenging aspect of the interplay of academic and industrial activity has been the continuous relationship between researchers and "real–world," "traditional" developers, which produced essential feedback on the definition of a truly usable and effective model-driven development methodology, which is (hopefully) reflected in the current status of WebML and its accompanying tools.

In this chapter we will overview the core features of WebML and some of its extensions and briefly comment on the usage experience. The chapter is organized as follows: Section 9.2 presents an overview of the WebML methodology and, in particular, introduces the WebML notations for the definition of conceptual schemas. Section 9.3 describes the implementation of the methodology and the architecture of the development tool supporting it. Section 9.4 presents extensions of WebML for supporting Web service composition and publication, workflow-driven Web applications, and context-aware Web applications. Section 9.5 shortly summarizes some of the lessons learned in the application of model-driven development with WebML in industrial projects. Finally, Section 9.6 presents the ongoing and future work and draws the conclusions.

9.2 THE WEBML METHODOLOGY

WebML is a visual language for specifying the content structure of a Web application and the organization and presentation of such content in a hypertext (Ceri et al., 2000, 2002).

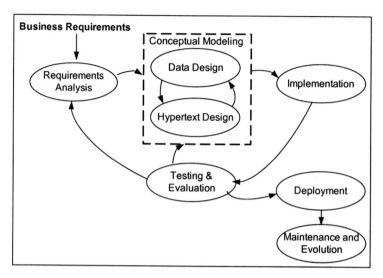

Figure 9.1. Phases in the WebML development process.

As reported in Figure 9.1, the WebML approach to the development of Web applications consists of different phases. Inspired by Boehm's spiral model (Boehm, 1988) and in line with modern methods for Web and software applications development (Beck, 1999; Booch et al., 1999; Conallen, 2000), the WebML process is applied in an iterative and incremental manner in which the various phases are repeated and refined until results meet the application requirements. The product life cycle therefore undergoes several cycles, each producing a prototype or a partial version of the application. At each iteration, the current version of the application is tested and evaluated and then extended or modified to cope with the previously collected requirements as well as the newly emerged requirements. Such an iterative and incremental life cycle appears particularly appropriate for the Web context, where applications must be deployed quickly (in "Internet time") and requirements are likely to change during development.

Out of the entire process illustrated in Figure 9.1, the "upper" phases of analysis and conceptual modeling are those most influenced by the adoption of a conceptual model. The rest of this section will introduce the WebML notations for the definition of conceptual schemas. It will then illustrate the different activities in the WebML development process, with special emphasis on conceptual modeling activities. Some issues about implementation through automatic code generation will be discussed in Section 9.3, by showing how conceptual schemas defined during the design phases can be translated into a running application using WebRatio.

9.2.1 Requirements Analysis

Requirements analysis focuses on collecting information about the application domain and the expected functions and on specifying them through easy-to-understand descriptions. The input to this activity is the set of business requirements that motivate the application development. The main results of this phase are

- the identification of the **groups of users** addressed by the application. Each group represents users having the same characteristics or playing the same role within a business process, i.e., performing the same activities with the same access rights over the same objects. The same individual user may play different roles, thus belonging to different groups.
- the specification of **functional requirements** that address the functions to be provided to users. For each group of users, the relevant activities to be performed are identified and specified.
- the identification of **core information objects**, i.e., the main information assets to be accessed, exchanged, and/or manipulated by users.
- the decomposition of the Web application into **site views**, i.e., different hypertexts designed to meet a well-defined set of functional and user requirements. Each user group will be provided with at least one site view supporting the functions identified for the group.

Analysts are expected to use their favorite format for requirements specification; for instance, tabular formats can be used for capturing the informal requirements such as group or site view descriptions; UML use case diagrams and activity diagrams can also be used as standard representations of usage scenarios and activity synchronization. In particular, functional requirements might be captured by activity flow, showing sequence, and parallelism and synchronization among the activities to be performed by different user groups.

9.2.2 Conceptual Modeling

Conceptual modeling consists of defining conceptual schemas, which express the organization of the application at a high level of abstraction, independently from implementation details. According to the WebML approach, conceptual modeling consists of data design and hypertext design.

Data design corresponds to organizing core information objects previously identified during requirements analysis into a comprehensive and coherent data schema, possibly enriched through derived objects.

Hypertext design then produces site view schemas on top of the data schema previously defined. Site views express the composition of the content and services within hypertext pages, as well as the navigation and the interconnection of components. For applications where different user groups perform multiple activities, or for multichannel applications, in which users can adopt different access devices, hypertext design requires the definition of multiple site views, addressing the user groups involved and their access requirements.

The models provided by the WebML language for data and hypertext design are briefly described in the following. A broader illustration of the language and its formal definition can be found in Ceri et al. (2000, 2002) and at http://www.webml.org.

9.2.2.1 WebML Data Model

Data design is one of the most traditional and consolidated disciplines of information technology, for which well-established modeling languages and guidelines exist. For this reason, WebML does not propose yet another data modeling language; rather, it exploits the entity-relationship data model, or the equivalent subset of UML class diagram primitives. The fundamental elements of the WebML data model are therefore entities, defined as containers of data elements, and relationships, defined as semantic connections between entities. Entities have named properties, called *attributes*, with an associated type. Entities can be organized in generalization hierarchies and relationships can be restricted by means of cardinality constraints.

In the design of Web applications it is often required to calculate the value of some attributes or relationships of an entity from the value of some other elements of the schema. Attributes and relationships so obtained are called *derived*. Derived attributes and relationships can be denoted by adding a slash character (/) in front of their name, and their computation rule can be specified as a logical expression added to the declaration of the attribute or relationship, as is customary in UML class diagrams (Booch et al., 1999). Derivation expressions can be written using declarative languages like OQL or OCL.

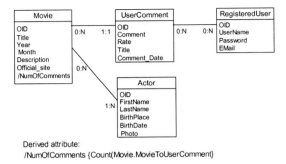

Figure 9.2. A fragment of data schema of the Movie database Web application.

Figure 9.2 shows a small fragment of the data schema of the Movie database example, containing the entities **Movie**, **UserComment**, **RegisteredUser**, **Actor**, and their relationships. The entity **Movie** contains one derived attribute **/NumOfComments**, which is computed as the value of the expression **Count(Movie.MovieToUserComment)**. This expression counts the number of comments associated with a movie according to the **MovieToUserComment** relationship role between the entities **Movie** and **UserComment**.

9.2.2.2 WebML Hypertext Model

The hypertext model enables the definition of the front-end interface, which is shown to a user in the browser. It enables the definition of pages and their internal organization in terms of components (called *content units*) for displaying content. It also supports the definition of links between pages and content units that support information location and browsing. Components can also specify operations, such as content management or user's login/logout procedures. These are called *operation units*.

The modular structure of an application front end is defined in terms of site views, areas, pages, and content units. A *site view* is a particular hypertext, designed to address a specific set of requirements. It consists of *areas*, which are the main sections of the hypertext, and comprises recursively other subareas or pages. *Pages* are the actual containers of information delivered to the user.

Several site views can be defined on top of the same data schema, for serving the needs of different user communities or for arranging content as requested by different access devices like PDAs, smart phones, and similar appliances.

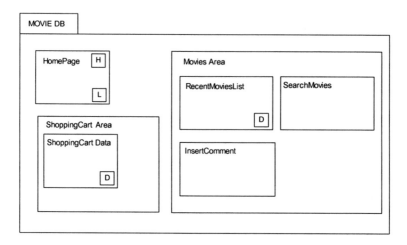

Figure 9.3. Example of site view modularization based on areas and pages.

Figure 9.3 gives an example of the organization of pages and areas in a site view, considering a fragment of the Movie database Web application. The site view is composed of a *home page*, which is the first page accessed when the user enters the application. The site view also comprises two areas: the **Shopping Cart** area, including only one page through which the user manages his current shopping cart; and the **Movies** area, including three pages that show the list of recent movies, support the search of movies, and allow the user to enter comments.

Pages and areas are characterized by some relevance properties, which highlight their "importance" in the Web site. In particular, pages inside an area or site view can be of three types:

- The **home page** (denoted with a small "h" inside the page icon) is the page at the default address of the site view, or the one presented after the user logs into the application; it must be unique.
- The **default page** (denoted with a small "d" inside the page icon) is the one presented by default when its enclosing area is accessed; it must be unique within an area. In the example in Figure 9.3, the **Shopping Cart Data** page and the **Recent Movies List** page are default pages for their enclosing areas. This implies that the two pages are entry points for the two areas.
- A **landmark page** (denoted with a small "l" inside the page icon) is reachable from all the other pages or areas within its enclosing module. For example, in Figure 9.3 the home page is also a landmark page, meaning that a link to it will be available from any other page of the site view.

Table 9.1. The Five Predefined Content Units in WebML

Data Unit	Multidata Unit	Index Unit	Scroller Unit	Entry Unit

Page composition. Pages are made of *content units*, which are the elementary pieces of information, possibly extracted from data sources, published within pages. Table 9.1 reports the five WebML predefined content units, representing the elementary information elements that may appear in the hypertext pages.

Units represent one or more instances of entities of the structural schema, typically selected by means of queries over the entity attributes or over relationships. In particular, *data units* represent some of the attributes of a given entity instance; *multidata units* represent some of the attributes of a set of entity instances; *index units* present a list of descriptive keys of a set of entity instances and enable the selection of one of them; *scroller units* enable the browsing of an ordered set of objects. Finally, *entry units* do not draw content from the elements of the data schema, but publish a form for collecting input values from the user.

Data, multidata, index, and scroller units include a *source* and a *selector*. The source is the name of the entity from which the unit's content is retrieved. The selector is a predicate, used for determining the actual objects of the source entity that contribute to the unit's content. The previous collection of units is sufficient to logically represent arbitrary content on a Web interface (Ceri et al., 2002). However, some extensions are also available, for example, the *multichoice* and the *hierarchical* indexes reported in Table 9.2. These are two variants of the index unit that allow one to choose multiple objects and organize a list of index entries defined over multiple entities hierarchically.

Link definition. Units and pages are interconnected by links, thus forming a hypertext. Links between units are called *contextual*, because they carry some information from the *source unit* to the *destination unit*. In contrast, links between pages are called *noncontextual*.

Table 9.2. Two Index Unit Variants

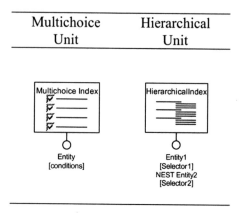

Multichoice Unit	Hierarchical Unit

In contextual links, the binding between the source unit and the destination unit of the link is formally represented by link parameters, associated with the link, and by parametric selectors, defined in the destination unit. A *link parameter* is a value associated with a link between units, which is transported as an effect of the link navigation, from the source unit to the destination unit. A *parametric selector* is, instead, a unit selector whose condition contains one or more parameters.

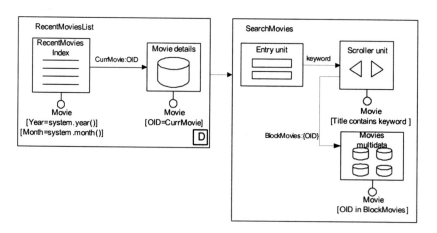

Figure 9.4. Example of contextual and noncontextual navigation.

As an example of page composition and unit linking, Figure 9.4 reports a simple hypertext, containing two pages of the **Movies** Area. The page **Recent Movies List** contains an index unit defined over the **Movie** entity, which shows the list of movies shown in the last month, and a data unit also defined over the **Movie** entity, which displays the details of the movie selected from the index. Two selectors (**[Year=system.year()]**, **[Month=system.month()]**) are defined to restrict the selection only to the movies of the current month and year. The arrow between the two units is a contextual link, carrying the parameter **CurrMovie**, containing the object identifier (OID) of the selected item. The data unit includes a parametric selector (**[OID=CurrMovie]**), which uses the input OID parameter to retrieve the data of the specific movie.

OIDs of the objects displayed or chosen from the source unit are considered the default context associated with the link. Therefore, OID parameters over links and parametric selectors testing for OID values can be omitted and simply inferred from the diagram.

An example of a noncontextual link is shown from the **Recent Movies List** page to the **Search Movies** page: This link does not carry any parameter, because the content of the destination page does not depend on the content of the source page.

The page **Search Movies** shows an interesting hypertext pattern; it contains three units: an entry unit denoting a form for inserting the keyword of the title to be searched, a scroller unit defined over the **Movie** entity and having a selector for retrieving only the movies containing that keyword in their titles (**[Title contains keyword]**), and a multidata unit displaying a scrollable block of search results. Through the scroller unit it is possible to move to the first, previous, next, and last blocks of results.

Automatic and transport links. In some applications, it may be necessary to differentiate a specific link behavior, whereby the content of some units is displayed as soon as the page is accessed, even if the user has not navigated its incoming link. This effect can be achieved by using automatic links. An *automatic link*, graphically represented by putting a label "A" over the link, is "navigated" in the absence of a user's interaction when the page that contains the source unit of the link is accessed.

Also, there are cases in which a link is used only for passing contextual information from one unit to another and thus is not rendered as an anchor. This type of link is called a *transport link*, to highlight that the link enables only parameter passing and not interaction. Transport links are graphically represented as dashed arrows.

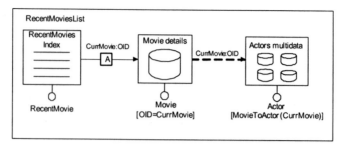

Figure 9.5. Example of automatic and transport links.

Consider the example in Figure 9.5, extending the content of the page **Recent Movies List** shown in Figure 9.4. The link between the index and the data unit has been defined as *automatic*: When the page is accessed, the details of the first movie appearing in the index will be shown to the user, without the need for her interaction. A multidata unit has been added to show the names of the actors playing in the selected movie. A *transport* link is used to pass the OID of the current movie to the multidata unit. This OID is used by the multidata unit in a parametric selector associated with the **MovieToActor** relationship defined between the entities **Movie** and **Actor** to retrieve only the actors associated with the current movie. Note that the automatic link admits the user's interaction for selecting a different movie and is thus rendered as an anchor; conversely, the output link of the data unit does not enable any selection and thus is defined as transport and is not rendered as an anchor.

Global parameters. In some cases, contextual information is not transferred point to point during navigation but can be set as globally available to all the pages of the site view. This is possible through *global parameters*, which abstract the implementation-level notion of session-persistent data.

Parameters can be set through the *Set unit* and consumed within a page through a *Get unit*. The visual representation of such two units is reported in Table 9.3. An example of use of the get unit will be shown in the next subsection.

Operations. In addition to the specification of read-only Web sites, where user interaction is limited to information browsing, WebML also supports the specification of services and content management operations requiring write access over the information hosted in a site (e.g., the filling of a shopping trolley or an update of the users' personal information). WebML offers additional primitives for expressing built-in update operations, such as creating, deleting, or modifying an instance of an entity (represented through the *create, delete,* and *modify* units, respectively) or adding or dropping a